PORTRAIT of JESUS?

OMEGA BOOKS

The OMEGA BOOKS series from Paragon House is dedicated to classic and contemporary works about human development and the nature of ultimate reality, encompassing the fields of mysticism and spirituality, psychic research and paranormal phenomena, the evolution of consciousness, and the human potential for self-directed growth in body, mind and spirit.

John White, M.A.T., Series Editor of OMEGA BOOKS, is an internationally known author, editor, and educator in the fields of consciousness research and higher human development.

MORE TITLES IN OMEGA BOOKS

PORTRAIT of JESUS?

THE ILLUSTRATED STORY OF THE SHROUD OF TURIN

Frank C. Tribbe

Second Edition 2006

Published in the United States by
Paragon House
1925 Oakcrest Aveune
Suite 7
St. Paul, MN 55113

First Edition 1983, Stein and Day Publishers

The Omega Books series from Paragon House is dedicated to classic and contemporary works about human development and the nature of ultimate reality, encompassing the fields of mysticism and spirituality, psychic research and paranormal phenomena, the evolution of consciousness, and the human potential for self-directed growth in body, mind and spirit.

Library of Congress Cataloging-in-Publication Data

Tribbe, Frank C.
  Portrait of Jesus? : the Shroud of Turin in science and history / Frank C. Tribbe.-- Rev. and expanded 2nd ed.
    p. cm.
  Includes bibliographical references and index.
  ISBN 1-55778-854-5 (pbk. : alk. paper) 1. Holy Shroud. I. Title.
  BT587.S4T74 2006
  232.96'6--dc22
                            2005037883

Manufactured in the United States of America
10 9 8 7 6 5 4 3 2 1

The paper used in this publication meets the minimum requirements of American National Standard for Information Sciences—Permanence of Paper for Printed Library Materials, ANSIZ39.48-1984.

For current information about all releases from Paragon House,
visit the web site at http://www.paragonhouse.com

Dedicated to the Memory of
Father Peter M. Rinaldi, SDB,
The Grand Old Man of Shroud Research

And to
Florence and Audre
For assistance, encouragement
And love

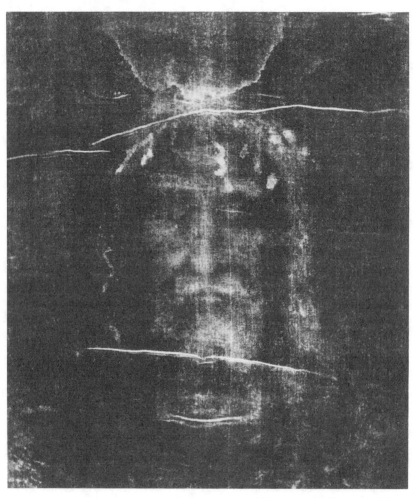

(Courtesy Holy Shroud Guild)

CONTENTS

ONE
WHAT IS THE SHROUD OF TURIN?
1

A short overview of public events concerning the Shroud, with the probable reasons for the attention it is getting. A description of the physical aspects of the Shroud and its present setting. How science came to be involved and its initial reactions.

TWO
EARLY HISTORY AND THE UNCERTAIN YEARS
13

A chronology of the Shroud's probable history and travels from A.D. 30 to 1204, and an overview of the historic facts, spliced with tradition, inference, and conjecture about the uncertain periods. The faces on cloth, such as the Image of Edessa and the Mandylion, are put in perspective.

THREE
THE ATHENS/BESANCON/KNIGHTS TEMPLAR CONNECTION
27

A review of the 153-year period (1204–1357) when the Shroud was unheard of and "missing"—from the fall of Constantinople until the first public exhibition near Paris—linking up the sequence of known facts to show inferences supporting the suggestions of custody of the Shroud during this period.

TWENTY
CONCLUSIONS: SCIENTIFIC, RELIGIOUS, AND PERSONAL
265

Many of the conclusions offered are personal, and each reader will have his own; belief and faith still have the final word. Science has no final answers; its evidence proves only penultimate conclusions, not ultimate ones. But the Shroud is important to every thinking person.

Illustrations

BLACK-AND-WHITE PHOTOGRAPHS

CHAPTER FIVE

CHAPTER SIX

General Editor's Foreword

Portrait of Jesus? is a a comprehensive and fully current account of the Shroud of Turin which, according to legend, was the garment which covered Jesus in the tomb after his crucifixion. First published in 1983, this revised edition brings the text up to date with the two decades of additional research and events related to the Shroud. Tribbe shows that the Shroud is an authentic first-century relic from the Near East, probably Palestine, and is therefore precisely what legend maintains. It is probably the most important holy relic in the world because, first, it has been authenticated through the most rigorous and thorough-going scientific research and, second, because it offers profound insight into the process of higher human development to enlightenment.

In 2003 Tribbe published *The Holy Grail Mystery Solved* (Galde Press, PO Box 460, Lakeville MN 55044, www.galdepress.com), which is intimately related to *Portrait of Jesus?* Tribbe shows that the Holy Grail is not a cup or dish. Nor, for those who have read *The DaVinci Code,* is it the bones of Mary Magdalene or even the Divine Feminine. Rather, it is the image of the man in the Shroud of Turin. The Shroud satisfies all the questions about the Holy Grail and the Knights Templar who initiated the Grail Quest.

In *The Holy Grail Mystery Solved,* Tribbe shows that "grail" comes from the Old French "greille," meaning the latticework frame which surrounded the face-image of the Man in the Shroud as it rested in a wooden box. The earliest historical records of how the Shroud was folded and stored (see p. 7 of the book) indicate the face-image was visible through an opening in the box—an opening framed with latticework. Tribbe also explains that the face-image of the Man in the Shroud was what the Knights Templar worshipped. That explains the central charge against the Templars when Philip IV of France suppressed the Order in 1307, namely, that they worshipped the image of a bearded man (see p. 37-38).

The term Holy Grail originated with the Knights Templar and was mistakenly applied by others to various objects such as a cup or dish. But the face-image was venerated by the Templars because it visibly demonstrated the central fact of Jesus's teaching: the conquest of death through ascension in holiness of spirit to recognition of our oneness with God. In the tomb, Jesus transubstantiated his flesh, blood and bone into the resurrection body or glorified body which is deathless. That event was, so far as modern science can explain it, a kind of controlled nuclear explosion involving a form of energy and radiation unknown to science, as Tribbe describes in *Portrait of Jesus?*. The result: Jesus attained victory over death via a body of light, the ultimate form of enlightenment.

Properly understood, Tribbe says, the Grail is enlightenment and the Grail Quest is actualizing our human potential for growth to that state of being which Jesus demonstrated. Jesus' attainment of the resurrection body which created the image of the Man in the Shroud is the highest form of enlightenment—literally becoming light. That is what Jesus taught and demonstrated, that is why he is called the Light of the world, His teaching-demonstration is for everyone; it is inherent in our human potential to become like Christ. Tribbe's scholarship places the Shroud in the context of the human potential for enlightenment and shows its significance for the entire human race, not in organizational terms but in psychophysical terms. That makes Jesus' work universal, not denominational. That means he didn't teach Christianity; he taught a system for enlightenment. *Portrait of Jesus?* therefore addresses the mission statement of Omega Books: higher human development and the nature of ultimate reality.

—John White

SPECIAL INTRODUCTIONS

1

Citing Scholarly Doubts as To Reliability of Carbon-Dating the Shroud Cloth in 1988

On October 13, 1988, the archbishop of Turin announced that three laboratories—in Tucson, Arizona; Oxford, England; and Zurich, Switzerland—had agreed that they carbon-dated the cloth of the Shroud of Turin to the early fourteenth century.

So, what effect did this bombshell have on the status of the Shroud with its mystical images, and upon its thousands of proponents, worldwide, who consider it to be the very burial cloth of Jesus of Galilee? And what effect did the announcement have on the dozens of scientists, historians, and professional researchers who, for the past fifteen years, have been exhaustively examining the cloth, its images, its history, and its associations? Basically, that announcement just expanded and extended the multifaceted controversy that has raged about this Shroud for several hundred years.

Shortly thereafter, on May 6 and 7, 1989, at Bologna, Italy, an international symposium on The Shroud and Iconography was held during which historical and various types of technical data were presented indicating the *impossibility* of a Middle Ages date for the cloth of this Shroud. Some two dozen varieties of such data are presented in the following pages of this book.

Thus, the relevant question becomes: What went wrong with the carbon-dating exercise in 1988? This question, among others, was specifically addressed at the Paris Symposium of September 7 and 8, 1989, where thirty-five reports concerning the Shroud were presented, covering sixteen hours of conference time. Six of those papers speak particularly to the crucial question of the carbon-dating exercise, and I will refer briefly to each of them, below.

But first, we should attempt a simple definition of "radiocarbon dating" that is used to date ancient artifacts by measuring their carbon 14 content: By scientifically measuring the extent to which any organic material (such as wood, bone, or linen cloth) has lost the very weak natural radioactivity it had during its life, we "carbon-date" it, to give us—in the case of linen—the date at which the flax from which it was made, "died" (was cut)—thus, the approximate year is determined in which the thread was spun from flax, and the linen cloth was woven from the thread.

Also, as a preliminary matter, we should note that archaeologists who are the principal end users of the carbon-dating service, rather uniformly point out that this procedure is complicated and sensitive, but *not* infallible; it is chiefly useful in dating *undisturbed* material, and then it must be removed and handled by using sterile tools and containers, and be rushed to the laboratory. If the C-14 date is inconsistent with other data, it is the first to be rejected.

Various facets of the dating exercise of 1988 were addressed in the following key papers at the Paris Symposium:

1.   Dr. Marie-Claire Van Oosterwyck-Gastuche, head of dating at the Museum of Central Africa, presented her paper "Radiocarbon: An Absolute Method of Dating?" in which she summarized the history of carbon-dating, indicating (a) that there were wide variations of results according to the effects of other things on the object, (b) that from 1500 B.C. there is a systematic change in C-14 dating, (c) that C-14 is especially inaccurate with linen samples, and (d) that microbe decomposition of cellulose that occurs in contact with humus acids distorts the aging results. She cited many examples of errors up to a thousand years, and explained why it was unrealistic to attempt a dating of the Shroud sample that was taken. She concluded by saying: "There is a mountain of facts demonstrating the inaccuracy of C-14 dating… [and] it is dishonest to say that science has spoken."

2.   Dr. John Jackson, professor of physics at the University of Colorado, presented the paper: "A Novel Mechanism of Image Formation on

the Shroud Which Is Consistent with All Observational Characteristics of the Image." By results of controlled experiments, he showed the impossibility of the image having resulted from an artist's drawing, molecular diffusion, natural radiation of the body, or by direct contact. He established the technical explanation of the image as resulting from cellulose degradation, which is a molecular change in the fibers, and proved that the image resulted from a cloth-covered body, based on mathematical intensity-distance calculations. However, he demonstrated that gravity caused the blood-marks to come while the cloth was *draped,* but for the body image the cloth was "slightly flattened" as if the "cloth physically collapsed *down into* the body region…" such as would happen if the body *disappeared* during the image-making process. His scientific findings imply radiation in the ultraviolet or x-ray range as the image-maker. Thus, despite the carbon-dating exercise, the overwhelming evidence favors authenticity. Dr. Jackson, after fifteen years of Shroud laboratory research, states: "What impresses and challenges me the most about the Shroud image is its resistance against explanation. Attempts to explain it as an artistic creation, or the result of a natural transfer process such as diffusion or direct contact, remain unconvincing."

3.   Dr. Arnaud Upinsky, mathematician, epistemologist, and president of the Euclidian Foundation, presented the paper, "An Epistemological Synthesis for the Shroud of Turin," which involved logic as a way "to distinguish the truth and the meaning of scientific results." He stated that science is interdisciplinary by definition so that no one result from one field can be valid on its own; thus, "if all scientific evidence up to 1988 is wrong (as suggested by the carbon laboratories) then clearly *no* scientific evidence is credible. It is not the credibility of the Shroud at stake but the credibility of science." Using thirty tables of factual data, he demonstrated "signatures of authenticity, and all of which exclude manual production… All elements of authenticity fit in with one another." He also saw significant weakness in the failure of the laboratories to publish their raw data.

4.   Professor Eberhard Lindner of Germany spoke specifically to "The Ambiguity of Radiocarbon Results," saying that perhaps the C-14 results are a hidden proof for Resurrection—since that event would have

been "a selective process of disappearance of protons leaving electrons which caused the image by radiation and the remaining neutrons causing an isotopic shift to C-14, thus affecting the dating result."

5. Dr. Alan D. Whanger of Duke University used slides of the April 1988 sample-taking ceremony to show that one of the major flaws in the carbon-dating exercise was that the sample taken from the Shroud included sixteenth-century threads from the seams rewoven into the Shroud.

In addition to these data, I must note that, having myself spent a lifetime in study of the Shroud of Turin, it is highly gratifying to observe that it is the scientists and researchers with the highest credentials and the longest periods devoted to examination and study of the Shroud data who are the most certain of its genuineness in spite of the carbon-dating reports. Also, as a churchman, I am of course solaced to observe that on April 28, 1989, Pope John Paul II, responding to a journalist, reminded that the Church has never spoken on the Shroud's authenticity, but for himself said, "I think it is a relic" (thus, just not an icon).

I can wholeheartedly recommend this book. When it was first published, I wrote the author: "If I tell you that I read it all at one sitting last night, it is because it is true, and also simply because I could not put it down. I stand amazed at the scope of your research, at the way in which you tell the story, at the many, well-selected illustrations! I can only say of your book, it will be a classic on the Shroud of Turin in the English language!"

—*Peter Rinaldi, S.D.B.,*

, 1993.

Father Peter Rinaldi, vice president of the Holy Shroud Guild (USA), though a native of Turin, Italy, continued to divide his professional life between that city and New York. Father Rinaldi may accurately be described as the premier Sindonologist of the world. It was his effort, almost single-handedly, that obtained permission for the American scientists of STURP to spend 120 hours continuously examining the Shroud in 1978, at the conclusion of its public exhibition. Father Peter M. Rinaldi, S.D.B., died in Turin on February 27, 1993, at age eighty-two; the above Special Introduction was his last formal writing on Shroud studies.

In *Shroud News* for February 1993, Rex Morgan wrote:

No mere obituary can do justice to the life and work of a man such as Reverend Father Peter Rinaldi, SDB. One needs to read all his books, all his articles and the literature about his life to gain a proper perspective of his contribution. His life as a Roman Catholic priest of the Salesian Order of Don Bosco and as the leading personality in Shroud studies for nearly sixty years is legendary. His activity of the Shroud front spans the entire period of modern study and discovery and awareness of the cloth. He had known Secondo Pio who first photographed the Shroud in 1898, opening up the whole modern age of study, as well as knowing all the major earliest participants, most of them, to us, only names in the literature: Barbet, Enrie, Tonelli, Vignon, Weuenschel, he knew them all. His long life had bridged the early twentieth century studies and the extraordinary period of scientific rediscovery of the Shroud in the 1970s.

2

Underscoring the Highly Significant Historical Research of the Shroud

Beyond the preponderance of scientific evidence supporting the authenticity of the Turin Shroud there lies a substratum of historical evidence similarly identifying the Shroud as the actual burial wrapping of Jesus the Christ. Once the findings from scientific study of the cloth and its surface debris in 1978 were published, little more could be said by Shroud science. Historical and iconographical research, however, has continued to uncover more written and pictorial evidence of the antiquity of the Shroud and its image. These documents discredit some opinions of the Shroud's history but dramatically confirm others. While not yet perfectly in focus, the picture is becoming ever clearer that the Christ-image on the Turin Shroud was the prototype for the first artistic portraits of Jesus with beard and long hair.

Most important, this new documentary evidence for the Shroud's early date flies in the face of the fourteenth-century date attributed to the cloth by recent radiocarbon methods, themselves susceptible to drastic unexplained errors.

In general, Ian Wilson's hypothesis has been reinforced during the last decade. His theory identified the Shroud, folded within a frame, with the Edessa Mandylion and established the existence of the Shroud at least as early as the fourth century. In 1984, Robert Drews' *In Search of the Shroud of Turin* argued that there was in Edessa a Gnostic community. This proto-Christian group did not have the usual Hebrew animosity against images. It was they, Drews urged, who retained a Christ-image in Edessa.

The year 1985 saw the appearance of A. M. Dubarle's survey, *Histoire Ancienne du Linceul de Turin,* in France. Dubarle covers the early history of the Shroud up to 1204. It is a work of immense scholarship. One of his contributions was to point up the importance of the 1192 Budapest Pray manuscript. It depicts a nude Jesus, hands in the same attitude as on the Turin Shroud, lying upon a cloth whose design resembles the herringbone twill of the Shroud. The cloth bears four marks in the same pattern as the burn-holes of unknown date still seen on the Shroud. This argues that it was modeled on the Shroud in or before 1192.

Brother Bruno Bonnet-Eymard has contributed much to our historical understanding of the Shroud through his publications in the periodical *Catholic Counter-Reformation of the 20th Century (CRC).* His scenario, which rejects Wilson's fourth-century date for the Shroud in Edessa, is that the burial wrapping remained in Jerusalem until the Persian conquest in 614. Taken for safety to Constantinople, it was removed to Edessa for the same reason during the iconoclast controversy of the eighth century. The Mandylion/Shroud returned to the capital in 944. Bonnet-Eymard has also drawn attention to an illustration in the Madrid manuscript of John Skylitzes, whose artist knew the Edessa image was much larger than a mere face-towel.

Gino Zaninotto contributed more than anyone to Shroud history in the 1980s. His research turned up a Roman "manual" for crucifixions, which identified the crucifixion technique manifested on the Shroud as first-century. His most important discovery was the sermon of Gregory, archdeacon of the Hagia Sophia, and one of the officiating clergy for the reception of the Mandylion in Constantinople on August 15, 944. Gregory's description of the image mentioned the blood and water from the wound in the side, a striking corroboration of Wilson's insight that the Mandylion/tetradiplon was already the same Shroud as in Turin today.

For the period between the Shroud's departure from Constantinople and its arrival in Lirey (1204–1355), there are few documents but numerous suggested itineraries, including Wilson's Templar thesis, now supported by Rex Morgan's evidence from Templecombe that the Christ-face wood panel was the lid of the Shroud's container (see Morgan's *Shroud News*). The thesis that the high-ranking crusader Othon de La Roche, prince of Athens, obtained the Shroud by 1205 and relayed it west to Besancon (France), where it was kept until 1349, has received new impetus by the researches of this writer *(The Shroud of Turin: Opposing Viewpoints),* and those of Bonnet-Eymard (see CRC). The silence of Geoffrey I de Charny and of the Lirey archives, the Shroud's "disappearance" after the cathedral fire in Besancon in 1349, the arrival of Jeanne de Vergy from that city to marry Geoffrey about that time, and the certain presence of the Shroud in Lirey soon after—all weigh in favor of a Besancon sojourn. Also in support of Besancon is the fact that only Besancon actually claimed to have the true Shroud. All other suggested possessors appear ignorant of the Shroud's existence.

Wilson has authored another potentially significant book, *Holy Faces, Secret Places* (1991), on Christ-images throughout history. Rev. Albert Dreisbach has researched numerous vague but suggestive references to the Shroud in the New Testament and in ancient apocrypha that may bear fruit. In 1993, this writer's "The Turin Shroud, Othon de La Roche, Besancon, and the d'Arcy Memorandum: An Elaboration and a Synthesis" appeared in Italian in the journal *Collegamento pro Sindone,* which established a series of links in a proveniential chain for the Shroud from 1205 to 1355. Also, this writer's "Philibert Pingon and the Shroud of Turin" (1993) uses the souvenir medallion bearing the crest of Vergy, found in the River Seine, to reinforce the thesis that Jeanne de Vergy of Besancon brought the Shroud to her marriage to Geoffrey I de Charny, first known private owner of the Turin Shroud in Western Europe.

—*Daniel C. Scavone, Ph.D.*
Professor of History
University of Southern Indiana

Dr. Scavone has had a lifetime interest in the Shroud of Turin and, with Wilson (cited above), is considered one of the two premier Shroud historians on the world scene. He has participated in several international Shroud symposia, has had a number of articles published on the topic, plus the above-noted book, *The Shroud of Turin: Opposing Viewpoints* (Greenhaven Press, 1989).

Author's Preface

The news media have often proclaimed the Shroud of Turin as a "Catholic relic." Such description is highly misleading.

At the time the Shroud of Turin was publicly presented in Lirey, France, in A.D. 1357, the only form of Christianity in Western Europe was Roman Catholicism (there were Eastern Orthodox churches in Russia and Asia Minor). Protestantism was nearly two hundred years in the future, and independent Christian denominations much further than that. Thus the owners of the relic would of necessity be Roman Catholics, as they still are today. But I would feel the present owners and custodians of the Shroud would be the last to assert as a parochial claim that the Shroud is strictly a "Catholic" relic. The Shroud is a Christian relic in the broadest sense, and the entire human race should be interested. For that reason, this presentation has been made as comprehensive as possible, and I have endeavored to keep the influence of my personal biases to a minimum.

My efforts in this volume to integrate, report, and analyze data are largely based on literary research from the papers presented at scientific meetings, articles in professional journals and proceedings, items from periodicals and news media, reports and publications of involved organizations, related materials from publications of bordering sciences, and all books in the English language that relate to the Shroud of Turin.

Three organizations lead research on the Shroud: the International Center for Sindonology in Turin; the American-based Holy Shroud Guild; and the American-based Shroud of Turin Research Project (STURP). Most of my research has been focused on their publications, the proceedings of their symposia, and the papers published by individuals who have worked under their aegis. Nevertheless, I am not in any sense a spokesman for those organizations or the persons affiliated with them, and the conclusions I state in this book are mine alone; I have had access only to materials and reports available to the public.

It is important to note that the STURP research group included agnostics, atheists, and Jews as well as committed Christians of various denominations, who performed crucial roles in the 1978 hands-on examination of the Shroud—and produced unanimous affirmative conclusions.

I report the data, findings, and opinions of others, make forensic evaluation, and draw logical conclusions, and shall state my personal opinions and beliefs. Although I have been favored by the friendly assistance of many people involved in the research who have helpfully reviewed and critiqued my manuscript, any error or misconception that might remain in the text is solely my responsibility.

To write comprehensively about the Shroud of Turin requires the presentation of a very complex story. As researcher-reporter-lawyer, I have attempted to do the following: to present facts and legend and distinguish between them; to present authoritative opinion and distinguish it from fact; to summarize scientific findings and put them into understandable lay-language; to evaluate conflicting opinions; and to evaluate criticisms, some valid and important and some that seem frivolous. I shall attempt to report objectively and to reach my own conclusions, labeled as such.

There are limits to what science can provide us in the way of validation of the Shroud, and there are limits to what the Roman Catholic Church (as owner-custodian of the Shroud) is willing to claim as to the authentication of this relic. However, using reasonable inference, logic, circumstantial evidence, and forensic reasoning, I can legitimately go beyond those limits and will not hesitate to do so. I also will go beyond scientific findings and religious scriptures for my data—including history, legend, apocryphal writings, archaeology, and other inspired writings.

Of necessity, the subject of this book considers the reality of a spiritual world, of God, and of a spiritual aspect of all men, and I subscribe to such views. The reader should be prepared at least to consider such factors, I hope with an open mind and suspended judgment. However, I will not engage in theological discourse or attempt to convert or to bring an evangelical message, though the implications of my data and reasoning may well draw the reader into thoughts along those lines. I have endeavored to avoid either a Protestant or a Roman Catholic viewpoint in my presentation; to the extent that a personal bias appears, it will more nearly be a Christian nondenominational viewpoint.

I have been a lifelong Protestant with ecumenical leanings (Methodist, Presbyterian, Baptist, Church of the Brethren). Although I have had minimal detailed knowledge about Catholicism, I am fully aware of the great debt that Protestants in particular and the world in general owe to the Roman Catholic Church—for Christianity would not have survived without it. Since my youth I've had an active interest in religious history and comparative religion, but I had little interest in, and minimal acceptance of, religious relics of Christianity until the development of my interest in the Shroud of Turin since the early 1970s.

I have always had a respect for, and interest in, historical tradition and legend concerning religion, and I hope that it has been a balanced and critical interest. I am neither a scientist nor a theologian, but have had a long career in research and investigative activity as well as in the analysis of technical material, the evaluation of evidence, and the application of logic and legal forensics. Throughout my forty years of government legal work, I was involved in the investigation of claims, many of which resulted in court action, and I participated in decisions about the prosecution and settlement of such matters. As a civilian lawyer for fifteen years in the Army Corps of Engineers, I learned to convert engineering and scientific findings into lay language. Those skills have all been utilized in this endeavor.

—*Frank C. Tribbe*

ACKNOWLEDGMENTS

For such merit as this volume may have, I owe a large debt of gratitude to a few people who have very diligently reviewed my manuscript, or parts thereof; they are: the late Father Adam J. Otterbein, president of the Holy Shroud Guild, and the late Father Peter M. Rinaldi, vice president of the Holy Shroud Guild, from their broad knowledge of sindonology and the Roman Catholic perspective; John W. White, author and editor of books in the field of consciousness studies, from a literary perspective; the late Dr. Alan D. Adler, professor of chemistry at Western Connecticut State College, from a senior STURP scientist's perspective; Dr. Daniel C. Scavone, professor of history at the University of Southern Indiana, for the historical perspective; Dr. Alan D. Whanger, of Duke University Medical Center, and his wife Mary, respecting their iconographical research; Isabel Piczek, one of the truly great artists and art-scientists in the world today.

Until 1972, I was aware of the Shroud's nature, but only in general terms, and knew that it was in Turin, Italy. From my travels in Europe and from my reading in religious literature I knew that many Christian churches enshrined relics of various kinds, including ones presumably related to the passion of Jesus. But this was a subject that had interested me very little, until then. Living in Washington, D.C., I had come to enjoy public lectures once or twice a year given there by retired colonel Frank O. Adams, who was a senior executive of A.R.E. (the Association for Research and Enlightenment), which had been founded in Virginia Beach, Virginia, by the great spiritual sensitive, Edgar Cayce. Consequently, in the early summer of 1972, I attended with high expectations an Adams lecture on the Shroud of Turin. Colonel Adams's illustrated presentation thrilled and intrigued me beyond all expectations. At the lecture's conclusion I eagerly bought his book, a set of slides, and a print of the Jesus face based on the Shroud Image, which Adams had commissioned. My interest has not waned since.

All books in the English language about the Shroud of Turin have been a treasure-house for my research (see the Selected Bibliography). My deep appreciation is acknowledged for the thorough research and careful marshaling of information by the earlier writers on this subject, whose records have been a primary source of data for me. Books of special help were: *The Shroud of Christ* by Paul Vignon, *Self-Portrait of Christ* by Edward A. Wuenschel; *Shroud* by Robert R. Wilcox, *The Shroud of Turin* by Ian Wilson, and *When Millions Saw the Shroud* by Peter M. Rinaldi.

Also, a very great debt is owed to the uncompensated scientists of the Shroud of Turin Research Project (STURP) and those affiliated with the International Center of Sindonology in Turin, Italy, as well as the independent researchers, whose papers, articles, and formal reports in periodicals, proceedings, informal reports, and special volumes have provided technical data and evaluations that gave totally new insights and thus made the writing of this volume worth the doing.

Above all others, my gratitude goes in full measure to my late wife, Audre, who initially urged that my lectures, articles, and reviews on the subject of the Shroud be expanded into a book, and to my present wife, Florence, who, in reviewing redrafts of this new edition, has given me insightful guidance as to what will likely be understood by the general reader, for whom this book is intended.

Of course, responsibility is mine alone for such errors, inadvertences, poor presentation, and illogic as may have persisted in my material in spite of careful review. I do indeed appreciate the contribution of ideas and data by all of the many persons of diverse skills throughout the past years (since the Shroud was first photographed in 1898), whose writings have stimulated me to an awareness of the broad implications of this controversial subject. I refer equally to the critics, skeptics, publicists, historians, writers, researchers, scientists, and churchmen. A few of their writings have seemed harsh and unreasonable; I hope that mine is objective and temperate. I can assure each person named or alluded to in my text, that my words in no instance are intended to demean or insult anyone, although I may strongly disagree with a few of them.

The gracious permission of the following persons and organizations for the use of quoted materials is very deeply appreciated:

Robert K. Wilcox for material appearing in chapter 15 from his book *Shroud* (Macmillan, 1977). Charles C. Wise Jr., for material in chapter 16 from his book *Picture Windows on the Christ* (Magian Press, 1979). The Holy Shroud Guild for material in chapter 13 from their summary announcement of October 11, 1981, and for many illustrations. Rex Morgan, for material from *Shroud News.*

All Bible quotations are from the King James Version unless otherwise noted.

ONE

WHAT IS THE SHROUD OF TURIN?

A LARGE piece of ancient linen, it apparently bears images of a bearded, naked, crucified man. That is the Shroud of Turin. In 1979 and 1980, "The Silent Witness," a documentary television program about the Shroud, aired on United States public television channels. In 1980 and 1981, *National Geographic* and *Harper's* magazines carried well-illustrated, major articles on the same subject. In April 1981 and again in April 1982, the ABC television news program *20/20* featured interviews and in-depth reports about the Shroud. Previously, in November 1973, Italian audiences saw the pictorial story of the Shroud on their principal channel, along with a special message from Pope Paul VI. Telecasts in Western European countries followed.

What has caused all this sudden interest? What was new? In Europe, the Shroud had been the subject of sporadic public interest and controversy since the turn of the century. Within the Roman Catholic Church hierarchy and clergy, and to some extent within its lay membership, knowledge of and interest in the Shroud as a religious relic had continued since 1357. Many had believed it to be the burial cloth of Jesus of Nazareth.

But for many Americans, Europeans, and others, popular interest in the Shroud of Turin stems mainly from events in 1976 and 1978. From 1969 to 1976 a secret commission organized by Turin church authorities examined and studied the Shroud. This work was primarily to inspect the Shroud for possible deterioration and also to explore the feasibility of subsequent extensive scientific testing of the Shroud. The report of the Turin Commission (to be discussed in chapter 7), written in Italian, was not released until 1976, and there has been no official English translation of it.

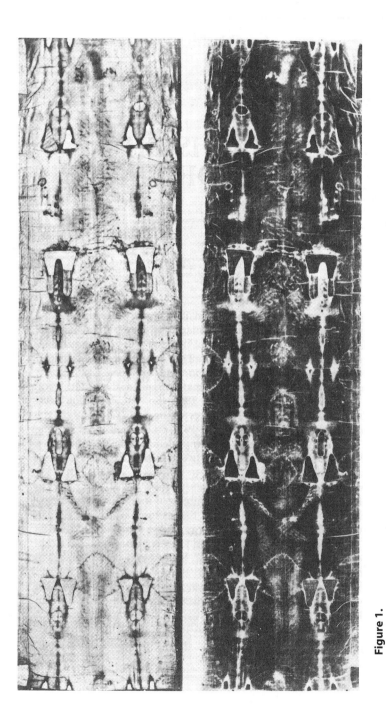

Figure 1.
The full Shroud. The upper photographic positive is off-white and is as seen when looking at it. The lower photographic negative is by far the more natural-appearing image of the Man of the Shroud. (*Courtesy Holy Shroud Guild*)

In the United States, information about the Shroud flowed primarily from events in October 1978. During the previous three years, a small group of U.S. scientists, trained mostly in the nuclear space probe and military technology, had, on their own time, been studying photographs of the Shroud taken by Europeans in 1931 and 1973.

Tentative conclusions and many questions resulted in these Americans traveling to Turin, seeking permission from Church officials for a thorough scientific examination of the Shroud.

Permission was granted, and the study was conducted during six days of intensive around-the-clock scientific activity, October 8–13, 1978. This historic effort has resulted in the publication of more than twenty scientific papers (see chapters 8, 9, and 10 for full discussion) that in turn have spawned dozens of syndicated newspaper articles throughout the country.

Along with a few Europeans, approximately thirty American scientists of various disciplines participated in the exercise. The group had recently incorporated itself as the Shroud of Turin Research Project (STURP). Their religious backgrounds and orientations were varied: A few were members of Catholic and Protestant churches, most of these men held little more than nominal religious beliefs; a few were Jewish; one or two were atheists; and most were agnostic or unconcerned about religion. All were involved because they were curious scientists intrigued by an apparent mystery that modern science might solve. STURP had no a priori plan either to validate or vitiate the Shroud's authenticity; objectivity was their watchword. However, a few later said that they had fully expected that an hour or so with the Shroud, using their very sensitive, sophisticated equipment, would doubtless prove its spuriousness. But no member of the group came away with such a conclusion, even tentatively. On the television program *20/20,* Dr. John Heller said: "How was the image produced? What produced it? And for that the answer is—it is a mystery."

What is the Shroud like? It is a piece of ancient linen cloth, presumably a burial shroud, fourteen feet three inches long by three feet seven inches wide. This sturdily woven cloth today would be a "second" since the various batches of yarn were not matched for color and texture, and frequently the weave-pattern from one day's work was not carefully blended into the next. It was hand woven in a three-to-one herringbone twill from fairly heavy yarn made of Near East or Mediterranean-basin flax, and the cloth is in an excellent state of preservation.

On the Shroud are indistinct images of the front and back views of a man. The two views are nearly joined at the head, as if the man's body had been wrapped in the cloth lengthwise, foot to head to foot. Optimum viewing distance is six to ten feet from the Shroud; closer or farther, the images fade out completely. Apart from being indistinct, the body images are, in an undefinable sense, "not natural." They are of a faint sepia color (light tan) on the off-white, yellowing old cloth.

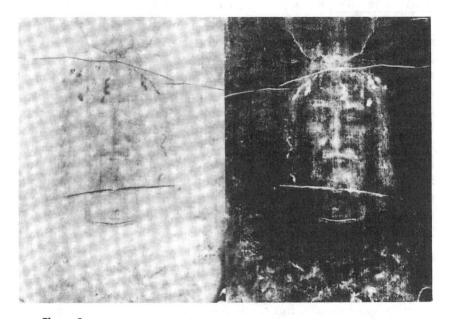

Figure 2.
The Shroud Face, positive (left) and negative. The horizontal streaks near the top and bottom are creases in the cloth. The blood rivulets are very noticeable, especially the one on the eyebrow. The full meaning of photographic negativity reversal can be observed: Usual negatives have a flatness that can be observed in the Shroud images as they look to the naked eye; however, a photographic negative of the Shroud shows gradations of tone, giving the body depth and contour as in a positive print—-these qualities that we call a "photographic likeness." *(Courtesy Holy Shroud Guild)*

Superimposed on these body images are darker markings resembling bloodstains, that are brownish red in color. These "bloodstains" are significantly seen at the wrists and feet, which exactly correspond to the blood stigmata of a classical Roman crucifixion. There also appear to be wounds covering the top of the head, the face, and one side of the body as well as several dozen smaller wounds on the back, all of which dramatically conform to the biblical description of Jesus' wounds. On the back, or dorsal, view, a narrow configuration extends for some eight or ten inches from the long hair of the head to a point midway between the shoulder blades. Some experts feel this may be a pigtail or ponytail hairstyle, as if the hair was caught and tied at the base of the skull—a common hairstyle among Jewish males in Palestine during Jesus' time. The Man's beard seems to show the twin points of the Nazarene style of that day.

In 1453 the Shroud was purchased by the Duke of Savoy, and the Savoy family owned it thereafter until 1983. The Savoys ultimately ruled over all of Italy, which was unified in the nineteenth century. Umberto II was deposed as king of Italy in June 1946 and lived in exile in Portugal until his death in 1983. He was titular head of the House of Savoy during his lifetime and owner of the Shroud, and regularly consulted with the archbishop of Turin, who was the Shroud's custodian. By his will, Umberto gave the Shroud to the pope of the Roman Catholic Church and his successors; the bequest was accepted by Vatican announcement of October 18, 1983. On February 7, 1984, the Vatican secretary of state announced that under the terms of Umberto's will, the Shroud was to remain in Turin, and that the archbishop of Turin would be the pope's personal representative for all future Shroud matters.

Throughout the known history of the Shroud its owners have always assumed (or known?) that this was the burial cloth that wrapped Jesus, and therefore it has been highly revered and closely protected. In Turin, it is now housed in the Cathedral of St. John the Baptist, in a special vault (reliquary).

For security reasons largely, there have been few public exhibitions of the Shroud in recent centuries. In this century it was hung for public display only in 1931, 1933, 1978, and 1998. In the nineteenth century

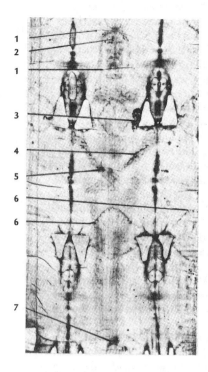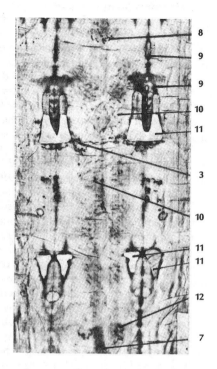

Figure 3.
Frontal (left) and dorsal views of the images on the Shroud, annotated. The photographer, Giuseppi Enrie (1931), did not get the extremities of the Shroud in his picture—particularly, all of the feet are not shown in the frontal view. *(Courtesy Holy Shroud Guild)*

1. Creases in the cloth
2. Rivulets of blood from thorn wounds on the forehead
3. Blood from the lance thrust
4. Blood flows down the arm from the wrist
5. Blood from the nail wound in the wrist
6. Waterstains
7. Blood from the wound on the right foot

8. Blood from extensive scalp wounds where contact with the cross mashed the cap of thorns into the flesh
9. Burn marks
10. Scourge marks from the metal flagra
11. Patches
12. Blood from the wound on the left foot

it was displayed publicly just five times. New exhibitions have been scheduled for 2000 and beyond.

When the Shroud was exhibited in 1898, a photographer, Secondo Pia, was authorized to record the vague and bizarre-looking stains on the cloth, which seemed to represent the front and back views of a human body. (He used glass plates 51 cm. by 63 cm., approximately 22 feet 2 inches by 25 feet 2 inches.) On May 28, 1898, when Pia looked at his wet negatives, he was shocked to discover a truly "natural" picture of a powerfully built, bearded man—the Shroud itself was a *negative;* Pia's "negative" was a photographic *positive.*

Photographic negativity simply means that the shades of light and dark are reversed, and rights and lefts are reversed. So, the Shroud is easily the world's oldest photograph, as well as being an archaeological artifact. Most of our knowledge about the Shroud has come as a result of the technique of photography and the photographic skills of just a few men: first Secondo Pia; next Giuseppi Enrie in 1931; then, G. B. Judica-Cordiglia in 1973; and, in 1978, there was Vernon D. Miller and a few associates.

The invention and development of photography was a *process* covering about a hundred years. Photographic negativity and positive printing were developed in 1816–22 by French physicist Joseph Niepce. He formed a partnership in 1829 with Louis Daguerre, but had died by the time the daguerreotype was promoted, beginning about 1840. Englishmen William Fox and John Herschel as well as Americans John Draper and Samuel Morse experimented with the process in the late 1830s, but only limited subject matter could feasibly be photographed under ideal conditions, and a half-hour exposure was usually required. F. S. Archer is credited with first making the process praticable in 1851. Despite great difficulties vis-à-vis the necessary on-the-spot darkroom facilities, Matthew Brady and assistants photographed thousands of Civil War scenes (1861–65). In 1888, Eastman introduced roll film. The ultimate developments in standard photography came in the 1930s, though improvements are still in process today.

Although an amateur, Secondo Pia was an enthusiastic and devoted photographer, who began an intense study of photography in the early

1870s. Nonetheless, according to my sources, photography was still in a primitive state in northern Italy at that time, and learning the techniques was no simple task; there were no schools or teachers for this skill, and professional photographers (who were most rare) would not willingly divulge their knowledge to a potential competitor. Pia had to buy equipment and manuals from a distance (mostly from France) and teach himself. Although he was a lawyer by profession, he also had his own photographic studio in Turin and in the period 1875–1900 established himself as the premier photographer of the area. Note that nevertheless he was still using glass plates in 1898. Well known in the city, it was only his status and reputation that overcame the Church's initial reluctance when he obtained approval for his proposal to photograph the Shroud Image. In Turin, in 1898, photography was a novelty and by no means an established and developed technique. Also, indoor photography (in the cathedral) presented special lighting problems. Electricity was available in the cathedral but not in most of the city, and Pia spent weeks experimenting in a loaned library to prepare to photograph the Shroud with electricity.

Might this be the cloth in which Joseph of Arimathea and Nicodemus wrapped Jesus of Nazareth as they put him in the tomb? Some churchmen, and now some world-famous scientists and historians, think so. Adam J. Otterbein's interest in the Shroud began in 1938 while he was a student of Reverend Wuenschel at Mount St. Alphonsus Seminary in Esopus, New York.[1] In 1951, Catholic clergymen Adam Otterbein, Edward Wuenschel, Peter Rinaldi, and William Barry formed the Holy Shroud Guild, which has served as the American focus for Shroud studies and the dissemination of information to the public about the Shroud.[2] This matches the European stimulus and informational focus maintained by the International Center of Sindonology in Turin (address in note 5 of chapter 9).

The year 1978 was the four hundredth anniversary of the Shroud's arrival in Turin, and in the fall of 1978 the Shroud was hung for public display in the cathedral at Turin for the third time in the twentieth century. Three and a third million people filed by to look at it. Groups of about a hundred at a time were admitted to the Shroud, where they

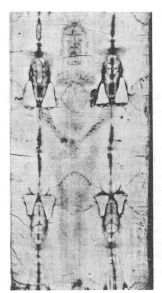 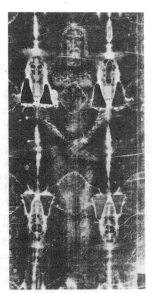

Figure 4.
The frontal view, positive (left) and negative. The longitudinal distractions on each side of the body image are burn marks and patches resulting from the 1532 fire, but only the shoulders and elbows were obliterated. *(Courtesy Holy Shroud Guild)*

Figure 5.
The cloth of the Shroud, magnified, showing the three-to-one herringbone twill weave. Handweaving irregularities and the failure to match adjacent lots of thread or yarn are easily seen. The dark marks are bloodstains. *(Courtesy Centro Internazionale della Sindone of Turin)*

were allowed a minute and a half with the relic. This exposition, August 26–October 8, was the longest ever held, forty-three days.

The Shroud of Turin Research Project (STURP)

As soon as the exposition closed on October 8, scientists, technicians, and Church authorities quickly moved the Shroud into a hall of the adjoining Savoy palace. There, in the palace hall, expensive and highly sophisticated scientific equipment had been set up by the American scientists in readiness for a concentrated study of the Shroud, which began immediately and continued around the clock for five days, concluding Friday night, October 13.

This was the first opportunity for American scientists to examine the Shroud. They had borrowed pieces of fabulous equipment, raised funds to finance the project, came at their own expense, and donated their time. They were under the nominal leadership of Dr. John P. Jackson, who was then on the faculty of the U.S. Air Force Academy and coleader of the Shroud of Turin Research Project (STURP), along with Dr. Eric J. Jumper. Once Church approval was given to the study, Church officials gave their cooperation unstintingly to the scientists. Scientific comment was free and uncensored; no Church official saw any paper or article prior to publication.

The body images on the Shroud the STURP team examined lie within a width of about twenty-three inches (the widest part is elbow-to-elbow since the hands are crossed at the pelvic area), leaving an unmarked border of ten inches on each side. These measurements are important when looking at a picture of the Shroud, because the most prominent visual characteristics are a series of burn and repair marks in longitudinal lines just outside the body images. These charred, burned, and scorched areas were caused by a fire in 1532. The worst damage was repaired by patches and darns. Most of the patches are light brown, though a few are white. The patching cloth is of a linen "square weave"—not herringbone—known as "Holland cloth" (the same as the backing on the Shroud), which is a linen shirting originally made in the Netherlands.

Thus, the row of damaged and patched areas down each side of the body are mostly much darker (and consequently more noticeable) than the body images of the light sepia color. Only the tips of the elbows and points of the shoulders of the body images are obliterated by the damage. At the time of the fire, the Shroud was folded (rather than rolled, as today) and the long longitudinal folds on each side of the body were the parts exposed to the melting silver from its casket. Also prominent are the water stains resulting from efforts to put out the smoldering fire.

In 1532, at the time of the fire, the Shroud was kept in a special chapel of a Savoy castle in the town of Chambery in southeastern France. For storage in its silver casket, the sides of the Shroud were folded in to the center and the length was folded on itself, making four layers about two feet by seven feet. Next it was folded in thirds, resulting in twelve layers about two feet square, and probably less than two feet deep.

The scientists continued to evaluate the data collected in those five days in October 1978, but many significant findings surfaced before the STURP team left Turin. We now know that the bloodstains, water stains, and charred and scorched areas did color the cloth quite deeply, sometimes completely through the cloth. The suspected bloodstains seeped into the threads of the cloth, and optical spectrophotometry and microchemical analysis confirmed that they do in fact contain traces of iron and hemoglobin as found in human blood. The scientists found that body images *did not penetrate* the linen. Extensive, highly sophisticated microchemical tests detected no pigment, pigment binders, or other foreign substances to a weight of less than millionths of a gram, thus totally demolishing any claim that paint had been used to create the image on the Shroud. It is a surface image that amounts to a darkening only of the top two or three fibrils of the crown (outside or top) of the thread. There was no seeping into the individual threads.

The phenomena of the body images seems to have been created by an "image-forming process," and the distance between the Shroud and the Man relates to tightness and darkness of the image; contact between Shroud and skin was not itself a significant factor in the image-making phenomena. The scientists are now certain that the body images were not formed by human art or artifice, nor by known natural means.

The Shroud Mystery

How were the images of the Man on the Shroud made, and when?
Who created the images? Was it nature? God? Jesus? The Christ Spirit?
A clever forger? The coins on the eyes of the Man of the Shroud. Can
they be dated? Can computers make a full, three-dimensional statue
from the images on the Shroud? Do the Shroud images match biblical
data? Historical data? Have artists known about the Shroud during the
"silent centuries"? Answers to these and many more important questions will be given in the following chapters. For the scientific-minded,
they will be as rigorous and objective as space-age science can provide.
For the religious-minded, they will be compatible with faith. For the
curious and undecided, they will provide much food for thought. But
in the end, for many there may still be an unanswered question—a
mystery that is central to Christian belief.

For the complete story of this fascinating and unique relic, we must
start back in A.D. 33 in Palestine. Where history leaves off—as it sometimes does—we will consult tradition, and when tradition is lacking we
will use logic and speculation. The seeming weakness of that chronology now seems very substantially overcome by the scientific findings to
be described in later chapters.

Until 2004, the chronology covers about 1,971 years. But only
during the last 647 years (since 1357) has there been open and continuously established custody to prove an uninterrupted history of the
Shroud. From 33 to 1357, its history is more conjectural. The Shroud
is referred to in both Church writings and secular literature going back
to the first century, and a sprinkling of Christians around the world,
mostly Roman Catholics, have continuously venerated it. But this early
reverence for the Shroud, based mainly on its legendary status, is based
on their faith—faith that it is indeed the burial cloth of the one they
call Lord, Jesus of Nazareth.

The Shroud of Turin is clearly the most important Christian relic,
the most exhaustively examined, the most nearly authenticated, and
yet the most controversial of religious relics.

TWO

EARLY HISTORY AND THE UNCERTAIN YEARS

SCIENTIFIC DATA from the study of the Shroud of Turin seem to make the Man on the Shroud a "perfect fit" for Jesus of Nazareth; certainly, no data are inconsistent with such a conclusion. Yet, legerdemain and deceit have become so common in our age that skepticism is almost an essential attitude, gullibility almost a sin. And, much as the faithful would like to believe in the Shroud, they are reluctant to risk believing in a fraud. A historic continuity must be demonstrated—like a perfect "chain of title." Forty-one years ago the idea of a perfect chain of title seemed an impossibility. In the last quarter of the twentieth century, however, the contributions of several researchers have changed matters significantly. The data and evaluations of British historian Ian Wilson in his *Shroud of Turin* and of American historian Daniel Scavone have been especially helpful in bringing certainty to those uncertain years of the Shroud's existence. However, a number of sources have been drawn on for this book.

We still must use reason and imaginative (though cautious) conjecture to fill in some of the blanks. The Easter morning visits of Jesus' followers to the Gareb Hill tomb owned by Joseph of Arimathea, as recounted in the Gospels, give us some clues. All four Gospels note that Mary Magdalene went into the tomb, perhaps accompanied by other women. The Gospels of Luke and John tell of Simon Peter entering the tomb, and the Gospel of John adds the "beloved disciple" as one who also entered. The two latter accounts make special and unusual comments about the observations of burial cloths. The descriptive words used are unclear and cryptic, and there are seeming inconsistencies among the accounts, but we can at least say that the cloths were especially observed and that something about them was powerfully compelling. Luke says that Peter "beheld the linen cloths laid by them-selves and departed, wondering in himself." In the Gospel of John it is reported that the beloved disciple "saw the linen clothes lying; yet went he not in. Then cometh Simon Peter following him, and went into the sepulchre, and seeth the linen clothes lie, and the napkin that was about his head, not lying with the linen clothes, but wrapped together in a place by itself. Then went in also that other disciple, which came first to the sepulchre, and he saw, and believed."

These passages will be considered in greater depth in chapter 5, but note that repeated and special emphasis is made in these two accounts about the cloths as if they were most unusual and very significant—it is stated that Peter "departed, wondering in himself," while the other dis-ciple "saw, and believed." Surely there was something very special about the cloth—possibly in the way it was lying and possibly in something visible on the cloth, or both. A recorded fact is that Braulio, bishop of Saragossa, Spain, from 635 to 651, in an Easter liturgy, used these cryptic words: "Peter ran…to the tomb and looked at the *recent traces on the linens* of the dead and risen man" (emphasis added). Because of the years of Braulio's bishopric, it is fair to speculate that he was refer-encing the Face-cloth (Sudarium) of Oviedo, Spain, on which (we now know) the bloodstains match perfectly with those on the Shroud of Turin (see chapter 11 for details).

Numerous stories have survived from those early years that point to the saving of the Shroud. Most are quite fanciful, and all we can really glean from them is the hint that the Shroud was saved and the narra-tor felt that an explanation was needed. For instance, the *Gospel of the Hebrews*, written sometime after 100, was subsequently lost; but it was in existence during the life of Saint Jerome (347–420), who was the principal translator of the Vulgate edition of the Bible. Jerome quoted from it that after Jesus' Resurrection—but before he appeared to his brother James—Jesus gave his sindon (shroud) to "the servant of the priest." The meaning of that phrase is too obscure to be helpful. Never-theless, the context of Jerome's quotation leaves no doubt that Jerome believed there was sound evidence for the reality of the preservation of this relic—but no image on it was mentioned. In another tradition, it was the angel at the tomb who had the foresight to hand the Shroud to Mary Magdalene for preservation. By another account, the fourth-century apostle Saint Nino, who had been raised in Jerusalem, reported that the common belief there during her youth was that Pilate's wife had given the Shroud to Saint Luke. In the year 120, Saint Braulio of Seville, Spain, wrote of the Shroud as a well-known relic at that time.

In any event, the certainty of Jesus' death Friday afternoon, his absence from the tomb Sunday morning, the declaration of the angel at the tomb, and the appearances of the risen leader that day would have heightened the excitement and hope of his followers, long before there was under-standing. In such an atmosphere, would it not have been quite likely, even natural, for one of the disciples or one of the women to have taken the cloths? Or for Joseph of Arimathea, who owned the tomb and had bought the Shroud? If for no other reason, to preclude so intimate an item as the Shroud from coming into the hands of the soldiers (who had just fled their guard duty, and were soon to return to the tomb)—the same soldiers who two days previously had divided Jesus' clothing amongst themselves.

If the shroud ("sindon") was so taken, due to whatever emotion, instinct, or panic-inspired thought, in a few days' time there would have been more sober afterthoughts. In spite of being "Followers of the Way" of Jesus, they still were Jews, and all their neighbors were Jews, raised under the strict Levitican taboos—one of which was that *everything* touching a corpse was ritually "unclean" and must be destroyed. In such circum-stances, it would be natural that the Shroud's existence would be kept a deep secret probably known only to a few, that the Shroud would be carefully concealed, and that it would not be mentioned in any records.

The above is based on inference and conjecture, but the next stage of the story has more substance. There is today in southern Anatolian Turkey a small, sleepy town called Urfa, doubtless hardly known even in Ankara or Istanbul. In Jesus' day it was the semi-independent city-state of Edessa, totally outside the Roman Empire and with allegiance to the kingdom of Parthia, whose capital was Ctesiphon on the Tigris River, far to the east. Prosperous Edessa, astride a major east-west caravan route, was ruled by King Abgar V from 13 to 50. Our best account of Abgar's story comes from Bishop Eusebius of Caesarea, who wrote his famous *History of the Church* about 325. Eusebius says he got the story by his own translation of Edessa archives from the Syriac into Greek.

Abgar, we are told, was suffering from an incurable disease. It may have been rheumatoid arthritis, plus leprosy, or possibly cancer. Having heard of the many healing miracles performed by Jesus, he sent a messenger to Jerusalem to search out Jesus and deliver a letter inviting him to come to Edessa and heal the king. Eusebius quotes the letter in full, and it includes these lines: "In my thoughts I have arrived at two possible conclusions, that either you are God and have come down from heaven to achieve these things, or you do these things because you are the Son of God.... I have heard that the Jews murmur against you and wish to do you harm. My city is quite small, but it is honorable, and there is a place in it for both of us."

Eusebius then quotes the letter of reply from Jesus:

> Blessed are you with your faith in me, although you have not seen me. Indeed, it has been written of me that those who saw me would not believe in me, so that those who have not seen me would have faith and life. With regard to what you have written, that I should come to you, it is necessary for me to accomplish here that for which I was sent and, after it has been done, to return to Him who sent me. But when I have been taken up, I will send one of my disciples to you, to cure your illness and to give life to you and yours.

Although Eusebius has always been considered one of the most reliable historians of the period, very little attention was paid to this story until Shroud researchers began examining old records. Tradition has it that, after the Resurrection, through the casting of lots, disciple Thomas, one of "The Twelve," was given responsibility for carrying Jesus' message to the nation of Parthia. From several sources we learn that, knowing of the correspondence between Abgar and Jesus, Thomas assigned Thaddaeus, one of "The Seventy" (see Luke 10:1), to go to Abgar in fulfillment of Jesus' promise and to carry the Shroud for deposit with Abgar for safekeeping. Also, Thaddaeus may have had a relationship with Joseph of Arimathea, who logically may have taken the Shroud from the Tomb.

Our most plausible records and legends for the next eleven and a half centuries concern only a "Face" of Jesus on cloth, but the theories and conclusions of Ian Wilson are logically persuasive, and recent research seems fully to validate them. Wilson presumes that the disciples compromised between their strong resolve to keep the Shroud relic and their fear of being caught possessing unclean burial cloths, by the simple expedient of making a framed picture of the Face only. This they could do by simply folding the length of the Shroud until they had a section three and a half feet wide and about two feet high, showing only the Face; this could be tacked into what we would today call a conventional picture frame, with heavy backing to conceal the folds of extra cloth. Most of the extant replicas dated prior to 1200 have these proportions (eight doublings of the Shroud would expose the Face on a cloth background 43 inches wide by about 21 1/3 inches high).

Some accounts say that when Thaddaeus arrived in Edessa and showed the Face to Abgar, the king was instantly healed. One can be skeptical about much of this story, but it is a fact that Abgar lived until A.D. 50 and that Edessa was known throughout the civilized world of that day as the first Christian city. Edessa had more than three hundred churches and monasteries to which pilgrims came from more than a thousand miles. Edessa was beyond the reach of Roman power, and this was also, doubtless, a drawing factor for Christians to want to worship there. The "Image of Edessa" was well known through all the neighboring countries as an important Christian relic, which was called "the true likeness of Christ" and the "image not made by the hands of man." One of their famous churches was the Church of St. Thomas, in which the body of the disciple was said to be enshrined after being brought back from India. Burials in another church included the bodies of Abgar and Thaddaeus.

If we had only Eusebius to support this link between the Shroud and Edessa, we might be chary of his claims, but there is more. During the 1840s a library of manuscripts was brought out of the desert of Lower Egypt from the Nitrian monastery, and many of them recount the Abgar story in the Syriac language. One such document is *The Doctrine of Addai the Apostle*, and Addai is the Syriac name for Thaddaeus. We also now know about a Byzantine icon in St. Catherine's Monastery on Mount Sinai, painted in 550, which so accurately reflects the facial contours of the Shroud of Turin that Dr. Alan Whanger of Duke University has counted more than forty-six points of congruity when he has superimposed the two faces. The icon depicts Thaddaeus holding the "Image [face] of Edessa" while King Abgar stands by, receiving a healing. (See chapters 11 and 19 for further discussion of the icon and Whanger's technique.)[1]

Christianity thrived in Edessa, and the original church of the city was reputed to be the first building built as a church anywhere in the world—it was later known just as "Old Church." However, this growth was short-lived. When Abgar V died in A.D. 50, about twenty years after declaring Christianity in his kingdom, he was succeeded by his first son, who ruled as Ma'nu V and who was also Christian. Ma'nu V died in 57 and was succeeded by his brother, Ma'nu VI, who had not embraced Christianity and immediately moved to suppress this fast-growing religion. His acts of suppression must not have been too vigorous, for Christianity was still vocal and making its presence felt politically in Edessa nine hundred years later. (Periods of fully sanctioned Christianity did follow in Edessa, the most famous being during the reign of Abgar IX, from 175 to 214.)

We have neither any of the original art nor any copies reflecting the first twenty-five-year period of the Image's fame in Edessa under Abgar V and Ma'nu V. This is partially because most of the Jews, who of course were the earliest Christians in Asia, would have shunned portraits of Jesus because Jewish law prohibited religious images, and, by the end of the first century, people who might have seen him in the flesh would have been dead. However, recent research disclosed that a "face of Jesus" discovered almost 160 years ago in the Roman catacombs matches perfectly with the Shroud face and dates to A.D. 50.

Lack of other copies in art of the Image of Edessa from about A.D. 33 to A.D. 57, and the scant references in written records concerning Jesus' burial clothes or any images on them throughout the entire first ten centuries of the Christian era, cannot be surprising. To the Jewish taboos respecting burial clothes and respecting religious images, and the intermittent Jewish and Roman persecution of all things Christian, must be added the destructiveness of the Eastern Christian iconoclasts during the eighth and ninth centuries as well as the great losses by fire and war, notably the burning of the great libraries of Constantinople

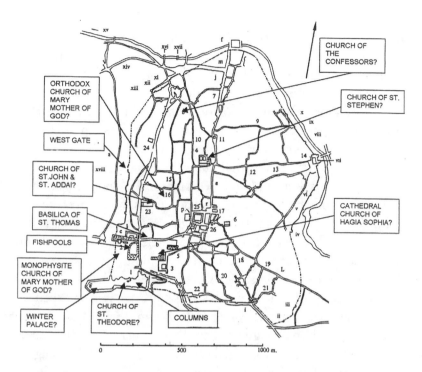

Figure 1.
City map of Edessa, Parthia, mid-first Century A.D., based on data of J. B. Segal *(Edessa, The Blessed City);* courtesy of Ian Wilson. Shows eight Christian churches, and the famous West Gate, above which the hidden Shroud was found in A.D. 525 after the disastrous flood of the River Daison. The Shroud of Jesus (Shroud of Turin?), sometimes known as the Mandylion or Face of Edessa or "achiropoietos" (not made by human hands), was reportedly kept in the Hagia Sophia from A.D. 33 to 57.

by the Crusaders. Those libraries certainly may have contained much evidence pertaining to the Shroud. Also, Alexandria was an important early Christian center whose great libraries suffered major destructions under Theodosius I in 391, and during its fall to the Arabs in 642.

From the year 57 on, nothing is heard of the "Image" for nearly five hundred years. Edessa seems to have maintained a semiautonomous status through the following centuries, but its allegiance shifted from time to time due to pressures from its powerful neighbors. Near the end of the second century, Parthian control of Edessa was replaced by Byzantine.

Constantine, the ruler of the area, had himself embraced Christianity and in 330 had moved his capital to Byzantium, which he renamed Constantinople, rapidly rebuilding it as a major Christian center.[2] There, the Byzantines encouraged religious of all kinds, and Constantine and his mother Helen sought religious relics throughout the empire to fill his new church buildings.

Nature was more of a concern to Edessa than politico-military threats. Situated on the banks of the Daisan River, the city was repeatedly subjected to disastrous floods, the worst ones occurring in 201, 303, 413, and 525. The one in 525 destroyed public buildings, palaces, churches, and much of the city wall, and drowned one-third of the population.

In the course of rebuilding, a secret chamber was found over the West Gate of the city wall. This gate was on high ground and was reputed to be the one through which Thaddaeus had ceremoniously entered with the Image. In the chamber was a chest containing the Image, still in excellent condition. It would seem that it had been sealed into the wall about 57 to protect it from Ma'nu VI's anti-Christian zeal and then was forgotten in later generations. Along with the Image was a tile bearing the same face, which may originally have been displayed over the gate.

By the time of the Image's rediscovery soon after 525, religious ideas had changed, and by the middle of the sixth century, strikingly "coincidental" with the rediscovery of the Image in Edessa, icons, mosaics, and paintings of Jesus' face began to appear throughout all areas of Christian-Byzantine influence.

Since the beginning of the twentieth century, Shroud researchers have noted the strong similarities in religious art between the Shroud face and art from the sixth, seventh, and eighth centuries. (Some specific comparisons will be made in later chapters.) Even a Syriac hymn, written about 569, is noteworthy because, with references to the enshrined Image, the song says "it contains the very essence of God."

One man, Pope Gregory, is probably responsible for the preservation of several excellent reproductions of the Image of Edessa. He had previously been papal legate to Constantinople about 578–82. Art in Italy credited to his prowess as a collector includes the Face in the apse of Sant' Apollinare in Classe, a church in Ravenna completed by 549, and the Face in the apse of the Church of St. John Lateran, Rome (sixth century), known as the face "not made by hands." The Emperor Justinian II (685–711) also felt strongly about the Image, and had it displayed (head and shoulders) on a coin, with his own likeness on the reverse side. (The coin, minted in 690, will be discussed in a later chapter.)

Artists' renderings of the face of Jesus that were created from the sixth to thirteenth centuries seem uniquely to stand out as a group because their commonality hints of a single subject that they copied. These include a 590 icon in St. Catherine's Monastery on Mount Sinai, a fresco of Christ Pantocrator in Daphni, Greece, and the Justinian coin. The "Face of Laon" in a church in Laon, France, is a glazed panel icon painted at Constantinople between 1201 and 1204. It is obviously copied from the Mandylion/Shroud, and its paleo-Slav inscription refers to the source as the "Image of the Lord on cloth." (The Image of Edessa while in Constantinople was known as the "Mandylion," a Byzantine word apparently used only to describe this Image. The word was derived from the Arabic, which was in turn derived from Latin. Literally, it could be taken to mean veil or mantle.) One artwork that definitely was made from the Mandylion because of the full trellis surround (discussed below) is known as Spas Nereditsa (Savior of Neredica) and dated 1199. The painter was of the school of Novgorod and the fresco was located in Moscow. Some paintings of the "Veronica" (discussed in chapter 18) seem copies from the Image/Mandylion.

The icon known as the Face of Laon was sent to Rome in 1249 by Jacques Pantaleon (of Troyes) while in the pontifical service (he became Pope Urban IV in 1261). In the upper corners of the icon are the Greek monograms "IC XC"—using the first and last letter of each word, it is the abbreviation of the Greek words *Ihcuc Xristoc,* Jesus Christ.

Although the Moslems took control of Edessa from the Byzantines in 639, the Christian population was tolerated, and the Christian cathedral of Hagia Sophia, which was built specifically for the protection and preservation of the Image, continued to house and periodically display the Image. During this period, from about 540 to 940 in the artworks throughout Christendom, one fairly common feature of the face of Jesus was a "trellis surround" that covers the width of the cloth, except for a central circle where the face is seen. This trelliswork has often been commented upon by art historians as a sort of hallmark. Such a device makes sense if this was indeed the folded Shroud, but is there a further explanation? Historian Ian Wilson thinks so.

According to Wilson, Thaddaeus's second in command, and successor as head of the Edessa church, was an artist of special abilities named Aggai. Aggai's previous duties had been to make for the king silks, robes, and headdresses, which in the Parthian tradition had been very elaborate. Apparently, upon embracing Christianity, Abgar V abandoned such fancy trappings as "pagan." His second son, Ma'nu VI, sometime after he became king in A.D. 57, demanded of Aggai (now head of the church), "Make me a headdress of gold as you did for my fathers in former times." Aggai refused and was executed. Cloth-of-gold robes and headdresses made for Parthian rulers did sometimes have, we know from pictures, a trellis-like pattern. Accordingly, it is not only reasonable but quite likely that Aggai made the cloth cover with gold trelliswork that was laid over the Image, leaving only the oval opening in the middle for the Face to be seen.

According to Noel Currer-Briggs in his book *Holy Grail and the Shroud of Christ* (ARA Publications, England, 1984), the term "Holy Grail" was in effect a reference to the casket into which the Shroud was folded and fastened, with only the Face visible. However, the term had in fact been coined to describe the grille-like (lattice or trellis) design of the cloth-of-gold overlay, with an oval opening in the middle to show the Face. The words *cratis* (Latin), *greille* (Old French), *grail* (Old English), *grail* (modern English), and *grill* (American-English) are all the same word.

A further speculation, based on logic, is that Ma'nu VI, upon becoming ruler, must have promptly ordered his father's tile-copy of the Image face taken from over the city gate. The artisan carrying out these orders may have been a Christian. Because of the nature and purpose of the plaque, Aggai would have been in attendance; in removing the plaque the workman may have accidentally broken through to a chamber over the gate. We can imagine that at that moment Aggai saw the answer to a problem—he brought out the cloth Image and put it and the tile in the chamber and watched the workman brick-up and seal the relics into the wall.

Sixth-century descriptions of the Image of Edessa referred to it as being "blurred." This compares favorably with direct observations of the Turin Shroud and contrasts with the sharper and more natural character of a photographic negative of the Shroud images. Whether for this reason or for mystical or theological reasons, it was frequently stated in reports from Edessa during the later centuries of the Image's stay there that the Face was too holy for ordinary gaze. Often the congregation was permitted merely to observe the clergy while the latter looked at the Face. This seems also to have been the attitude during its 260-year stay in Constantinople. There were private viewings for dignitaries and artists, and public displays (apparently of the full Shroud) during the months before the fall of the city when Constantinople was practically under siege and the morale of the defenders was of concern.

This restrictive attitude may have been the cause of several unrealistic reports and legends. Another cause could have been the increasing appearance of copies of the Face that were venerated as true relics. For whatever reason, in 670, Arculph, a French bishop, stated that he was present in Jerusalem when the "Lord's Shroud" was taken from a shrine and shown to a multitude of people; he had been allowed to kiss it, he said. In the eighth century, Saint John Damascene (in nearby Damascus) mentioned the Shroud of Jesus along with a list of other revered relics. Stephen III became pope in 769; a sermon that he preached at about that time (a text of which survives) seems to give validation to a *full shroud* as to the Image of Edessa, saying that the image impressed on the cloth is Jesus' *body*. The sermon continues:

> For the same mediator between God and men...stretched his whole body on a cloth, white as snow, on which the glorious image of the Lord's face and the length of his whole body was so divinely transformed that it was sufficient for those who could not see the Lord bodily in the flesh to see the transfiguration made on the cloth.

Yet, we strongly suspect that the disciple Thomas—and probably Thaddaeus and Aggai—was the last to know that the Image was a full burial shroud with Jesus' image on it, until the full dimensions and character of the cloth were discovered in Constantinople, sometime after its arrival in 944.

The Shroud was in Constantinople from August 15, 944, to April 12,

1204. Some sindonologists believe the discovery that the Face of Edessa, the Mandylion, was in fact a full burial shroud with front and back markings of a complete body on it, did not come until fairly late in this 260-year period. However, quite recently, history professor Dr. Daniel C. Scavone of the University of Southern Indiana has presented rather compelling evidence, based on reevaluation of *ten* documents from the 944–1247 period, that the discovery came within weeks, and perhaps days or hours of the arrival of the Face in Constantinople on August 15, 944. His study also presents strong data to the effect that indeed Abgar had received not just a facial image but a cloth that enabled the viewer to discern the form and stature of Jesus' entire body. And finally, he concludes that the Shroud did indeed leave Constantinople in April 1204, but he traces it as going to Athens, from whence it was sent in 1208 by Othon de La Roche, Latin duke of Athens, to his father, Ponce de La Roche, for custody by the archbishop of Besancon, France, who placed it in the Church there. Moreover, he suggests that it "disappeared" well before 1349, when the church of St. Etienne was struck by lightning and burned down. The "disappearance" will be explained in the next chapter. (Also see "The Shroud of Turin in Constantinople: The Documentary Evidence," by Dr. Daniel C Scavone, *Byzantinishee Zeitschrift,* October 1988.)

The belief and depth of commitment that the Image/Mandylion evoked in that period was so strong that a war was waged for possession of the relic. In the spring of 943, the Byzantine emperor Romanus Lecapenus sent his imperial army, under the command of Gen. John Curcuas, to besiege Edessa for the express purpose of bargaining with the Moslems to deliver the Mandylion under threat of battle. Curcuas offered the emir of Edessa twelve thousand pieces of silver, the release of two hundred Moslem prisoners, the sparing of the city from attack, and a guarantee of permanent immunity—all for delivery of the Mandylion. After discussions in Baghdad until the following summer, the Moslems finally agreed. However, the emperor's designee, the bishop of nearby Samosata, would not accept the Image until two known copies were delivered with it. The Byzantine army withdrew, and the Mandylion, after a short stay in Samosata, was delivered in Constantinople on August 15, 944.[3] At different times, the Mandylion was kept in Constantinople at three locations: the

Church of St. Mary of Blachernae, the Hagia Sophia, and the Chapel of Pharos in the Boucoleon Palace. In passing, it may be noted that when the Mandylion arrived, the emperor's sons were disappointed in it because the Face was so vague and unnatural. Another observer was Constantine Porphyrogenitus, who would shortly succeed as emperor. It was said that his attitude was much different because as an artist he could discern the portrait clearly.

In 945 the emperor Constantine Porphyrogenitus commissioned a special scribe to write a history of the Mandylion. The scribe, anticipating twentieth-century science by a full millennium, wrote that the image was made on the cloth by a "secretion without coloring or painter's art...; it did not consist of earthly colors."

Church records indicate that a special tile with a face on it was brought to Constantinople from Edessa in 968. Crusader Robert de Clari reported seeing the tile bearing the face of Jesus in a chapel of Boucoleon Palace during the years 1203–4; the tile was never again seen after the Fourth Crusade sack of Constantinople in 1204.

Numerous Church records and reports of the emperor's visitors attest to the presence of the Mandylion in Constantinople from 944 to 1204, and Scavone cites reevaluation of a Vatican manuscript (Codex Vaticanus Graecus 511), disclosing in 1986 that one Gregory delivered a sermon in Constantinople on August 16, 944, the day after the arrival of the Mandylion, in which he clearly described the *full body image* on the cloth. A Latin codex of about 1130 (presently in the Vatican Library) records a text of Jesus' message to Abgar, saying, "I sent you a cloth on which the image not only of my face but of my whole body has been divinely transformed." (Although highly significant since it speaks of a full-body image, of course, the codex presents us a further anomaly by suggesting that Jesus sends a message to Abgar *after* being in the tomb.) William of Tyre, a twelfth-century historian, records that he accompanied the king of Jerusalem on his visit to Constantinople in 1171, where the emperor Manuel I Comnenus showed his visitors *"the most precious evidence of the Passion of our Lord Jesus Christ, that is the cross, nails, lance, sponge, reed, crown of thorns, sindon, and sandals..."* (emphasis added). In 1201, Nicholas Mesarites, keeper of the relic collection for the emperor, stated that the collection included Jesus' "sindon with the burial linens...[which was] defying decay because it wrapped the mysterious naked dead body after the Passion."

There seems to be no doubt by 1203–4 that a full shroud was in the emperor's relic trove, because the history written by crusader Robert de Clari clearly describes a full sindon with a full image on it.

The connection that Ian Wilson postulates between the Image/Mandylion and the Shroud, by the technique of a full-folded shroud hidden by the picture frame and its backing, has been criticized by some researchers as being too far-fetched. But work by scientist John Jackson may have validated Wilson's theory. Using sharper photographs of the Shroud taken in 1978, Jackson sees visible creases of an eightfold pattern that fits such a theory exactly.

Wilson's other theory, which I call "The Knights Templar Connection," will be discussed in the next chapter, in bridging the Shroud's missing years of 1204 to 1357. Emperor Baldwin II (died 1273) of Constantinople, the last "Latin emperor," was so impoverished that he did sell many religious relics to King Louis of France (a relative), including one listed as the "holy towel." However, the recorded price indicates that this was a minor relic—it could have been a painted copy of the Mandylion face, of which there were many. The true Shroud would have brought a king's ransom and would have made Baldwin solvent—if not bankrupting Louis.

Regardless of how, when, and why the Image/Mandylion came to Edessa, it seems repeatedly documented and true beyond question that the Face was in existence in Edessa from about 33 until 944. Also, it seems certain that the full Shroud was in Constantinople, 944 to 1204.

Valuable as ancient records are, we must be chary of descriptions that observers in Edessa, Jerusalem, Constantinople, and Lirey have given of what they think they are looking at and of how they think it was made. Similarly, descriptions in inventories of treasury relics can be suspect. Moreover, inventories can be doubted as to what items are included or excluded, since the curator may have been ordered by his employer to state it as he did (governmental inventories may be made for an ulterior reason, even today). In the same vein, we cannot always assume the genuineness of relics pawned, sold, or given to monarchs.

THREE

THE ATHENS/BESANCON/KNIGHTS TEMPLAR CONNECTION

ISTORIANS AND religionists can understand and accept the secrecy about the Shroud during most of the 910 years from the crucifixion (A.D. 33) until the Shroud's probable arrival in Constantinople on August 15, 944, as secrecy would have been essential for the Shroud to survive. For nearly three hundred years, until about 313, Christians were persecuted because of their faith, and thousands were killed by the Roman authorities throughout the Mediterranean world. At the same time, this loose confederation of Christian churches was rocked and repeatedly threatened by internal schism, so that frequently Christian could not trust Christian. As early as 57, the apostle Paul had to remonstrate sharply with his much-beloved congregation in Corinth (I Cor. 1:13) because it had split into factions under separate leaders.

In 309 the Roman emperor Galerius stated that Christianity would be tolerated throughout the empire. This was confirmed in 313 through the Edict of Milan by the emperor Constantine, who, in 312, had become joint emperor with Licinius. Constantine became sole ruler in 324. His synod at Arles in 314 and council at Nicaea in 325 established his primacy in Church affairs, so that Christianity, in the process, became the official state religion. (During the rule of Constantine, the practice of crucifixion was abolished.)

In 330, Constantine moved his capital from Rome to Byzantium, which he rebuilt and renamed Constantinople. With his mother Helen, he set out to make the city not only a New Rome for administration of the empire, but especially to make the capital Christian, which had been an impossibility in Rome. They scoured the empire for sacred relics (especially from Jerusalem) and riches of every sort, until every city complained that they were being stripped for the adornment of Constantinople. The "unified" Roman Empire, but with two capitals, continued (at least in theory) for sixty-five years until 395, when the empire's division into East and West became permanent.

As the Roman Empire, divided and weakening from the early fourth century onward, began to lose control of the Near East, various groups, including the Moslems, the Egyptians, and the Seljuk Turks, began moving into the power vacuum. Pilgrimages to the Holy Land became more risky. Finally Jerusalem was taken by the caliph Omar in the early seventh century while Moslem generals were making conquests far and wide, including successes in Persia and in Syria at the back door of Constantinople. As if that were not bad enough, the Seljuk Turks began challenging Constantinople directly. In 1071 they defeated the Byzantine emperor Romanus IV in a battle at Manzikert, Armenia, resulting in the empire's loss of most of Asia Minor. Shortly thereafter, emperor Alexius I appealed to the West for aid.

Thus began the series of wars known as the Crusades, ten in number, spanning the years 1095 to 1291, that were authorized by the popes and undertaken by European Christians, often led by kings and other nobles. The Crusades were ostensibly to make safe the routes of pilgrimage to the Holy Land and the environs of Jerusalem, but they ultimately attempted conquest of much of the Near East and included looting for profit. (The popularity of a religious crusade and the romance of the idea of knighthood resulted in a number of other "crusades" within Europe itself that were accorded papal authorization for a number of purposes.)

Constantinople continued to be regarded nominally as a Christian capital into the early years of the thirteenth century, when Pope Innocent III authorized the Fourth Crusade of Palestine, under the leadership of Marquis Boniface de Montferrat of north Italy. However, that Crusade violated its instructions, never got near Palestine, and embroiled itself in regional politics. In order to install its own man, Alexius IV, as emperor, the Crusade besieged Constantinople. The Crusaders breached the city wall, overran, and sacked the city on

April 10–12, 1204, and looted it in three days as thoroughly as could be imagined.

Three disastrous fires raged during this brief period. No restraint was placed on the crusaders during those three days, and large amounts of jewelry and artwork disappeared into the hands of individual crusaders; however, thereafter some of the larger and more obvious items were seized from them by their leaders. The booty included considerable money, and the leaders set aside one hundred thousand silver marks, which were divided among the Crusaders. Many valuable items were melted down for their base metal, and jewels were ripped from their settings. Venice and many major cities of Europe today display art from the 1204 rape of Christian Constantinople.

The Byzantine Empire, centered in Constantinople, had been a bastion of Christendom for 900 years. After its fall in 1204, the succeeding "Latin Empire" lasted but 57 years. One result was that the schism between Orthodox and Roman churches deepened thereafter. Also, with the Byzantine power destroyed, succeeding centuries saw Eastern and Southeastern Europe overrun by Turkish/Moslem armies and by the Mongol hordes, vestiges of which are still troublesome to this day. (A careful recapitulation of these events is reported in *The Great Betrayal of the Fourth Crusade,* by Ernle Bradford, Dorset Press, 1967.)

Clear, written accounts of a *full* burial shroud related to the passion of Jesus appeared in the years 1201–3. The first was a statement by a Greek, Nicholas Mesarites, who was keeper of the emperor's relic collection in the Pharos Chapel of Boucoleon Palace in Constantinople. In 1201, during a palace revolution, he had to defend the chapel against a mob. In that connection, he wrote:

> In this chapel Christ rises again, and the sindon with the burial linens is the clear proof…still smelling fragrant of myrrh, defying decay, because it wrapped the mysterious, naked dead body after the Passion….

The use of the word "sindon" is very significant, for it probably always meant a full burial shroud that wraps the body and would not have been confused in those days with a chin-strap napkin or other burial linen.

The second eyewitness account came from French crusader Robert de Clari (1170–1216), a Picard "chevalier" of modest means who followed his liege lord, Pierre of Amiens (a town north of Paris), one of the leaders of the Fourth Crusade. Robert returned to Picardy in 1205 and gave some of his booty to the Benedictine abbey of Corbie, near Amiens. He wrote or dictated his "History of Those Who Conquered Constantinople," covering principally the years 1198–1205, probably with the encouragement of the monks at Corbie. In his *Chronicles* he described his daily visits in Constantinople while the army, camped outside the walls, awaited its promised payment for deposing Alexius III and seating his nephew, Alexius IV, on the throne of Constantinople. Robert wrote specifically of the period 1203–4. His text was written in Old French, which was in use until about 1650, and included these lines:

> There was another church which was called My Lady Saint Mary of Blachernae, where there was the SYDOINES in which Our Lord had been wrapped, which every Friday, raised itself upright, so that one could see the form of our Lord on it, and no one, either Greek or French, ever knew what became of this SYDOINES when the city was taken.

It was said to have been hung on display for the purpose of strengthening the people's resolve to resist the siege, since the Blachernae Palace was a rallying place for the citizens of Constantinople in times of distress.

Translators have caused controversy over the French word *figure,* rendered as "form," above. Dr. Peter Dembowski points out that in Old French, *figure* can be freely and properly translated thus: "One could see clearly the 'form,' or 'outline,' of the 'body' of Our Lord"—only after 1650 could it have meant "face." Also, *sydoines,* he notes, is a masculine singular noun, meaning sindon, from the Greek for "shroud." The sometime translation as sudarium or "napkin" is totally in error.

Dr. Peter Dembowski, whose expertise is cited above, has written a book (in French) on the Chronicle of Robert de Clari. Dembowski emphasizes that Robert may have been a humble and simple knight, but he was certainly not childish or naive, as others have classed him. Rather, Robert had undeniable literary and historiographical pretensions and was an excellent and "natural" storyteller.[1]

Dembowski's translation of the paragraph from de Clari's chronicle, and especially of the word *figure,* is fully supported by Dr. Raymond Andes, another expert in Old French.[2]

The French Crusaders took Constantinople twice. The first time (July 1203) they assisted the young Alexius IV in gaining the throne. The "Latins" lived both outside and inside the city walls for several months in 1203, and Robert doubtless saw the Shroud hanging full length many times. Later that year the French were expelled by an "anti-Latin" coup by Murzuphlus Ducas who, having assassinated Alexius IV, proclaimed himself Alexius V. The second assault on the city by the Crusaders was in April 1204. Robert's phrase, "when the city was taken," obviously refers to the second assault.

The quotation (above) from Robert de Clari's account concludes that the statement, "and no one, either Greek or French, ever knew what became of this SYDOINES when the city was taken." Doubtless, that was true as to rank-and-file Crusaders, but the handful of leaders who divided the major spoils between themselves knew. The three principal ones were Dandolo, Baldwin, and Boniface.

The doge of Venice, Enrico Dandalo, who had provided 450 ships (including 50 galleys) and financing for this Crusade, got the "lion's share." He received fifty thousand silver marks for financing the Crusade, specific islands, ports, and harbors in the Ionian and Aegean Seas and in the Levant, plus Crete, and three-eighths of the city of Constantinople. The doge lived only until 1205.

Squabbling and negotiation and pressures for two or three months finally resulted in Baldwin, earl of Flanders (French), being elected the new emperor of Constantinople (crowned on May 16), with his realm to include most of Asia Minor and Greece as far south as Mount Olympus. When he died the following year (as a result of unsuccessful fighting against a combined Greek and Bulgarian force), he was succeeded by his brother, Henri of Hainault, as emperor. Boniface, marquis of Montferrat (north Italy), was awarded central and eastern Greece, including Athens, Thessalonica, Salonica, and part of Asia Minor. The last "Greek" emperor of Constantinople, Isaac, had died in January 1204, and his widow Margaret, sister of the king of Hungary, had stayed on in the Boucoleon Palace with the emperor's wealth, including the Shroud of Edessa and other great Byzantine relics and treasures. The first week in May, Boniface married the widow, who took the name Mary-Margaret.

After Baldwin was crowned, Boniface and Mary-Margaret promptly left the city for their territory of Thessalonica, together with their entourage, which included Othon de la Roche, a Burgundian, who, during the last weeks of the siege and occupation, had been commander of the military district where the Shroud of Jesus was kept. Thereafter, by October 1204, Othon had become lord of Athens, and two extant documents written in 1205 establish that the Shroud was then in Athens (see Shroud Symposium reports from Daniel C. Scavone, 1992–96).

In 1208 the documents in Besancon (Champagne Province, France), state that Ponce de La Roche had then received the Shroud from his son, Othon, in Athens, which Ponce delivered to Archbishop Amedee de Tramelay for safekeeping in the Church of St. Etienne. After some twenty-five years in Athens, Othon returned to his home in Burgundy (circa 1230), where he died in 1234. The Church of St. Etienne was totally destroyed by fire in 1349.

But, in about 1343, Othon's great-great-grand-daughter, Jeanne de Vergy, went from Besancon to Lirey, where she married Geoffrey de Charny in 1352. She presumably took the Shroud with her to Lirey, for it was her dowry and, beginning in 1357, she and Geoffrey jointly exhibited the full Shroud to huge crowds for several weeks. Medallions of that exhibition were sold as souvenirs. The Lirey church had been built by Geoffrey with papal authority and financial support from King Philip VI, apparently for the purpose of housing the Shroud for the exhibition.

The Shroud's sojourn in Besancon, 1208 to 1343, spawned a dramatic sidelight involving the Knights Templar, a military/religious order created by papal authority for service in the Crusades. To understand the very involved legal/political activities of 1306–14 and the relevant religious activity of the Templars during the preceding century (1208 to 1306), it will be well to review the organization's history.

Originally calling themselves the Knights of the Temple of Solomon, the Knights Templar was formed in the Champagne Province in about 1118 by Hugh de Payens and others, with the purely military function of protecting pilgrims going to and from the Holy Land. They were one of several great orders (the Knights Hospitalers and the Teutonic Knights were others) that arose out of the Crusades. The Knights Templar fought with distinction in the Second Crusade (1147–49) and all later ones. Soon the Templars became one of the most powerful organizations in Europe: They appointed their own bishops; held monastic privilege responsible only to the pope; and maintained their headquarters for a considerable time in Jerusalem. The combination of special privileges and chivalrous adventure attracted many nobles to membership and attracted lavish gifts and powerful friends because they combined the two great passions of the Middle Ages—religious fervor and military prowess. The Templars were very prominent in the forces of the Fourth Crusade at Constantinople, which was led mostly by French, Flemish, and Italian nobles.

From 1187 to 1291 the Templars operated from Acre (a port in northern Israel) and then retreated to the island of Cyprus. At this time the Templars became the leading moneylenders of Europe, served as bankers to several kings, and the order became more worldly, more decadent, and more hated and feared. In 1307–8, King Philip IV of France, with the support of Pope Clement V, began arrests, persecutions, and confiscations against the Templars, ostensibly to get financial support for his Flemish war. Many were tortured to extract confessions of performing sacrilegious practices. The question of Templar sacrilege is charged repeatedly during this period but is never specified with certainty. Nonetheless, at ceremonies for Templar initiates, it was said they were required to prostrate themselves before "something" that gave the initiates a momentary vision of God. During the Middle Ages, Templar secrecy was occasionally breached, and a common story involved vague references to a "head" that had an important role in their worship ceremonies. The definitive *History of the Military Order of the Templars*, written by de Puy (Paris, 1713), provides considerable support for the existence of some special image of veneration and of many copies of it for local ceremonies.

At dawn on October 3, 1307, all Templars in France were arrested on orders of the king. A search was made for "the idol," but it could not be found. The leaders, including the last grand master, Jacques de Molay, were tried by ecclesiastic judges. On March 19, 1314, Jacques de Molay and the Templar master of Normandy, Geoffrey de Charnay, were burned at the stake for "heresy."

In the interval between the Templars' arrests and the executions of de Molay and de Charnay, the Church held the Council of Vienne (1311–12), during which the pope dissolved the Templar order by a papal bull. At that time there were more than twenty thousand Templars in Europe, owning vast areas of land and paying no taxes; many were far wealthier than kings. Until the order was abolished, each Templar wore a red cross on a white field; their surcoats were emblazoned with the eight-pointed cross—a badge that guaranteed them immunity wherever they went.

Late in this century, Shroud researchers have apparently evolved part of the explanation for Templar Shroud involvement. In 1185 the Templars acquired a property in Templecombe, southern England, which they used as a recruitment and training center for new members. They had dozens of such centers throughout Europe. In a 1951 storm, the ceiling plaster collapsed in an outbuilding of those Templecombe premises, revealing (behind what had been a false ceiling) a thin wooden panel bearing a painted face in a late medieval style that has since been matched to the Shroud of Turin face. The panel bore hinge-marks and a keyhole, indicating the likelihood that it had served as a lid or cover which, it is supposed, may have concealed one of the many Templar copies-on-cloth of the Face of the Turin Shroud. Testimony at the Templar trial stated that they had copies of a mysterious Face—facilitating their "heresy"—at a large number of their centers. Father Peter M. Rinaldi, in his 1972 book *It Is The Lord*, reports that forty-two copies of the Turin Shroud Face are known in Europe today, many of which may have belonged to the Templars. More recently, art researcher Isabel Piczek has recorded fifty-two proven copies of the Shroud Face.

Thus it seems clear that the trial testimony regarding "worship of a bearded face" at the Templar ceremonies was based on an element of truth, but the Templar leaders, respecting their oaths of secrecy, stood mute at their trial rather than explain that the Faces were copies of what was believed to be a self-portrait made by Jesus at his Resurrection, and thus involved respectful and proper worship and no heresy.

During the Shroud's 135-year stay in Besancon (1208–1343), there would have been ample opportunity for the Templars to have artists make many copies of Jesus' face for their ceremonies (per research of Daniel Scavone).

Some thirty years after the executions of de Molay and de Charnay, Geoffrey de Charny obtained grants from King Philip VI and King John II of France for construction of first a chapel and then a collegiate church at Lirey (near Paris), in which "the Shroud" would be housed and exhibited. After a final grant to Geoffrey's widow in 1356 (the year Geoffrey I died), the church was completed and furnished. A series of exhibitions of the Shroud was held the following year at Lirey, and huge crowds attended.

In 1453, Geoffrey's granddaughter Margaret accepted, in exchange for the Shroud, certain valuable estates of land from the Duke of Savoy, whose seat later was moved to Turin, Italy, and whose family was destined to become the rulers of Italy.

Ian Wilson's explanation for the Shroud's missing 153 years (1204 to 1357) is "the Knights Templar connection." This connection, though logical, depends completely upon inference, for neither public nor private records nor Templar admissions provide any documentary proof. The points that lead to this inference are:

(1) The Mandylion had been known as a "face" (or bust portrait) only, but during the period 1201–4 it was disclosed and exhibited in Constantinople as a full burial sindon—a shroud bearing the image of a man. An intimate circle had known of the Shroud's true nature for some time. Various competing explanations (some very fanciful) had

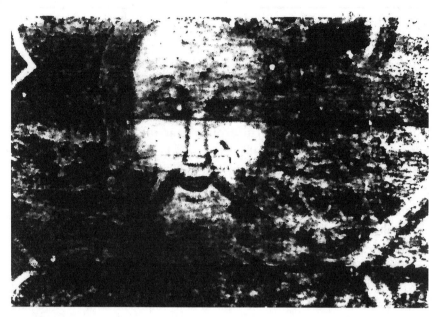

Figure 1.
The Templecombe Face, found in 1952 in southern England—a "match" for the Shroud of Turin Face.

been given from time to time about how the Mandylion was created. However, once the full sindon was seen, with its front and back views of a naked, tortured, and crucified male body, the significance and importance of the Shroud would have been immediately recognized, making it a religious relic beyond all price.

(2) The Templars were prominent—but not leaders—in the Fourth Crusade, participating in the looting of Constantinople. In the weeks preceding the breaching of the city's walls by the crusaders, they had been unwelcome guests roaming the city, and many would have been well aware of the great prize, the Shroud, that had been seen by de Clari and doubtless many others, especially the leaders.

(3) That the Crusaders took fantastic quantities of loot during the sack of the city has been well established, both by eyewitness reports and by careful historians such as Edward Gibbon, who described how the Crusaders' mules and horses were laden with "wrought silver and

gilt carving which they had torn down from the doors and pulpits of the churches." The breach of the city walls had, incidentally, been made not far from the Blachernae area where the Shroud had hung. The Templars had so much booty that a treasury was created to hold it all.

(4) That the Shroud was either hidden or taken during the looting seems likely; Robert de Clari's last comment was, "No one, either Greek or French, ever knew what became of this sydoines after the city was taken." But, of course, someone knew. This might just have been the story the crusader hierarchy wanted believed, so that the Shroud could be quietly diverted.

(5) With the arrival of the Templar treasury at their temple in Paris in 1306, the situation changed drastically. Beginning at this time, rumors were being heard all over Europe about some mysterious object the Templars were said to be hiding and worshiping idolatrously at secret ceremonies. Templar history as written in the mid-nineteenth century by the Frenchman Michelet described a certain "bearded head, which they adored, kissed, and called their Savior." Translations of records of the trial of de Molay and de Charnay refer to an "idol" that they "venerate as God." These are strange statements if the Shroud (or its copies) was not involved, but very understandable if it was. Public whispering and criminal charges of idolatry and heresy brought the Templars down. The Templars were completely destroyed in 1314. All of their possessions that could be found were confiscated by the king of France and by subordinate secular rulers, even though formal Templar regulations provided that in the event of dissolution their assets should go to the Knights Hospitalers.

In 1353, Geoffrey de Charny and, subsequently, his widow (in 1356) quietly though not secretly obtained grants from King Philip VI of France for construction of the church at Lirey for the express purpose of housing and exhibiting the Shroud. It was an entirely different line of kingly succession.[3] Philip IV, who had taxed the clergy as well as harassed the Templars, died the same year (1314) that he ordered de Charnay executed, and in the next fourteen years he was followed in quick succession by Louis X, Philip V, and Charles IV. But this was the end of the main line of Capetian kings of France. With the coronation of Philip VI (who ruled from 1328 to 1350), the house of Valois, a younger branch of the Capetians, commenced. From 1337 to 1453, however, the kings of France were plagued by the so-called Hundred Years' War with England. The English occupied much of France from time to time during these years. John II (John the Good) ruled from 1350 to 1364, and it was he who provided the grants to Geoffrey and later to his widow. John was in England in captivity from 1356 to 1360, with the dauphin, who was later to succeed to the throne as Charles V (1364 to 1380) serving as regent. These latter incidents may explain why it was possible for the local bishop and then the canons of Lirey to make so much trouble for the de Charnys in connection with the Shroud.

Thus, it might seem that the affairs of the de Charnay/Charny families and of the Knights Templar were intertwined with those of the Shroud, and that the appearances and disappearances of the Shroud from 1204 to 1357 fitted exactly with their movements and interests. This scenario does depend entirely upon a series of inferences. Contrariwise, Dr. Scavone's proposal explaining the Shroud's "missing" 153 years (1204 at the fall of Constantinople until its first public exhibition in Lirey in 1357, "the Athens/Besancon scenario") is now supported by the written evidence he has identified to establish its residence for the appropriate years in both cities, and seems to solidly fit all the circumstances.[4]

Two researchers came to approximately the same conclusion as Scavone, but with more tenuous reasoning and no significant date: The Reverends Patrick O'Connell and Charles Carty, in a 1974 booklet[5] suggested that Othon, who had been commander of the military district that included Constantinople's Blachernae Palace where the Shroud was kept, "received it as part of his recompense" and sent it at once (1204) to his father in Besancon. They speculated that at the church fire in 1349 the Shroud was slightly damaged (scientific data cannot accept that claim). They speculate further that in removing it from the burning church it was stolen, but then given to King Philip of France, who gave it to Geoffrey de Charny, and that two years later a copy of the same was obtained without informing the parishioners of the substitution. Finally, they speculated that this copy still exists in a Church of St. Gomaire, Belgium (conversely, we do not know that the Shroud Face copy in Besancon was taken to Paris in 1794 by members of the French Revolution, where it was destroyed).

It has been speculated that the Templar de Charnay was of the immediate family of Geoffrey de Charny and thus provided the supposed ownership link in the Shroud's move from Constantinople to Lirey, but no data have ever been found to support such theory. Moreover, there is no known basis for suggesting that de Charnay could have legitimately acquired the Shroud *in* Constantinople. Also, Scavone's Athens/Besancon scenario involving the de la Roche and de Vergey families, which *is* supported with data, is inconsistent with the Charnay/Charny nexus.

We do know that the de la Roche/de Vergy/de Tramelay families of Besancon were closely related (as per Scavone), and that Jeanne's coat of arms would not have been on the Lirey exhibition medallion unless *she* had a *real* interest in the Shroud. There seems no basis on which de Charnay of Champagne Province could have acquired ownership of the Shroud, but I suggest that he may have had a meaningful involvement in the Shroud saga; because he may have introduced his wealthy neighbor Jeanne de Vergy, to his remote relative Geoffrey de Charny, who was financially restricted but was a favorite of the king, with a brilliant diplomatic and military record.

Although Wilson's "Knights Templar connection" must be dropped in favor of Scavone's "Athens/Besancon scenario," concerning the missing 153 years, Wilson must be given high marks as the first to recognize the "Face of Edessa" and the "Mandylion" as the true Shroud, and thus establishing continuity from A.D. 33 to 1204.

We know that under the pressure of siege for more than a year, and the extra demands of the wily bishop of Samosata, the Moslems of Edessa gave up the Image/Mandylion *plus two artists' copies of it* in August 944 to the emperor of Constantinople.

We know that a *full shroud with image on it* was displayed in 1203–4 in Constantinople. Historians have counted more than forty copies of the Shroud during the fourteenth, fifteenth, and sixteenth centuries.

Indeed, there is no reason to doubt the possibility—even the likelihood—that the Byzantine emperors of 944 to 1204 had copies of the Shroud painted once they knew of its full length and image. Nor, for that matter, is there reason to doubt that copies were made by the Latin emperors of 1204 to 1261. How many kings or custodians of relics in those chaotic times knew the true nature of the real Shroud and would have recognized a copy for what it was?

It seems likely that Philip the Fair was anything but in his treatment of the Templar masters, and that their worship before Shroud copies, though in secret, was probably totally Christian.

"Confessions" obtained by torture have always made the Templars' convictions highly suspect. Even Voltaire, challenging the French government's actions against the Templars, asked whether the leaders of the order could have behaved as accused after having fought for Christianity in the Near East, where many died in Moslem prisons rather than renounce the Christian faith.

General histories and public records do not indicate whether there is any connection between the medieval Order of Knights Templar, created and later dissolved by papal authority, and the Order of Knights Templar of the Masonic Lodge. Freemasonry (Order of Free and Accepted Masons) had its beginnings in the fourteenth century and began to flower in the eighteenth century. The Order of Knights Templar is prominent in the organization, as is the Order of De Molay, an organization for boys. Is there a secret Templar record still in existence in some forgotten archive that tells the untold story of the Shroud from Constantinople to Lirey?

FOUR

Solid History for 661 Years

USING PUBLIC events for our datings, we normally consider that the de Charny ownership of the Shroud began with the first exposition in the Lirey church in 1357. However, ownership by Geoffrey I de Charny and deposit of the Shroud in the Lirey church probably occurred a little earlier (Scavone suggests 1343).

As early as 1343, Geoffrey applied to King Philip VI for funds with which to build a chapel in Lirey, and to have five chaplains; this act might hint of a future need for housing the Shroud. Everything we know of Geoffrey's private life is consistent with that of a man who had ongoing plans. It is unlikely the Shroud came to him unexpectedly.

Apparently his plans moved forward in 1349 when, on April 16, he advised Pope Clement VI that his Lirey chapel "was built" [*sic*]. He petitioned that it be upgraded to a collegiate church, and he specified particulars, including a staff of five canons with salaries stipulated. His requests were granted, but fulfillment of his plans was delayed by his capture and imprisonment by the English in 1350. The following year, King John II paid an enormous ransom for his release, and in 1352 he was married to Jeanne Vergy. In 1353 the church construction was apparently completed.

A penultimate step appears to have been taken in 1354, as evidenced by his petition on January 30 to the new pope, Innocent VI, for broadening the charter of his collegiate church. Under the new specifications, it was to have six canons, one of whom was to be elected dean, plus three clerics. The stipend of the clergy was to be doubled from the amount Clement VI had approved. It was also specified, for the first time, that Geoffrey and his heirs were to be buried in the cemetery of the church. Other terms were increased accordingly, including special indulgences for pilgrims "from all over the world." This sounds very much as if something significant had just happened. John II also added to the church's income at this time.

In succeeding decades, three separate papal bulls recite the fact that *Geoffrey* de Charny *placed* "the Shroud of Our Lord Jesus Christ… bearing the effigy of our Savior" in the church of Lirey. Clearly the Shroud was in the church at Lirey *before* Geoffrey died in September 1356. Some type of ceremony, perhaps a dedicatory service, took place early in 1356, because on May 28, 1356, Henri de Poitiers, bishop of Troyes, sent Geoffrey a letter of praise and approval about the ceremony. (Oddly, this is the same bishop who, in late 1357, stopped the exposition of the Shroud.)

When Jeanne de Vergy, widow of Geoffrey I de Charny, completed construction of the collegiate church in Lirey and began the expositions of the full shroud we know as the Shroud of Turin in 1357, history

Figure 1.
The Lirey Medallion. This metal bas-relief, a pilgrim's medallion, was found in the Seine River in 1855 and has been dated to 1356–57. It clearly shows the head-to-head body images of the Shroud and probably was issued to commemorate the Shroud's installation, dedication, and exposition at the Lirey church. The coat of arms at lower left is that of Geoffrey I de Charny, who died in September 1356, and at lower right of his wife Jeanne. The medallion would have been sold to those attending the exposition after the dedication. *(The Cluny Museum, courtesy Musees Nationaux, Paris)*

records that huge crowds of pilgrims came to view the relic. It has been suggested that one of the reasons for her action was to derive some personal revenue, since Geoffrey's extended military service for France and the king, plus his imprisonment by the English, had depleted his modest resources. Doubtless the Lirey church benefited by donations received in lieu of admissions to the exposition, but we also have tangible evidence of a profitable sideline that we may reasonably speculate was operated by Jeanne. In the Cluny Museum in Paris reposes a bronze pilgrim's medallion in commemoration of the exposition. The medallion, dated 1356–57, was found in the Seine. On it was cast in bas-relief a depiction of the Shroud (front and back images, head-to-head) and the coat of arms of both Geoffrey and Jeanne. Such a souvenir could not have been made and sold without advance papal authority. The letter from de Poitiers and the medallion strongly imply that the Shroud was received by the Lirey church in early 1353, and that it was probably dedicated at a special service early in 1356.

The opportunities for the pilgrims to view the Shroud continued, perhaps daily, for some weeks or months, until they were stopped later in 1357 by order of the bishop of Troyes (the capital of the Department of Aube). Bishop Henri charged that the cloth was a forgery and that he had the confession of the painter who had made it, but he left no records indicating that he had made any investigation or had discovered any such facts.

Jeanne later remarried, and her new husband was uncle of the churchman who became Pope Clement VII. In 1389, thirty-two years after the first exposition, Jeanne quietly obtained permission directly from Pope Clement and began a second exposition of the Shroud at Lirey in April of that year. Henri's successor, Bishop Pierre D'Arcis, wrote an angry memorandum to the pope, insisting that the exposition be stopped; he cited the position of his predecessor but provided no data in support of the charge of forgery. Clement must have been fully briefed on the matter by Jeanne's representatives and been on her side, for he immediately ordered D'Arcis to desist and keep silent under threat of excommunication—surely a very abrupt action and a harsh threat to an official in the hierarchy of the Church. What can we make of this?

The Middle Ages were times of rough politics, some of which were quite odious, in the upper echelons of the Roman Church. Also, this was a period of great abuses in commercial traffic of religious relics, with frequent charges of forgery and fraud. The copying of relics was a common thing then, and historians have counted more than forty "true shrouds" that were in various churches, chapels, and shrines during the Middle Ages. Copying per se is not wrong; in a good art museum today, one will frequently find artists at work before a masterpiece, making a copy on commission. Some, if not most, of the copying of the Shroud may have been merely a method of "sharing the wealth," without any intent to deceive or misclaim, since it would not then have been feasible to have traveling exhibitions. Nevertheless, some clergy may have exaggerated the claims for their relics, taking advantage of the naivete, gullibility, and ignorance of their parishioners. We may note also that Clement, either because of lingering doubts or to give D'Arcis an "out" he did not choose to take, required that the Shroud be labeled as a "representation" of Jesus' burial garment.

It is perhaps worthwhile at this point to summarize the question of "ownership" of the Shroud of Jesus. The Gospel of Mark reports that Joseph of Arimathea "bought" the Shroud. From apocryphal accounts we can fairly assume that he tacitly gave it (by the hand of Thaddaeus) to be the first church of Edessa, whose ownership continued during the independence of the city. For a time after the fall of Edessa to the Moslems in 639, Christianity was tolerated, but at some point this important relic was seized by the government. In 943 the Christian emperor Byzantium sent an army to surround the city and demand the Mandylion, the Face of Edessa; in August 944 the Moslem ruler gave up the relic. Thus it was owned by the emperor until Constantinople fell in 1204. As a spoil of war, ownership of the Shroud came to Othon de la Roche, duke of Athens, who passed it to his great-great-granddaughter, Jeanne de Vergy, of Besancon, France (Othon's home area), who took it as dowry to her husband, Geoffrey I de Charny of Lirey, France. After his death, Jeanne passed it to her son, Geoffrey II de Charny; his daughter Margaret sold it to Duke Louis of Savoy in 1453; the Savoys became rulers of all of Italy. At the death of Umberto II (last

Savoy king, exiled to Portugal) in 1983, he willed the Shroud to the Vatican. At no time was the legality of ownership of any of the above-named owners questioned.

Unfortunately, early in the twentieth century the D'Arcis accusation resurfaced in the Shroud criticisms of French scholar Canon Ulysse Chevalier, whose claims were then seconded in 1912 by prominent English Jesuit Herbert Thurston. Chevalier reported the discovery of a 1389 D'Arcis memo to the pope in which he claimed an unnamed artist had admitted to his predecessor, Bishop Henri de Poitiers, to have painted the Shroud image.[1] However, the bottom line is plain and clear: The Shroud of Lirey and the Shroud of Turin are the same cloth, and some of the best scientists in Europe and America have emphatically certified that it was not painted or otherwise fabricated by medieval artifice.

At the 1991 Saint Louis University symposium, one of the papers read was by Brother Bruno Bonnet-Eymard of the Little Brothers of the Sacred Heart, France. He provides what is perhaps the first exhaustive study of the controversial "1389 Memorandum of the Bishop Pierre d'Arcis"; the report was based on his own direct study of the original archives of the Diocese of Troyes, which happens to be his own residence and but a few miles from the town of Lirey.

It is most unfortunate that earlier writers, notably Canon Ulysse Chevalier (1902) and English Jesuit Herbert Thurston (1912), did not bother to make a study, rather than superficially checking secondary records, thus giving fodder to Shroud critics since then.

From the archival documentation, Bonnet-Eymard firmly concludes that the "historic" paper was neither an official "memorandum" nor was it "of bishop Pierre d'Arcis." It was no more than a draft by some clerk on the bishop's staff and was never adopted by the bishop, was not ever dispatched to Clement VII, the "Avignon anti-Pope," nor was it acknowledged by Clement, and was not a part of the papal archives; more specifically, Clement did not refer to that paper when he wrote D'Arcis on January 6, 1390, so his mandate on Lirey and the Shroud was not a "reply" to the so-called d'Arcis memorandum.

The paper in question, states Bonnet-Eymard, "is in fact an anonymous, unsigned, undated and unsealed copy done on paper [not parchment], lacking the marks [and heading] of an authentic archive document." And to substance, "those confessions and that painter are nonexistent." He sums up: "One conclusion stands out even now—1355 is the baseline date for the Holy Shroud's presence at Lirey. By that date it was in its reliquary in the treasury of the Collegial Church of Lirey, where it was known and inventoried as an authentic and holy relic with the canonical approval of the ordinary, Henri de Poitiers, bishop of Troyes."

And in 1993, Madame Hilda Leynen of Antwerp, by research at the Bibliotheque Nationale in Paris, fully confirmed Brother Bonnet-Eymard's conclusions that the so-called 1389 "Memo" of D'Arcis was in fact a fraudulent nonmemo crafted by Chevalier from a clerk's draft in poor Latin, never dated nor signed nor sent to the Vatican, and with no official copy either in Troyes or in the Vatican.

Two points are worthy of this note: Bishop Henri de Poitiers vacillated by first praising the de Charnys' exhibition of the Shroud in Lirey, and then trying to stop them. Also, the late Dr. John A. T. Robinson of England also believed the Chevalier claims at first, but he kept on reading and convinced himself that the Shroud and its images were genuine. Most important, Dr. Scavone observes that even as a draft, it hints of a "hidden agenda" on the part of all major players concerned. It may be, he suggests, that the unnamed painter for de Poitiers that "D'Arcis" cites may, in fact, have painted the *new* Besancon shroud of 1377 by copying the true Shroud of Lirey.

Lirey was and is a very small village, nearly one hundred miles southeast of Paris and twelve miles from Troyes. Because the Hundred Years' War with England was under way (1337–1453), with English troops at times ranging all over the northern half of France, Jeanne was understandably concerned about the safety of the Shroud, as were the canons of the Lirey church. Nevertheless, the Shroud stayed in Lirey until 1418, but exhibitions were intermittent because of Church disputes. The local bishop's ban had been effective from late 1357 until 1389, when Clement VII became pope and silenced Bishop D'Arcis. After the death of Geoffrey I de Charny in 1356, and the initial efforts of his widow Jeanne, their son Geoffrey II took responsibility for the Shroud. When he died in 1398, his daughter Margaret assumed this responsibility.

Because of France's loss at the Battle of Agincourt, bands of marauders came even closer to Lirey, and so the canons agreed that Margaret should take the Shroud to a safer place. In July 1418 she took it to the de Charny castle at Montfort in southwestern France. After a short stay there, she moved it again to St. Hippolyte sur Doubs in southeastern France, where her current husband, Humbert of Villersexel, was lord. The Shroud remained there until 1449, and was exhibited to the public each of those thirty years. During this time many copies were made of the Shroud.

In 1438, Humbert died, leaving Margaret childless, as had been true with her first husband. In 1443 the canons of Lirey insisted that the Shroud be returned to them; they apparently felt that the war's threat to its security was no longer serious (even though the war did continue for another ten years). But Margaret apparently had developed a personal attachment for the Shroud, and, of course, she was its undisputed owner. Besides, the Lirey church was a wooden structure, now nearly a hundred years old and in very poor condition. For whatever reasons, Margaret ignored the demands of the canons, which they repeated periodically.

In 1449, Margaret authorized showings of the Shroud at Liege and Hainault, Belgium, but did not return it to St. Hippolyte sur Doubs. She was at this time nearly seventy years of age, with no relatives she could trust to properly care for the Shroud. Her nearest relatives were a nephew by marriage, a half brother, and a cousin. The canons of Lirey were becoming more persistent; in 1443 they had had her summoned before the parliament of Dole. At that time she returned all relics and other property, except the Shroud, that she and Humbert had been keeping for the church. And in 1446, 1448, and 1451 she avoided a more severe court judgment by paying for church upkeep costs to the Lirey canons.

Margaret's trip to Belgium in 1449 was apparently an effort to find suitable heirs for the Shroud. When that effort did not succeed, she moved it to the south of France. In March 1453, in Geneva, she signed a contract with Duke Louis of Savoy, by which she passed title in the Shroud to the House of Savoy in exchange for certain estates in land. Margaret was not dealing with strangers because both her father, Geoffrey II, and her second husband Humbert had been knighted with the Order of the Collar by earlier Savoy dukes. Moreover, the piety of the Savoys in those years seems to have been a major motivation. Among other things, Louis's father had become Pope Felix V. Perhaps most of

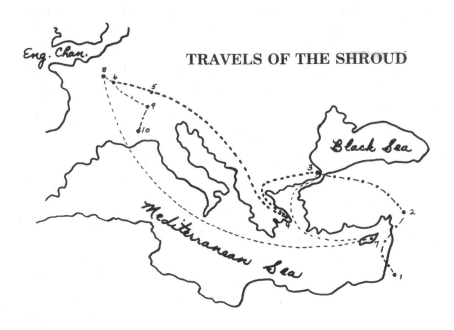

Figure 2.
Travels of the Shroud

1. Jerusalem
2. Edessa
3. Constantinople (Istanbul)
4. Athens
5. Besancon
6. Lirey
7. Cyprus
8. Paris
9. Chambery
10. Turin

Legend
Known itinerary _._._._
Probable route ------
Possible route ---------

Drawn by Mary Lu Lewis

all, Margaret saw in Duke Louis and his wife Anne (who was a princess in her own right) a rising dynasty, wealthy and powerful enough to give security to the Shroud. Her judgment was eminently sound, as the Savoys ultimately became the kings of Italy. Four years later, in 1457, Duke Louis made a cash gift to the canons of Lirey in settlement of their claims. Margaret died in 1460.

Closely associated with the Savoys at the time was Franciscan friar Francesco della Rovere, who became Pope Sixtus IV. In 1471 he published a monograph, *The Blood of Christ,* in which he flatly stated that "the Shroud in which the body of Christ was wrapped…is now preserved with great devotion by the Dukes of Savoy, and it is colored with the blood of Christ." Thus, for the first time the Shroud was given full recognition by the Holy See.

In 1453 the Shroud was publicly seen briefly in Geneva in connection with the negotiations between Margaret and Louis, but not again until Good Friday 1494, when it was exhibited at a Savoy castle in Vercelli, Italy. We are not told exactly when the Savoys placed the Shroud in their Chambery castle in southeastern France, but for more than thirty years they worked to embellish the ducal chapel there and dedicated it for the Shroud in 1502. The chapel was then named Sainte Chapelle of the Holy Shroud. For the next thirty years there were annual expositions at Chambery as well as a special one in central France in 1503.

A crisis happened on the night of December 4, 1532, when a fire broke out in the chapel's sacristy. It engulfed the chapel and ravaged parts of the castle proper before it was brought under control. At considerable risk to themselves, four men rushed into the burning chapel, broke through the grille of the Shroud's crypt, and carried the Shroud in its silver casket out through the flames. The casket had become so hot that the Shroud was deeply scorched along its longitudinal folds by molten silver, and holes were burned through its various layers, by the melting silver dripping onto the Shroud. Nuns from the Order of Poor Clares worked on the Shroud for the next two years, patching, darning, and reinforcing the burned areas. They also put a linen backing behind the entire Shroud to strengthen it. Nevertheless, many scorch marks still remain, and together with the patches (mostly of darker linen) they are the first thing an observer notices, since they are considerably darker than the image of the Man on the Shroud.

After the repairs had been carried out, a papal commission examined the Shroud to validate its integrity, especially since there had been rumors that the Shroud was totally destroyed. At the same time (1534) a brief exposition was held at Chambery to reassure the public. It was shown also at Turin (1535), Milan (1536), and Nice (1537). At this time French troops in the area created a risk to Chambery, and the Shroud was taken to another Savoy castle in Vercelli, Italy, for safekeeping from 1537 to 1561. Its final stay at Chambery was from 1561 to 1578. There were annual expositions of the Shroud for most of the time it was either in Chambery or Vercelli.

When peace finally came to the region in 1559, Savoy duke Emmanuel Philibert determined to move his capital and the Shroud to his palace in Turin, Italy. But it wasn't until 1578 that a pretext finally presented itself for the final move of the Shroud without public outcry. The highly revered archbishop of Milan had vowed to make a pilgrimage on foot to the Shroud, but his poor health and advanced years would have made the long journey to Chambery over the mountainous terrain of the Alpine foothills a dangerous venture. The duke announced that the Shroud would be taken to Turin (today, a two-hour bus ride from Milan) to facilitate the archbishop's pilgrimage. The Shroud was never returned to Chambery.

From 1578 to 1898 (320 years), ten expositions of the Shroud were held in Turin. In the 1690s a magnificent chapel in baroque-style architecture was built between the Cathedral of St. John the Baptist and the Savoy palace, joining the two into a single building complex with chapel entrances from both sides. The Shroud was placed in its new reliquary, locked behind the grille above the high altar. The final exposition of the nineteenth century, in 1898, to celebrate the fiftieth anniversary of the unification of Italy, made history that eclipsed all its previous ceremonies, because the exposition brought forth new truths of science. These in turn reintroduced the probability of the Shroud's supernatural character, with an excitement reminiscent of the first century.

Figure 3.
The Cathedral of St. John the Baptist in Turin has been the home of the Shroud since 1578. *(Courtesy Centro Internazionale della Sindone of Turin)*

In the late nineteenth century, photography, recently invented, was improving its technical processes, with results not significantly inferior to simple photography today. The unique and crucial feature of the photographic process was the "magic" of photographic negativity, whereby light passing through the camera's lens exposed the picture the camera "saw" onto its sensitized plate or film. When the exposed plate or film was developed in the darkroom (using a "fixing" chemical reagent), it became a permanent negative for the contact printing of pictures (positive prints). However, the key to the negative's secret was the reversal of all values; on the negative, darks were light, lights were dark, lefts were right, and rights were left. Photographic negativity is not optically natural; the reversal process is confusing, and one can hardly identify his own recent pictures when looking at the negatives.

A local Turin lawyer, Secondo Pia, was an amateur photographer, and, in connection with the exposition of 1898, he was authorized to make photographs of the Shroud's bizarre images of a man, which seemed so vague and unnatural. Technical problems the first day precluded any results at all. The second day everything seemed to go well,

Figure 4.
The altar in the Cathedral of St. John the Baptist, surmounted by the Shroud's reliquary. The grille in the center of the altar protects the Shroud's casket and is secured by three locks, for which the keys are kept by three officials. *(Courtesy Centro Internazionale della Sindone of Turin)*

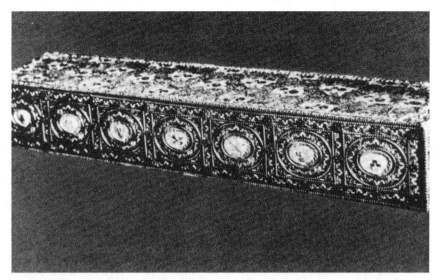

Figure 5.
The silver casket in which the Shroud is kept. The Shroud is covered with red silk and then rolled on a wooden spool. *(Courtesy Centro Internazionale della Sindone of Turin)*

Figure 6.
The Shroud is displayed outside the cathedral in 1931. *(Courtesy Centro Internazionale della Sindone of Turin)*

and Pia rushed to his darkroom with the glass negative plates and immersed them in the developing solution. As he lifted the first plate up to the dim red light for an initial visual check, he was so startled by what he saw that he almost dropped the plate—his negative plate was not vague and unnatural as he expected. It showed a natural-appearing picture of a man. Contrary to the science of photography, the negative was *a photographic positive*—so the Shroud image must itself be a "photographic negative"!

The facts and circumstances force one to posit an *intentional* (photographic) negative image, incredible as that thought certainly is. In chapter 2, I note that in sixth-century Edessa the image was described as "blurred," and later I point out that the emperor's sons were disappointed in the Face because it was so vague and unnatural, but another observer said that "as an artist he could discern the portrait clearly." Modern sculptor Weyland said, "The width of the Face on the Shroud must be felt, rather than traced, because there exists no outline."

Using Pia's pictures, a few scientists began at once a detailed study of the Shroud images and their meanings. From the Greek word *sindon* (full burial cloth) they have come to be known as sindonologists. The results of their studies in sindonology have been reported in books, scientific journals, and proceedings, and through occasional symposia.[2] French biologist Paul Vignon was the earliest sindonologist, and his book *The Shroud of Christ* was published in London in 1902. A Sorbonne anatomist, Yves Delage, was briefly involved, but scientific scorn of the French Academy of Sciences soon put his efforts to rout. A most impressive early researcher was Dr. Pierre Barbet, a Parisian physician, autopsy surgeon, and professor of anatomy, who was the first to develop crucifixion experiments and to use fresh cadavers for demonstrations. His 1950 book *A Doctor at Calvary* was translated into English and published in 1953. Expositions in 1931 and 1933 provided the opportunity for more and better photographs by photographer Giuseppi Enrie, which restimulated the sindonologists.

World War II presented a new danger for the Shroud as northern Italy underwent convulsions of political and military unrest. So the Shroud was secretly taken in 1939 to a chapel in Avellino in southern Italy for safekeeping. It was returned to Turin in 1946. The war was disastrous for the Savoys. Umberto II, as king of Italy, was caught in a political-military net from which he could not extricate himself. Although his father's premier, Mussolini, was toppled, the Fascist Party, though underground, remained a significant factor. The Communists could not tolerate either the Fascists or the Royalists. The Allied Military Command and the Allied Military Government decided that a "clean slate" would be easier to deal with, and so Umberto was permitted to quietly leave Italy and establish a residence in exile in Cascais, Portugal, near Lisbon. He remained the titular head of the House of Savoy, however, and the Savoys still owned the Shroud. Accordingly, the family's representative at Turin participated with the archbishop of Turin in all decisions about the Shroud.

FIVE

THE BIBLICAL STORY OF THE SHROUD

A LL FOUR Gospels tell of Jesus' trial, crucifixion, death, burial, and Resurrection. To get a comprehensive picture, we need to integrate all four—but is that possible since the timing seems not to be consistent? The Book of John has Pilate delivering Jesus to the soldiers to be crucified at the sixth hour (19:14–16), while Mark has Jesus already nailed to the cross at the third hour (15:25). This can be rationalized when we realize that the Jews and the Romans used two different systems of timekeeping. The synoptic Gospels use Jewish time, while "John" (the writer's identity is uncertain) uses Roman time throughout his Gospel, probably because the Book of John is written for non-Jewish readers. The writer is always explaining Jewish customs to his readers.

After their return from Babylonian captivity, the Jews started their days at sunset and arbitrarily set twelve "hours" of night, until sun up, and then twelve "hours" of day until sun down. The length of their "hour" depended on the time of year; in winter the nights would be close to an equivalent of fourteen hours and the days ten hours; in summer the lengths were reversed. Jesus' passion came at Passover time, which was near the spring equinox, and so the "hours" for the period we are considering would commence at about 6 A.M. and 6 P.M., respectively.

The Romans' day began at midnight and the evening at noon, two twelve-hour periods, but the length of their hours varied with the seasons, just as with the Jews.

Thus we find no difficulty in fixing a chronology for that crucial Friday. The arrest in Gethsemane on Thursday may have been near midnight, and the farcical "trials" throughout the balance of the night shuttled from the council of Jews, to Pilate, to Herod, and back to Pilate.

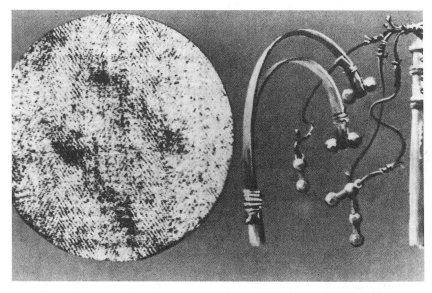

Figure 1.
Roman lashes (right) with the barbell-shaped metal flagrum. The Shroud cloth enlargement shows lash marks. *(Courtesy Holy Shroud Guild)*

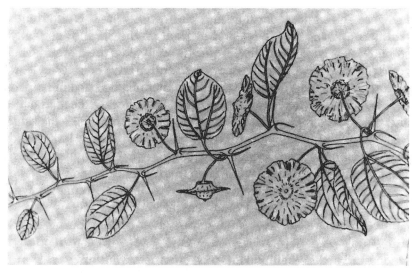

Figure 2.
The Syrian Christ thorn. *(Courtesy Frederick T. Zugibe, M.D.)*

Figure 3.
The crown of thorns on the sculpture by Charles Villandre *(Courtesy Holy Shroud Guild)*

There were no *formal* or *legal* trials of Jesus. Neither Herod nor Annas had any authority at all. The hearing before Caiphas did not meet the legal requirements of the Great Sanhedrin sitting as a court (which it did, twice a week), and obviously was only intended to have the "color of formality" to mislead the public. Technically, the arrest of Jesus was probably legal. Pilate had no legal need to hold a formal hearing or trial. Although he initially was disposed to treat the Sanhedrin's informal charges as a trivial matter, the subtle threats (blackmail?) by Annas to report the matter to Rome were enough to persuade him—because he had already been reprimanded twice by Rome, because Jesus' actions at the temple might jeopardize money payments to Rome, and because possible armed involvement by Zealots could not be precluded deriving from Jesus' acts. Thus, regardless of Pilate's reluctance and his motivation ultimately, his authority and procedures were clear and his action was a *Roman* crucifixion.

Pilate ordered that Jesus be scourged. Usually (but not always) this was accomplished by tying the victim's wrists to an iron ring set about knee level, so that he would be bent over; or, facing or backed to a column, the wrists would be tied overhead. There were probably two scourgers, standing on each side, with whips five or six feet long ending in two leather thongs tipped with metal. As the scourging whips fell across the victim's back, they would wrap around his body at times, lacerating his body front and back, so that scourge marks soon covered all of his body except the head, feet, and forearms. This is what the markings on the body of the Man on the Shroud do show.

It was uncommon for the Romans to *both* scourge and crucify a person. Why was it done to Jesus? It has been conjectured by some scholars that Pilate thought by excessive scourging and beating of Jesus, the Jewish council would be satisfied (see Luke 23:16 and 22). They weren't. But the scourging, and the beating with fists and stones by soldiers and the rabble (clearly evident on the Shroud), certainly hastened Jesus' death on the cross. In analyzing the Shroud and Shroud pictures through microscopes, scientists have counted at least 120 blows with the two-tailed lashes. Each tail had a barbell-shaped metal flagrum (tip) that fell on the Man of the Shroud; scientists have found there were more than 220 flagrum bruises that broke the skin. Jewish law permitted flogging only to a maximum of forty lashes, and the Pharisees in their piety reduced that number to thirty-nine. Roman law and practice knew no limitation in this respect, and so we can be sure it was a Roman scourging inflicted on a non-Roman. It was against the law to scourge a Roman citizen.

The Gospels are not consistent as to when Jesus' scourging and beating took place. "John" says it was just before Pilate rendered sentence and ordered him taken to be crucified. Matthew says it was just after Pilate's final order. Mark says the scourging was before and the beating after Pilate's order. In any event, it was just after sunup, in the first hour of the Jewish daylight period (between 6 and 7 A.M.) that Jesus was scourged, beaten, sentenced, and started carrying the crossbeam of the cross toward Golgotha.

American pathologist Robert Bucklin examined the Shroud while in Turin and concluded that abrasions over both shoulder blades could have been made by carrying a heavy object, such as the horizontal bar of a cross; he estimates that the object might have weighed 80 to 100 pounds.[1] That weight may not have been greater than that of a double-yoke for oxen, and as a carpenter Jesus would regularly have had to carry and position heavy timbers. The difference would be that throughout Thursday night, with no sleep, he took a scourging of 120 lashes, a beating about the face, and the trauma of sharp thorns mashed into the scalp where the nerves have no padding of protection between skin and skull. Scientists also note that for the Man of the Shroud the shoulder bruises came *after* the scourging and that cuts on both knees indicate probable falls while carrying the cross.

Figure 4.
Dr. Charles Villandre's crucifixion statue. Dr. Barbet said that Villandre was a "past-master in sculpture as well as in surgery." *(Courtesy Holy Shroud Guild)*

The crucifixion took place at the third hour of the Jewish daylight period (9 A.M.). From the sixth to the ninth hour (noon until 3 p.m.) there was total darkness, according to Matthew, Mark, and Luke. Jesus' death came at the ninth hour of daylight (3 P.M.), at which time the synoptic Gospels report the Temple veil being torn from the top to the bottom. Matthew says also that at that time there was a violent earthquake, causing rocks to split and graves to open. The other three accounts are silent about these latter phenomena. Did they happen? Present-day archaeo-astronomers have no scientific validation of such an event, but persistent legends and a few secular records seem to indicate that it was so—that an intense darkness did come that afternoon without any prior prediction of an eclipse, nor could scientists of the day provide any explanation. The historian Tertullian wrote that the records of Rome reported a complete and universal darkness that frightened the Senate, then meeting, and threw the city into turmoil. Phlegon wrote of a great darkness across Europe. Grecian and Egyptian records state that the darkness was so intense even their astronomers were alarmed and that an enormous earthquake occurred in Nicaea (near Byzantium/Constantinople/Istanbul). The Jordan River and Dead Sea lie along one of the world's most active "fault lines," noted throughout history for its earthquakes.

Figure 5.
A Roman spike such as was used in crucifixions. *(Courtesy Robert K. Wilcox)*

Nations of the Near East used crucifixion as a punishment long before Roman rule, and the Romans used it for about four hundred years—exclusively for non-Romans and especially for slaves and the worst criminals. The Roman historian Tacitus wrote extensively about crucifixion techniques, disclosing the wide variety of methods their ingenuity and cruelty devised. The cross was usually in the conventional form we know, but sometimes the crosspiece was on top of the upright and occasionally a Y-shaped or an X-shaped cross was used. Sometimes the wrists were nailed, and other times they were tied to the crosspiece with leather thongs. Occasionally, a small seat was provided for the buttocks. The feet might be perched on a small shelf or be nailed to the cross; the feet might be nailed separately or both with one spike. The single spike might go sideways through the two heels (with the knees twisted to the side) or one foot might be placed on top of the other for the spike to pierce.

Pierre Barbet's *A Doctor at Calvary* (Doubleday, 1950, 1963) includes a chapter, "Crucifixion and Archaeology" (pp. 37–71), that is probably the best on the subject that is readily available in English; he refers to numerous ancient writers including Tacitus, Tertullian, Livy, Josephus, Mommsen, Plautus, Cicero, Quintilian, Philo, Empiricus, and Eusebius. He also praises the exhaustive study of crucifixion by Father Holzmeister in four issues of *Verbum Domini* (May, July, August, September 1934), the review of the Pontifical Biblical Institute.

Modern data have added to our knowledge of first-century crucifixions and have provided further validation of details found on the Shroud of Turin. In 1968, during routine construction excavation in Jerusalem, workmen broke into an ancient Jewish cemetery. A group of burials, precisely dated to the Roman-inflicted massacre that occurred with the Jewish revolt of A.D. 70, were preserved in stone burial chests called ossuaries, which were reburials containing only the bones after the flesh had decayed. One of these, Jehohanan ben Ha'galgol (identified by the name written in Aramaic on his ossuary), had been crucified. A seven-inch nail was still sideways through his heel-bones, through a block of acacia wood, and had splinters of olive wood (the upright of the cross) still adhering to its tip. Nails had also been driven through his wrists, where the radius bones were noticeably worn, doubtless by grating on the nail as Jehohanan pulled himself up so he could breathe. The tibia and fibula bones of his calves were crushed, to hasten his death by preventing the push-up from his feet to permit breathing—as was done to the thieves executed alongside Jesus. Archaeologist Vasilius Tzaferis and Hebrew University pathologist Nicu Haas examined Jehohanan's bones (reports by both men are contained in *Israel Exploration Journal,* 1970).

All four Gospels tell us that Joseph of Arimathea wrapped Jesus' body in a linen cloth and laid it in a tomb. Joseph of Arimathea's tomb was a new one, previously unused, hewn into the face of a cliff of solid rock. Its entrance was barred by a movable stone, which probably could be rolled (with much effort) in a groove or trench. A stone bench cut into one of the walls would have been the resting place for Jesus' body. Mark and Luke say that Joseph took the body down from the cross. Matthew, Mark, and Luke (the synoptic Gospels) tell us it was a tomb carved from rock. John's account adds that Nicodemus brought burial spices and assisted Joseph. None of the accounts say whether the body was wrapped at the cross or in the tomb. From the King James Version:

> Matthew 27:59–60—And when Joseph had taken the body, he wrapped it in a clean linen cloth, and laid it in his own new tomb, which he had hewn out in the rock....
> Mark 15:46—And he bought fine linen, and took him down, and wrapped him in the linen and laid him in a sepulchre which was hewn out of a rock....
> Luke 23:53—And he took it down, and wrapped it in linen, and laid it in a sepulchre that was hewn in stone....
> John 19:38–42—He came therefore and took the body of Jesus. And there came also Nicodemus.... and brought a mixture of myrrh and aloes, about an hundred pound weight. Then took they the body of Jesus, and wound it in linen clothes with the spices, as the manner of the Jews is to bury...and in the garden a new sepulchre...there laid they Jesus....

The Gospels of Luke and John, describing the empty tomb, comment on the appearance of the linen cloths, and on the reaction of Peter and the "other disciple" to the sight of it. From the King James Version:

> Luke 24:12—Then arose Peter, and ran unto the sepulchre; and stooping down, he beheld the linen clothes laid by themselves, and departed, wondering in himself at that which was come to pass.
>
> John 20:4–8—And the other disciple…stooping down, saw the linen clothes lying; yet went he not in. Then cometh Simon Peter following him, and went into the sepulchre, and seeth the linen clothes lie, and the napkin, that was about his head, not lying with the linen clothes, but wrapped together in a place by itself. Then went also that other disciple, which came first to the sepulchre, and he saw, and believed.

In chapter 2 it is suggested that the taking and saving of the Shroud by Jesus' followers would have been an instinctive act, and that it is quite reasonable and logical that the New Testament gives no hint that the Shroud still exists. However, early Church writers seemed to have no doubts on the matter. For instance, Bishop Braulio (635–651) of Saragossa, Spain, wrote: "At the time, many things were known to have happened which are not written down; for example, concerning the *linteaminibus* [sindon; shroud] and the *sudarium* [chin-napkin] in which the Lord's body was wrapped—we read that it was found but we do not read that it was preserved. Yet, I do not think that the apostles neglected to preserve these and such like relics for future times." In other chapters similar quotations are furnished from such as Saint Jerome (347-420), Saint John Damascene (675–749), Saint Braulio of Seville (circa 120), and Eusebius of Caesarea (circa 263–340).

The scriptures clearly imply that Jesus was given a hurried and temporary burial—"the Sabbath drew on," says Luke (23:54). Dusk was falling and further work with the corpse would soon be illegal. That only minimal steps were taken seems clear from Luke's statement that "the women…beheld…how his body was laid. And they returned [home], and prepared spices and ointments" (23:55–56), implying that the body had not been fully or formally anointed. His body was laid upon a "clean linen cloth" purchased by Joseph of Arimathea, perhaps purchased on the spur of the moment (Mark 15:46; Matt. 27:59).

It seems probable that the shroud and body were profusely spread with spices provided by Nicodemus (John 19:39) to slow down the process of decay. This was said to involve a large quantity of myrrh and aloes, probably in powdered or granule form, and they put it "with" the grave clothes, doubtless packed around the body. According to Mark (16:1), the women purchased aromatic oils after the Sabbath was past (Saturday night); Luke (23:56) says spices and perfumes. These were evidently in liquid form to "anoint" the body Sunday morning (Mark 16:1), when the body could first be properly washed and prepared.

Luke particularly notes that the burial linens were in the empty tomb when Peter rushed into it that Easter morning, and "beheld the linen clothes laid by themselves" (24:12). John is more specific and tries to describe the position of the shroud, and the chin strap or napkin probably used to keep the mouth closed (20:7), and he clearly implies that the cloths were not in disarray, as they certainly would have been if the body had been removed hastily or surreptitiously either by the disciples, or by thieves or enemies—or if Jesus had revived, got up, and walked away. John's words would be consistent with the case of the burial cloths being carefully folded, but they would also be consistent with *collapse* of the cloths without them being touched by human hands—and this is what the evidence of the Turin Shroud points to. The latter interpretation would seem more appropriate scripturally because the writer of John says that the "other disciple" "saw, and believed" (20:8). (In fact, the Shroud of Turin is called by some the "Fifth Gospel.")

Compare the case of the raising of Lazarus (John 11:44). He had been properly buried, but, when called, he was able to walk out of the tomb unassisted, though he first had to be "unbound"—probably the removal of the "Sudarium," the chin strap (sometimes translated as hand-kerchief), and the untying of the hands and feet. (The Jewish Mishnah instructs that the chin of the corpse is to be tied up [Shabbath 23:5], as does the Code of Jewish Law [Laws of Mourning, chapters 351–52].)

One can speculate that New Testament writers purposely avoided categoric mention of the saving of the Shroud relic, out of fear for its safety on the one hand, and on the other because of the Jewish prohibitions against touching the burial clothes and against images of a human, and respecting charges of idolatry—a very real concern in the early Church, that even extended to church decorations other than geometrical designs, which is the Moslem precept even today. Also, we should note that all of the eleven disciples were probably from Galilee, and thus were "fundamentalists" who would have been concerned about those Jewish taboos. But, Joseph of Arimathea had bought that Shroud, and had wrapped Jesus in it, violating religious taboos as he did so, and put Jesus in his own tomb—and so it is he, I suggest, that would instinctively have taken the Shroud from the tomb on Easter morning, and then preserved it when he found those mystical images on it.

As following chapters will discuss, scientists have now found that there is real blood on the Shroud, and that the bloodstains did soak completely through the cloth (as distinguished from the body image that is lightly imprinted on only the tops of the threads of the cloth), but the question has arisen in the minds of some sindonologists as to whether the body of Jesus was washed before being put into the tomb. Three views have been expressed. Because the Gospel of John states that Joseph and Nicodemus followed Jewish burial custom, some consider that this must mean a ritual washing of the body. Because the bloodstains on the Shroud in large part reflect the experiences on the cross, some hold that washing must not have been accomplished for it would have obliterated those vital marks. That philosophy also points to the lack of time. Jesus died at about 3 P.M. and the spear-thrust came thereafter, according both to the Bible and to the interpretation of the Shroud. Then Joseph went back to Jerusalem, sought out Pilate, and asked for the body. Pilate was surprised that Jesus was dead so soon; accordingly, he sent an inquiry to the captain in charge of the crucifixion. Once that assurance was brought back, Pilate gave his assent. It is possible that the Shroud and spices would have to be bought or picked up from his residence and, with the other materials, be taken to the tomb on Gareb Hill. Next, the soldiers might have to be importuned to take Jesus down from the cross, including the extracting of the nails. Consequently, by the time Joseph and Nicodemus got the body, it may well have been five o'clock. Proponents of the no-washing theory point out further that proper ritual washing would have required aromatic perfumes mixed with warm water; outside the city walls and under these circumstances this would seem impractical.

A third evaluation has been proposed by Lavoie, Lavoie, Klutstein, and Regan in an article appearing both in the *Sindon* journal (Turin) and *Shroud Spectrum International* (Nashville, Indiana). They have researched the Bible, the Mishnah, the Talmud, and the Code of Jewish Law and report that when a Jew died a violent death and his body was bloodied in connection with the death, Jewish law *forbade any washing* of the body. Thus, they conclude that to follow Jewish burial custom would have certainly meant "no washing" in Jesus' case.

Interesting as these views are, I feel impelled to take a very different position: As will be discussed in later chapters, all scientists studying the Shroud appear to agree that contact between body and shroud was not a significant factor in the making of either the body images or the blood images on the Shroud of Turin, and one of the reasons is that there is not the slightest sign on the Shroud of smearing of *any* of the bloodstains—*each* bloodstain is precise and unsmeared. Now, in taking Jesus' body down from the cross and extracting the spikes, the soldiers certainly would have taken no special care or precautions in handling the body. The spear-thrust must have resulted in one or more quarts of blood flowing down the side of the abdomen, thigh, calf, and foot. The body must have been so bloody from head to foot that it would be very difficult to handle it at all. Regardless of what preparations Joseph and Nicodemus had made, doubtless it would have been necessary for them to carry the body (weighing approximately 170 pounds, scientists have estimated) in their arms for fifty to a hundred yards, over possibly rough and rocky ground. At most, they might have had a carrying cloth to cover the naked body at the cross, to soak up some blood, and make the carrying a bit easier. They would not likely have done more at the cross, with a curious crowd still standing around. Would Matthew describe burial on "a *clean* linen cloth"? Because the cloth on which he was carried from the cross would not have been clean.

These two (Joseph and Nicodemus) were members of the powerful Sanhedrin, and they had probably cast the only votes that morning favoring Jesus. They were followers of Jesus who had many times heard him say, "You have been told of old…, but I say to you…"—indicating that many rules of Judaism were outmoded in Jesus' view. I suggest that taboos of what was unclean would have little concerned them that afternoon in the tomb, with only an hour until the Sabbath. They probably had stopped at the tomb with supplies before going on to the cross, and now, using wet cloths, they wiped the body clean. Next, they spread half of the length of the clean shroud on the stone bench cut into one side of the tomb, and laid the body on it. Finally, they spread the powdered or granule-form myrrh and aloes copiously over the body to delay decomposition and brought the other half of the shroud over the head and draped it down to the feet. A few small bags of the spices may have been added along each side, to hold the shroud snugly in place. They expected the women to come Sunday morning with scented warm water, oils, and liquid spices, when a ceremonial cleansing and formal burial would be possible (which might include ritualistic acts such as shaving the head and beard and cutting the fingernails; also, hands and feet might be bound with strips of cloth). Note that none of these special actions and anointings would have been permissible under the strict Jewish law cited above regarding violent death, yet, obviously, Jesus' followers intended to do it anyway, because their plans are specified by Mark (16:1) and Luke (23:56; 24:1).

The actions of Joseph and Nicodemus of washing the body (as I have speculated) may have caused a pool of blood to collect at Jesus' side under the spear wound and at the feet. Those are the *only* bloodstains that show on the Shroud of Turin that might have been formed *after* he was taken from the cross. No other blood flows on the Shroud run toward the sides of the body, as if he were lying on his back as the blood flowed. Instead, all of the other blood flows run approximately from head to foot, as gravity would take the blood as he hung on the

Figure 6.
A method of wrapping with a shroud, as shown in a sixteenth-century paint-ing by Giovanni Battista della Rovere. *(Courtesy Centro Internazionale della Sindone of Turin)*

cross—and there were no blood smears on the Shroud. A further dis-cussion of this anomaly will be presented in a later chapter.

The probable actions and attitudes of the eleven disciples and other key followers of Jesus at the time of his death are important to a possible understanding of the enigma of the Shroud, and it is worthwhile puzzling over such matters even though any conclusions must be speculation at best. Both Nicodemus and Joseph of Arimathea were Pharisees and members of the august Sanhedrin on the one hand, and "closet Christians" on the other. At the crucifixion, they boldly revealed themselves as "Christians." Apocryphal accounts indicate that, as a result, Joseph was either banished or had to flee from the country. Their actions in asking for Jesus' body and in burying it can fairly be taken to indicate that they had abandoned Judaism as their religion, or were willing to do so. Then, however they managed to carry Jesus' blood-smeared body from the cross to the tomb (and I have suggested *a temporary* cloth wrapper), at this point their Jewishness would not have precluded a simple wiping away of the blood with wet cloths before they laid him on the new shroud that was spread on a stone bench in the tomb.

It surely is significant that Matthew reports Joseph of Arimathea as wrapping the body of Jesus in a *"clean* linen cloth" (both the King James Version and the New American Standard Version use this language, while the New English Bible says "clean linen sheet"; the Jerusalem Bible uses "clean shroud" and the Revised Standard Version says "clean linen shroud"). Thus the translators are nearly unanimous on use of the word "clean." Why would Matthew have denominated the shroud as "clean" when we cannot conceive of Joseph's use of a *soiled* shroud? If a temporary "shroud" or "carrying cloth" was used at the cross to cover the naked body, soak up some of the blood, and make the carrying easier, then it makes sense for Matthew to especially comment on the use of a *clean* shroud in the tomb.

This would *not* have been *a proper Jewish ritual* washing for burial, but would have reflected only practical necessity and simple decency as well as their new role as Christians. Also, a Jewish burial would not have involved preservative spices—that was not in accordance with Jewish custom. Conversely, *as Christians,* Joseph and Nicodemus wanted preservation of the body so that a more respectful anointing (not a Jewish anointing) would be feasible on Sunday morning. Again, it is sheer speculation as to what that anointing would consist of and how it would be done. But the Gospel accounts make it clear that the ointments were procured by the women on Saturday evening and were carried by them to the tomb on Sunday morning—even though the question is "moot" since there was no body to anoint.

I have quoted from and cited Judaic theologians, Jewish Bible scholars, Jewish archaeologists, and other Jewish authorities as appropriate for a full understanding of the background, mores, and instincts of both Jesus' followers and critics. However, I repeat that in my view his followers would be acting primarily as "Christians" rather than as Jews "under the Law." For this reason it is not appropriate to test the presumed actions of those followers against the various requirements of the Jewish law. Repeatedly, we see that the followers of Jesus are strongly influenced by their Jewishness, and yet in crucial moments will move away from those taboos and mandatory requirements whenever Christian concepts seem more important.

And to further amplify the religious milieu of the situation, it is worth noting that the wealthy, Rome-oriented Sadducees controlled the Sanhedrin, but permitted the more numerous Pharisees to dominate the religion of the Jews. Hillel was a Pharisee leader who died in A.D. 10. Gamaliel was his grandson and was *raban* (chief presiding officer) of the Great Sanhedrin. Hillel founded the Bet Hillel liberal school of Pharisaic teaching that has survived *to this day*. However, from 30 B.C. to A.D. 70 it was very subordinate to the conservative school of Bet Sammai Pharisees, which did not survive the holocaust of A.D. 70 in Judea. Harvey Falk, in his *Jesus the Pharisee* (Paulist Press, 1985), concludes that Jesus was a Bet Hillel Pharisee and that "charges of the Bet Hillel against Bet Shammai were word-for-word the same as those made by Jesus against *the Pharisees*."

Burial practices of the Jews were further verified in the last decades by excavation of a Jericho cemetery that had been in use during the first centuries B.C. and A.D. (And see *First Century Burial Customs of the Jews,* by Father Joseph Marino, St. Louis Priory, 1987.) All such data is fully consistent with the information now deduced from the Shroud of Turin. One skull, buried there, contained two coins from the reign of Herod Agrippa (41–44), demonstrating the sometime practice of putting coins on the eyelids.

Vera Barclay of Great Britain notes that the nearby Dead Sea Qumran community (second century B.C. to A.D. 70) graves have been extensively excavated, and they have found skeletons in the exact position of the Man on the Shroud: stretched out flat on the back, face up, hands folded over the pelvic region, with elbows protruding at the sides. This would be inconsistent with an Egyptian-style burial that required close winding of the body with strips of cloth.

During this century, archaeology has consistently demonstrated the historical accuracy of both the Jewish Bible and the New Testament, sometimes in surprising detail. This conclusion has become better known with the modem advent of such periodicals as the *Biblical Archaeology Review,* bringing science to the general reader. The negative aspect of this conclusion is equally impressive. The prominent American archaeologist and biblical scholar Nelson Glueck once wrote: "It may be stated categorically that no archaeological discovery has ever controverted a Biblical reference. Scores of archaeological findings have been made which confirm in clear outline or exact detail historical statements in the Bible."[2] With considerable success, he, like some others, used the Bible as a starting point and "map" in his search for unknown sites.

Some of the historical and archaeological record may one day support the Bible even more fully if the work of Immanuel Velikovsky in redating the Egyptian chronology is generally accepted, because then (seemingly) much of our vast archive of Egyptology might dovetail with and validate large segments of the Bible story.

Dr. John A. T. Robinson, well-known British theologian, writes that one of the things that shook his "natural predisposition to skepticism about the Turin Shroud" was that it could not easily be harmonized with the Gospels' accounts as to the grave-clothes; that "no forger starting, as he inevitably would, from the Gospel narratives... would have created the shroud we have." Yet, the single long cloth covering the whole body, back and front, though not what a forger would have thought of, "makes complete sense of the texts and fully comports with what other ancient evidence we have." He points out that the Greek words of the New Testament are not inconsistent with the Turin Shroud: Matthew (27:59) and Luke (23:53) most accurately say that Joseph and Nicodemus "folded" *(enetylixen)* the linen cloth around the body; Mark says they "wrapped" *(eneilesen)* him in it; the Gospel of John is more vague, saying that they "bound" *(edesan)* the body.[3]

Herbert Thurston, British Jesuit, crystallized the issue in these terms: This was either the impression of the body of the crucified Jesus of Nazareth, or it was designed as a counterfeit of that impression. A number of the detailed findings respecting the Shroud exactly fit Jesus as we know his story. Could all of these findings also fit someone else?

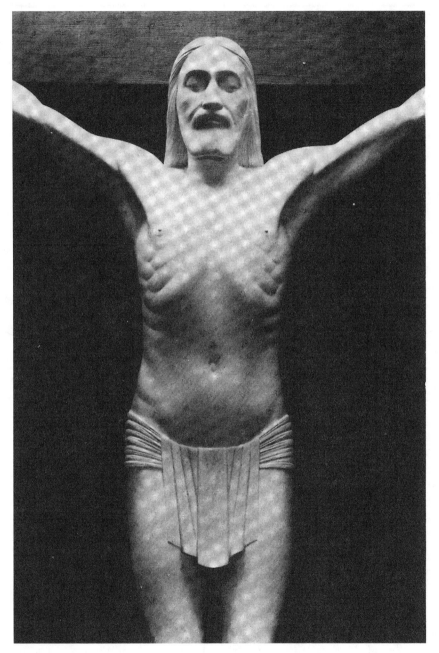

Figure 7.
Rev. Peter Weyland's crucifixion statue in plaster. *(Courtesy Holy Shroud Guild)*

Thurston, an early skeptic as to the Shroud's authenticity, said: "In no other person since the world began could these details be verified."[4]

Is it the Shroud of Jesus? Why else should the Shroud have been protected and revered for centuries unless each possessor had a basis for believing so? There is no inconsistency of the Shroud with the biblical accounts. Jesus was given an expensive burial in a new rock tomb, using expensive linen and burial spices, even though his execution was as a slave or criminal. His burial was incomplete. The body on the Shroud fits those facts—and it did not decompose (which *would* have marked the Shroud). The body and the Shroud were separated before decomposition, yet the bloodstains were not smeared. The Man of the Shroud was "crowned" with *a cap* of thorns, the oriental style for a crown. He was stabbed in the side, his legs were not broken. He had been excessively scourged and beaten about the face. All of these items fit the biblical account of the trial, execution, and burial of Jesus of Nazareth.

The Face of the Shroud, negative in sepia. There is a water stain at the top; creases top and bottom; blood rivulets on the forehead and hair. *(Courtesy Holy Shroud Guild)*

The Transfiguration. This mosaic, dated about A.D. 540, is in the apse of the Church of the Virgin, Monastery of St. Catherine. The mosaic has been untouched since it was made under the rule of Justinian I (527–565). The monastery is on Mount Sinai in the south-central Sinai Peninsula. *(Courtesy of St. Catherine's Monastery, especially Archbishop Damianos, and Father Gregory, head of the Sacred Council)*

King Abgar V (A.D. 13–50) receiving the Face on Cloth from the disciple Thaddaeus. St. Catherine's Monastery water damage is noticeable on the painting. *(Courtesy of St. Catherine's Monastery)*

Christ Pantocrator, apse of the Daphni church, Greece, a mosaic made about 1100. "Pantocrator" was the Byzantine term meaning omnipotent lord of the universe and mighty ruler. The water damage on the lower left has been repaired with plaster. *(Courtesy of John Gitchell)*

Christ Pantocrator, a twelfth-century mosaic in the apse of the Cefalu Cathedral, Sicily. *(Courtesy John Gitchell)*

Christ Enthroned, Monastery of Chilandari, Mt. Athos, Greece. The paint on this thirteenth-century Serbian icon is noticeably chipped, though negligibly so on the face. *(Courtesy John Gitchell)*

A twelfth-century mosaic of Jesus, National Museum, Florence, Italy. *(Courtesy John Gitchell)*

(below) The Veronica as painted by Gabriel Max. We know the history of the actual Veronica only from 1000 to 1527, while it was in the Vatican. Max, a German painter (1840–1915), copied the Veronica in 1874 from an existing painting and called it *Jesus Christus.* The original of his painting hangs in Prague in a private collection. *(This photograph was made, with permission, from a photographic copy of the painting at the Truth Center Foundation in Seattle, Washington, courtesy Dr. Mary Martin-Bacon.)*

(above) Face of Laon, cathedral in Laon, France, dated 1201–4. Notice the trelliswork surround. *(Courtesy John Gitchell)*

(above) Dr. Jackson briefs the STURP team of scientists in a hall of the Savoy Palace just before the five-day examination of the Shroud begins. *(Copyright 1978 Ernest H. Brooks II)*

(right) Dr. Jackson (left foreground) and other STURP members, wearing white gloves, smooth the Shroud on the special frame; magnets will hold it in place. *(Copyright 1978 Ernest H. Brooks II)*

(below) Pilgrims view the Shroud in Turin during the 1978 exposition *(Courtesy Holy Shroud Guild)*

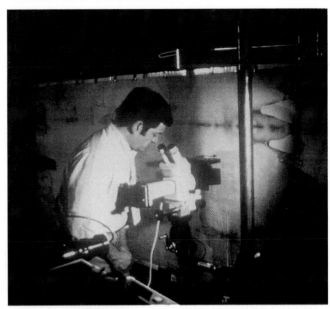

A STURP scientist making close-up pictures of the Shroud by photomicroscopy. *(Copyright 1978 Vernon Miller)*

An ultraviolet fluorescence experiment on the Shroud is shown in process. *(Copyright 1978 Ernest H. Brooks II)*

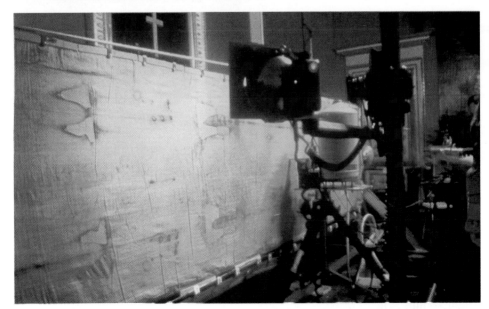

(right) Mark Evans of the STURP team taking pictures of the Shroud through a photomicroscope. *(Copyright 1978 Barrie M. Schwartz)*

(bottom) Scientists in Turin check the Shroud as equipment is being set up for their five-day intensive examination of it. *(Courtesy Holy Shroud Guild)*

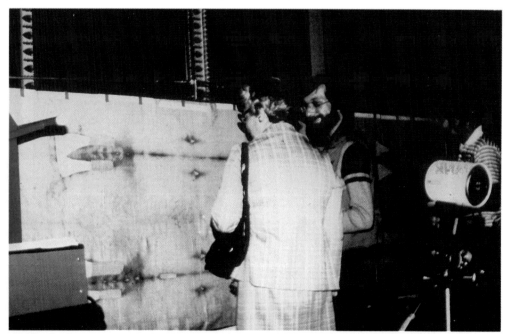

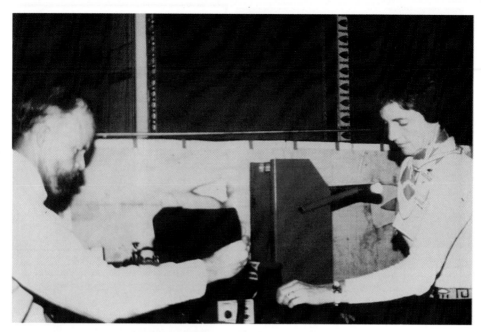

The Doctors Gilbert using a densitometer.
(Courtesy Holy Shroud Guild)

This laminated cardboard statue was made by STURP scientists using a three-dimensional projection from Shroud image photographs. *(Courtesy Holy Shroud Guild)*

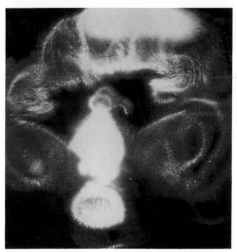 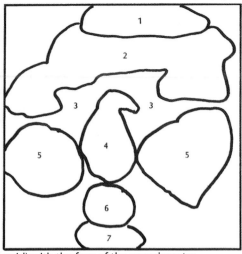

A Kirlian-type photograph made by contact (Polaroid) with the face of the experimenter, Cecile Ruchin. When a color Polaroid picture is taken by contact (for instance, of a human finger tip) the electrical impulse takes more than the physical subject (fingerprint, etc.). It seems to capture an "energy" emanation that gives accurate information about the health, emotions, and thoughts of the person whose fingerprint was placed on the film rawstock. Some have speculated that this "spiritual energy" might have a relationship to the "energy" that created the Shroud images. *(Courtesy Cecile Ruchin)*

1. Right brain: orange-white
2. Forehead: whitish-blue
3. Eyes: black
4. Nose: white

5. Cheeks: dark blue
6. Lips: reddish-white
7. Chin: dark blue

(left) A clear Pontius Pilate coin in good condition. *(Courtesy American Numismatic Society)*

(right) This Pontius Pilate coin, more typical, is struck off-center. The letters TIBE should be lower and at the left margin of the coin. *(Frank Tribbe)*

(above) Magnified weave of the Shroud cloth, showing the body image at the tip of the nose. *(Copyright 1978 Mark Evans)*

(below) Magnified weave of the Shroud cloth, showing a bloodstain on the lower back of the Man of the Shroud. *(Copyright 1978 Mark Evans)*

(above) This magnification of the Shroud cloth shows a burn mark that occurred before the 1532 fire. *(Copyright 1978 Mark Evans)*

(below) A tack used in some earlier exposition caused the rust showing on the magnification of the Shroud cloth. *(Copyright 1978 Mark Evans)*

The Guadalupe Madonna in Mexico City, as it appears today. This is one of a group of photographs taken in May 1979—the first photographs made of the image while removed from its glass-covered frame. All previous ones were taken through the glass. The paisley-like pattern on the robe was an added feature, says scientist-photographer Callahan, because the lines go straight across instead of "dipping" into the "folds" of the garment. *(Courtesy Dr. Philip S. Callahan)*

A painting by Philip Serna Callahan after the Guadalupe Madonna, which attempts to show the original image plus the overpainted areas. Figure A (upper left) represents the customary undersketch that is missing from the tilma, upon infrared inspection. The left half of the figure is as it was originally, while parts of the right portion show added stars and sunbursts, as it appears now. B is the background that was put on the rough tilma without the use of sizing to fill the crevices of the fabric. C is the rose-colored robe, and D is the blue cloak. Callahan shows faint outlines that were the original fingers, which were painted out to make them shorter (as an Indian's would be). The rock on which the Madonna stands is now overpainted and one sees a crescent moon held up by cupid. (Courtesy Center for Applied Research in the Apostolate)

Ris Phillips's Face of Jesus *(Courtesy Patrick Walsh Press)*

Ariel Agemian's Face of Jesus in sepia *(Courtesy of the Confraternity of the Precious Blood)*

SIX

MEDICAL EVALUATION OF THE SHROUD

DR. PIERRE Barbet of Paris researched the medical aspects of the Shroud for many years, beginning in 1931. He was an outstanding surgeon (surgeon general of St. Joseph's Hospital, Paris) and a professor of anatomy, with an enormous medical knowledge. He was one of the first to point out, in two respects, the difference between the body images and the bloodstains on the Shroud. First, the body images have a mist-like quality with no sharp lines, whereas the bloodstains are richer and darker in color and have more precise lines. Also, the bloodstains appear as positive images while the body shows as a photographic negative, as Secondo Pia discovered. Barbet's study and experimentation resulted in far-reaching conclusions: For example, he found that all of the blood-flow lines, coagulation patterns, and other characteristics of the bloodstains on the Shroud are natural and typical in every detail.

Barbet was perhaps the first to discover that the Shroud image clearly shows that the nails went through the wrist, not the palm, and modern research has validated this as the Roman crucifixion technique. By experiments on fresh cadavers, he demonstrated that nails through the palms would tear out in a few minutes from the weight of the body. Neither artists, physicians, nor clergy of the Middle Ages were aware of these facts and assumed that the nails went through the palms. Although the Gospels specify *hand* wounds, "hand" is translated from the Greek word *cheir,* which can also mean wrist and forearm.

The Shroud image seems to have no thumbs on either hand. Dr. Barbet's experiments showed that driving a nail through the "space of Destot" in the wrist lacerates a nerve, which causes the thumb to bend sharply into the palm.

Dr. Barbet also found that it was impossible to transfer human blood to linen cloth with anything like the precision shown on the Shroud. If the blood was too wet (thin) when it came in contact with linen cloth, it would spangle or run in all directions along the threads. If it was not wet enough, it would leave only a smudge. The perfect bordered, picturelike clots on the Shroud, it seemed, could not be reproduced by staining. Thus, even the bloodstains could not have happened *just* by contact with a bloody body.

Because of the different lines of blood flow from the wrist wounds, and the forcibly contracted and enlarged respiratory muscles of the trunk that could be clearly traced on the Shroud image, Barbet was convinced that the Man of the Shroud had died rather quickly of suffocation. The weight of the body hanging from the wrists, with the arms at about 65-degree angles above the horizontal, permitted the filling of the lungs with air but precluded the expelling of it. Asphyxiation forced the man to push up from the nail through his feet, bringing the arms nearer to shoulder level (at least to a 55-degree angle), and thus permitting him to exhale. Then pain and fatigue would cause body sag and return of suffocation. If the Man of the Shroud was Jesus, then, being weakened by the night long torture before the crucifixion, he was able to achieve suffocation-relief very few times before fatal asphyxiation occurred. Barbet's experiments convinced him that the Shroud imprint image made very certain the early death of the Man of the Shroud while still on the cross.

Barbet concluded that the spear entered the chest between the fifth and sixth ribs, and most medical experts since have agreed with that appraisal of the wound.

The positioning of the left foot over the right, for a single spike, and the location of the spike wound, again are validated both by anatomical truth and by research data on Roman practices.

Dr. Pierre Barbet's masterful evaluation of the medical aspects of the Shroud of Turin *(A Doctor at Calvary)* has been criticized because the arms and hands of the Man of the Shroud seem preternaturally long. However, four mystics (Anne Catherine Emmerich of Westphalia, 1774–1824; María de Agreda of Spain, 1602–65; Bridget of

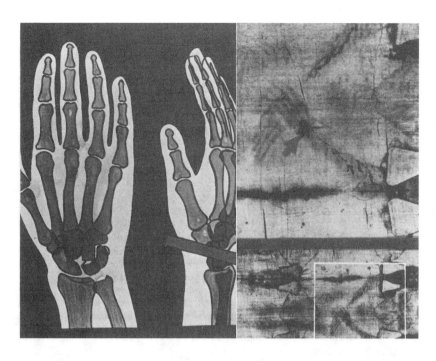

Figure 1.
An enlargement of the wrist wounds on the Shroud (above) and an artist's conception of the penetration of the wrists. *(Courtesy Holy Shroud Guild)* A three-dimensional relief of the crossed hands (below). *(Courtesy Giovanni Tamburelli, C.S.E.L.T.)*

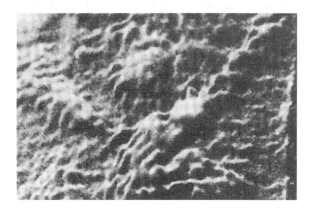

Sweden, 1303–73; Teresa Neumann of Bavaria, 1898–62) *repeatedly* "observed" Jesus' crucifixion on the video-screen of their minds and dictated detailed descriptions of it to their priests who published the accounts—AND, all four *saw* the soldiers cruelly stretch his arms, dislocating the joints, as they spiked his wrists to the *patibulum.* (See "The Shroud of Turin, Mystical Visions and Retrocognition" by Frank C. Tribbe, in *SINDON* no. 34, December 1985, Centro Internazionale della Sindone of Turin, Italy. Also, note the significance of David's prediction in *Psalms 22:* "My God, my God, why hast thou forsaken me?... and all my bones are out of joint...")

There seems to be no doubt, scientifically, that the left foot was spiked on top of the right foot, and the bent knee (frozen in rigor mortis) verifies this observation. However, Shroud scientist Dr. Joseph M. Gambescia of Philadelphia, upon close examination of the Shroud bloodstains at the feet (frontal and dorsal images), concluded that there was more than one nail used. Following this suggestion, archaeologist Paul G. Maloney, vice president of ASSIST (Association of Scientists and Scholars International for the Shroud of Turin) made lifesize glass transparencies of the foot images to superimpose, front and back of each foot, demonstrating the verity of Gambescia's observation. He then obtained an amputated human foot and the expert assistance of a forensic pathologist, while Maloney drove square Roman-type nails through the foot. These procedures clearly demonstrated that the right foot was first spiked to the upright of the cross from the front of the ankle, exiting through the heel; thereafter, a second nail penetrated the center of the left foot and "tacked" it onto the center of the right foot and thence into the cross. Thus two spikes were used, both going through the right foot. And consequently, the left foot was free to pivot up and down as the Man of the Shroud changed positions, causing the strange blood patterns noted by Gambescia. Maloney's paper covering this was presented April 7, 1989, at a Ferris State University conference at Big Rapids, Michigan; it was then presented at the International Conference on the Shroud and Iconography held in Bologna, Italy, May 6 and 7, 1989.

Shroud data show that the crown of thorns worn by the Man of

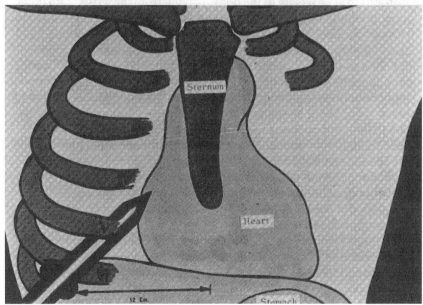

Figure 2.
An enlargement of the side wound on the Shroud (top) and an artist's conception of the spear thrust. *(Courtesy Holy Shroud Guild)*

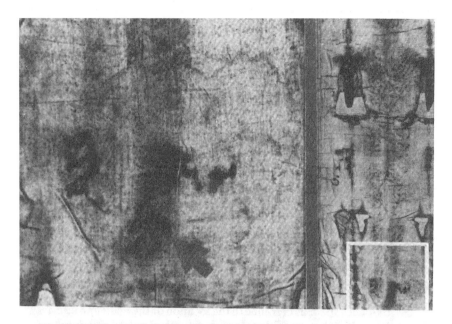

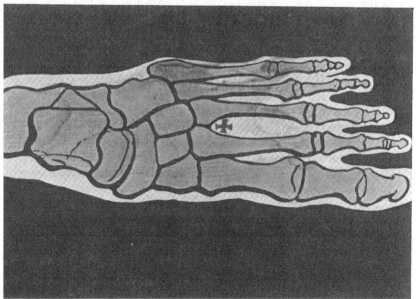

Figure 3.
An enlargement of the wounded feet on the Shroud (top) and an artist's conception of where the spike would have been located. *(Courtesy Holy Shroud Guild)*

the Shroud was a cap, not a wreath or circlet. In Greece and Western Europe the latter seems favored, but in the Orient, when crowning kings, they always used a caplike crown, sometimes called a miter, that enclosed the entire skull.

Most medical men who have examined the Shroud, the photographs of the Shroud images, and the reports of Dr. Barbet agree that the wounds of the Shroud image came by transfer in some fashion from a human body and could not have been faked. Dr. Barbet's report of his research and findings is contained in his book *A Doctor at Calvary.*[1]

The views of early-twentieth-century medical men like Yves Delage of the Sorbonne have been largely supported by later ones like Pierre Barbet, and present-day Robert Bucklin of the Los Angeles Medical Examiner's Office and pathologist Frederick Zugibe of New York State.

Physicians Giuseppe Caselli (during the 1939 Convention of Holy Shroud Studies), Pierre Barbet (in his 1950 book), and Sebastian Rodante (issue no. 1, 1982, of *Shroud Spectrum International)* have carefully examined the blood flows on the forehead of the Man of the Shroud, with special reference to the location of the veins and arteries of the scalp. They are able to conclude with absolute certainty that each discernible rivulet of blood shows distinctive characteristics of either venous flow or arterial flow *in every case* correct for the location of the thorn-puncture from which the rivulet starts. They point out that arterial blood flow is always to be distinguished by the spurts of blood that emerge from a wound due to the heart pulses; conversely, the thicker venous blood flow is slow and steady and coagulates more quickly. Most striking is the observation of Dr. Rodante that knowledge about the circulation of human blood and the difference between arterial blood and venous blood was discovered only in 1593 by Andrea Cesilpino, thus demonstrating once more that the Shroud images contain data that could not possibly have been known to an artist or forger in the Middle Ages or earlier.

STURP member Robert Bucklin (Los Angeles medical examiner) has said that his examination of the wound images and apparent blood flows on the Shroud indicate that they accord with what the Gospels say of the wounds of Jesus and they appear as a knowledgeable anatomist

Figure 4.
An enlargement of the back wounds on the Shroud. *(Courtesy Holy Shroud Guild)*

might expect them to. If the Shroud was faked by transfer from a statue it would mean that the "statue would have been done before much was known about the anatomy of circulation."[2] Also, the blood flows were not smeared, as would have been true if the Shroud was wrapped and unwrapped around some statue or mold.

J. Malcolm Cameron, British Home Office pathologist, notes[3] that the arms of the Man on the Shroud were forcibly bent across the lower abdomen to break the postmortem rigor (muscle stiffening) of the shoulder girdle (a common problem for morticians regardless of the cause of death, in order to get a body into position for burial). Drs. Jackson and Jumper of the STURP scientific team noticed, when their computer projections were developing three-dimensional images from the Shroud data, that the head was bent forward as a result of rigor mortis. Knees bent by the rigor are also observable, especially the left. Moreover, their three-dimensional images have further special value for medical studies of the Shroud because they show, for instance, the degree of swelling in the right cheek, and the overextension of the chest and abdominal muscles.

Did Jesus die on the cross or after he was taken down? This has often been raised by skeptics and critics of the Shroud. Scientists studying the Shroud no longer have doubts on that point, for a variety of reasons. Professor Giovanni Tamburelli of Turin University has used the computer in his study of blood flows on the Shroud. For instance, he has found that all streams of blood on the face flow *down* the face; none of them flow toward the ears or back of the neck or head. Thus it is clear that the death of the Man of the Shroud caused the blood to stop running while he was still on the cross. If he were alive when removed from the cross, the blood would have still been flowing, and as he lay on his back it would have flowed toward his back. Tamburelli also noticed a drop of blood from the right nostril that did not fall because its weight was not sufficient. The drop was pointed, not round, proving that the blood ceased to flow because of death while he was still on the cross.

Another significant characteristic is that the Shroud bloodstains have a "halo effect" that is typically suggestive of the separation of blood and serum, which happens after the heart has already stopped— evidence of death on the cross.

Monsignor Giulio Ricci, an Italian artist, summarized the views of himself and five medically expert sindonologists (Hermann Moedder, Germany; David Willis, England; Anthony Sava, Frederick T. Zugibe, and Robert Bucklin, USA) who agreed with Dr. Barbet that the Man of the Shroud was definitely dead before he was taken from the cross and that it must have been a real corpse that had suffered real wounds of crucifixion. Various signs of rigor mortis were noted. One contrast was observed, that the head wounds were clearly premortem while the wound in the side was postmortem. The latter, typically, oozed with gravity, but showed no sign of force from a pumping heart. Incidentally, this wound appears on the left side of the image, which means that it was on the Man's right side.

After death, blood separates into a watery serum and a thick, cellular mass. Barbet, Moedder, Bucklin, and Willis all concluded that the lance had pierced both the pleural cavity and the right side of the heart of the Man on the Shroud, and that most of the blood had come from the heart while most of the water was from the pleural cavity of the chest. This does not preclude that some blood could have come from the pleural cavity and some water could have come from the sac that surrounds the heart, the pericardium.

Sava and Zugibe suggest that the spear may only have penetrated the pleural cavity, which, together with the pericardium sac, was probably filled with blood and water due to internal hemorrhaging as a result of the scourging and other trauma of the previous hours.

Zugibe also concludes[4] that even if the body of Jesus was washed before being wrapped in the Shroud in the tomb, the wounds could have oozed blood sufficiently to leave some of the major stains we find on the Shroud of Turin. As an experienced medical examiner, he states unequivocally that "blood does *flow* from a dead individual, particularly if death occurs violently."

How the blood stained the Shroud is still a mystery. Some claim that a corpse will bleed very little—not as much as shown on the Shroud. However, Dr. Derek Barrowcliff, British Home Office pathologist, says: "It can be demonstrated in the mortuary that a short stab wound or cut on the back of the scalp [of a corpse]... or indeed a cut into any dependent part, will bleed freely, continuously, unimpeded by any of the natural mechanisms such as spasm of blood vessel or clotting of the blood which in the living would tend to arrest bleeding. Blood will flow from an open vein as long as the normal laws of gravity operate upon the hydrostatic pressure."

More recently, the work of Drs. Alan D. Adler and John H. Heller, chemical engineers in Connecticut, leads them to conclude that the blood traces in the Shroud are of mammalian, primate, and *probably* of human, blood. Professor P. L. Baima Bollone reported in *Sindon* journals[5] that by the use of fluorescent antibodies he has demonstrated the presence of human globulins in the Shroud "bloodstains." Globulins are a type of protein found in blood serum. Adler and Heller have tested for human albumin, and in large measure have confirmed and extended Baima's observations.[6]

Dr. Hermann Moedder, a radiologist in Cologne, Germany, used volunteer university students in a simulated crucifixion experiment.

He found that his volunteers would lose consciousness in about twelve minutes of hanging if there was no arrangement that would permit them to push up from their feet. Suspension from the wrists causes the pectoral muscles of the chest and the intercostal muscles of the abdomen to become paralyzed so that they cannot force air out of the lungs.

New York medical examiner Frederick Zugibe also conducted a series of simulated crucifixion experiments with volunteers. He recorded a wide variety of observations, medical tests, and evaluations while the subject was suspended. These included data respecting pain, breathing difficulties, blood/oxygen content, lung pathology, carbon dioxide elimination, lung ventilation, blood lactic acid, heart rhythms,

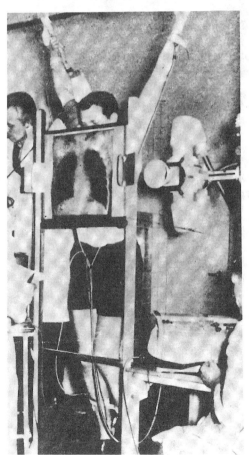

Figure 5.
Dr. Hermann Moedder's crucifixion experiment. A fluoroscope shows breathing impairment. *(Courtesy Hermann Moedder)*

Figure 6.
Dr. Frederick Zugibe's crucifixion experiment. Note the push-up support given the feet. *(Courtesy Frederick T. Zugibe)*

blood pressure, cardiac activity, and blood chemistries, plus a psychological evaluation. Although the experiments were conducted in an air-conditioned room, heavy sweating was so intense that it ran off the toes to form a puddle on the floor. Shoulder pain was severe. The most common position was with the body fully arched and the top of the head against the cross. Using suspensions of up to forty-five minutes, Zugibe found no signs of asphyxiation or significant breathing distress. However, photographs show that he did give his volunteers a solid foot support from which they apparently could push up to facilitate breathing. He does not comment on this point, which would be a significant deviation from the situation used by Moedder.

Dr. Barbet tells of German torture by crucifixion at the Dachau concentration camp during World War II. He says that the condemned man was hung up by his hands, with his feet some distance from the ground. In a short while his breathing difficulty became intolerable, and the man overcame this to some extent by drawing himself up by his arms, and holding himself up for one-half to one minute. The executioners tied weights to his feet to prevent his pulling up to breathe. Asphyxia then came on rapidly, but at the last moment they would remove the weights so he could get some relief. After an hour of this cat-and-mouse action by the jailers, his thoracic frame had swelled to its maximum and the epigastric hollow was extremely concave. Profuse sweating stained the ground and his hair and beard were drenched, although the temperature was at freezing. Death came in about three hours. After death, the body had an extreme rigidity from the previous cramping, and the head fell forward.

What was the cause of Jesus' death—asphyxiation or heart failure? It is doubtful that an absolute diagnosis can be made from the Shroud data, or that it matters. Both factors were undoubtedly present. Dr. Frederick Zugibe is sure that the trauma of Gethsemane, plus those injuries as seen on the Shroud, would have caused internal hemorrhaging in the chest, loading the heart sac (pericardium) and pleural cavity above the diaphram with blood and serum, putting an intolerable strain on the lungs and heart. Either could have failed. I would opt for asphyxiation simply because most experts find precise evidence in the Shroud image that the abdomen muscles were excessively swollen, and the 3-D projections confirm this.

Dr. Zugibe says that if he were writing a death certificate for the Man on the Shroud, the cause of death would read:

> Cardiac and respiratory arrest due to severe pulmonary edema due to cardiogenic, traumatic, and hypovolemic shock due to crucifixion.

One can hardly quibble with his diagnosis of combined causes.

Unfortunately, from Zugibe's fairly conservative and well-written book, many news reporters chose to feature just one point, of less than three pages, in the book: They picked up his speculation that Jesus may have died of a very obscure heart ailment known as Marfan's syndrome, which involves a rupture of the aorta artery near the heart. Zugibe labels it "a scientific speculation" based upon the skeletal structure and age of the Man of the Shroud. Perhaps the media focused on it in order to take literary license and say that Jesus died of "a broken heart."

The medical data on the Shroud implicitly raise one enigma—stigmata cases. For several hundred years a sprinkling of these cases have been recorded, including some famous persons who were later canonized as saints, and some of whom were recorded even in our present generation. The phenomenon of stigmata usually involves a highly religious person who, in his late youth or young adulthood, begins to bleed either periodically or continuously from areas where one or more of the five wounds of Jesus on the cross were located. All recorded cases involve bleeding from the center of the palms. One of the more famous recent cases involved Padre Pio, a Capuchin monk in eastern Italy who died about thirty-six years ago. He had all five wounds of stigmata, and they bled continuously from about the age of twenty. This was both an embarrassment and a handicap, as he had to wear special fingerless gloves all of the time. Officials of the Vatican and even popes disbelieved the reality of Pio's stigmata for several years while he underwent treatments and examinations, but the stigmata were real.

Teresa Neumann, a stigmatist of our era, who has also had many visions of Jesus' passion, has said: "Do not think that Our Savior was nailed in the hands where I have my stigmata. These marks have only a mystical meaning. Jesus must have been fixed more firmly on the cross."

If the Shroud and current historical research are right and Jesus was nailed through the wrists, why are the stigmata in the middle of the hands? I suggest that there is a psychological factor involved in the stigmata: The person knows that the Bible says "nailed through the hands," and he may sometimes be influenced by knowledge of other stigmatics. I further suggest that when knowledge of the medical evidence of the Shroud becomes well known in churches worldwide, more and more stigmata cases in the future *will* involve wrist wounds.

SEVEN

THE TURIN COMMISSION AND RESEARCH OF 1969–73

U PON THE assent of the Holy See and of King Umberto II of Savoy, Cardinal Pellegrino (archbishop of Turin) appointed a special commission of Italian experts to examine the Shroud, advise him about its storage and preservation, conduct limited tests, and recommend a program of extensive scientific testing. Initially the commission consisted of four churchmen, seven technical experts, representatives of the governmental Ministries of Education and Finance, and a photographer.

The commission convened in the Royal Chapel of the Holy Shroud, a part of the Cathedral of John the Baptist in Turin, and on June 16 and 17, 1969, conducted all-day sessions of preliminary examination, photography, and nondestructive testing of the Shroud. Examinations were made visually and with the microscope, by normal light, an ultraviolet light, and by infrared light. The commission's conclusions recommended more extensive examinations and testing, including attempts to date the cloth, photographic and spectroscopic analyses, tests of selected threads and small samples of the cloth, and documentary videotaping of the relic.

On October 4, 1973, the Shroud was displayed in the Royal Chapel while Italian television crews conducted a series of photographic tests to ensure that television exhibition would be feasible. Then on November 22 and 23, 1973, television photography of the Shroud was conducted, and at 9 P.M. on the twenty-third the first televised exhibition of the Shroud was aired in Italy.

On November 24 the commission reconvened, with substantially the same personnel as convoked in 1969. Added to their number were two French scholars, Professor Gilbert Raes of the Ghent Institute of Textile Technology in Belgium, and Dr. Max Frei, a criminologist, botanist, and pollen expert from Zurich, Switzerland.

The Shroud was clamped to a frame, set up vertically for initial examination (later it was laid out on a table that was first covered with sheets). While held vertically in its frame, the photographer outlined it with a much larger piece of black cloth, and daylight from the windows was blacked out. Using six cameras, photographer Gian Cordiglia took pictures in black-and-white, color, ultraviolet, and infrared. His early shots were rushed to his studio for developing so that adjustments could be made before taking more pictures in the afternoon. Although much of his work did not turn out well, his color photos were the first ever taken, and they were very helpful in the early American work that was just beginning.

The Church authorities were helpful, especially in two respects: first, in permitting Dr. Frei to use "sticky-tape" to lift off surface debris for subsequent laboratory study; and, second, in allowing twelve short lengths of thread and two very small samples of cloth to be taken for laboratory testing by three different facilities.

The work of the commission basically involved textile studies covering five activities:

1. Direct examination of the Shroud (including the removal of thread fragments and cloth samples and the lifting of surface debris by sticky-tape) with various equipment.

2. Examination in the laboratory of surface materials (by Dr. Frei).

3. Examination of thread and cloth in the laboratories (Professor Raes, Belgium; Professors Mari and Rizzatti, Institute of Forensic Medicine, University of Modena; Professor Filogamo, Institute of Human Anatomy and Histology, University of Turin).

4. Examination in the laboratory of photographs of the Shroud made during firsthand examination.

5. Examinations in the laboratories of simulated materials and of control and contrast materials.

Four nuns from the nearby Institute of the Daughters of St. Joseph (all proficient in darning and embroidery) carefully removed thread fragments and cloth samples under the direction of the experts, and then repaired the minor (but not visible) damage to the cloth. A grid map had been made of the Shroud so that a meticulous record could be made of the locations from which the thread fragments (none more than 1 1/2 inches long) and cloth samples were taken.

Included in the direct examination was a detailed recording of the repairs previously made to the Shroud and its backing. They recorded 31 patches and 48 darns. It was noted that all of the patches were made with plain-woven linen, some of which is white and some brownish. This was the first comprehensive listing of the repairs, but it was done more thoroughly five years later by the American team using x-ray equipment that showed even more.

Dr. Raes reported that the Shroud's linen cloth is woven with a three-to-one herringbone twill and is sewed with linen thread; he stated specifically that warp threads, weft threads, and sewing threads of the Shroud were all linen. If dated to the first century, it would have been an expensive piece of cloth for those days. Using polarized light for microscopic viewing, he could identify "traces" of cotton fibers known as fibrils, which, upon testing, were found to be of "Gossypium herbaceum" type, a cotton which had existed in the Middle East of the first century. A fibril is a hairlike strand of material; a number of fibrils are twisted together to make a thread. Threads of the Shroud itself are about fifteen-hundredths of a millimeter in diameter. The Shroud body image is colored only two or three fibrils deep into the thread.

In June 1984 in Manchester, England, a paper presented by Mrs. Eve Cockburn of the Palaeopathology Association, Detroit, reported that a scrap of cotton fibers was attached to the linen funerary wrappings of an Egyptian mummy, Pentu, reliably dated to 170 B.C.

Some critics of the Shroud had heretofore said that there was no clear evidence for the use of cotton in Egypt as early as the first century A.D.

The cotton traces meant that it was woven on a loom that had previously been used to weave cotton cloth; this finding makes it almost certain that the Shroud linen was woven in the Middle East, since raw cotton was unknown in Europe until the ninth century, when it was first planted in Spain by the Moors. Cotton was first woven in Venice and Milan in the fourteenth century; cotton cloth was not even seen in England until the fifteenth century. Cotton was grown in China and India in antiquity and was expertly woven in India several centuries before the Christian era; by the first century A.D. it was grown extensively in Mesopotamia and Egypt.

Leviticus 19:19 states: "neither shall a garment mingled of linen and woolen come upon thee." Notes in the Jerusalem Bible (Doubleday, 1966) indicate that this was in essence a prohibition against magic, with incongruous compounds. The Mishnah of the Talmud, which contains interpretations of scriptural ordinances as compiled by the rabbis about A.D. 200, makes it very clear that cotton may be added to linen without fear of a transgression of this prohibition known as the "mixing of kinds," but the slightest amount of wool mixed with the linen would not have been tolerated. Thus, there can be no question that the cloth of the Shroud would have been perfectly proper and acceptable as burial linen for a Jew in the first century A.D. Dr. Raes concluded that this piece of linen *could* have been manufactured in the first century A.D., but he could not say with certainty that it *was.*

This cloth is a twill and therefore is different from Egyptian cloth, known as plain weave (one thread over, and one under), of the first century. The three-to-one twill weave with herringbone pattern has been found in fabrics of the Middle East dated to the first three centuries of the Christian era, but it was more common in silk than in linen. This weave was unknown in France even in the fourteenth century. It was the consensus of the commission that twill weave originated in either Syria or Mesopotamia. British textile expert Elizabeth Crowfoot (later consulted) placed the Shroud linen as of Syrian origin, according to historian Ian Wilson. The commission also noted that Monsignor P. Savio reported to them that a mummy found in Antinoopolis (present-day name, Sheik of Abade), Egypt, and dated between A.D. 136 and 200, was wrapped with bands of a twill weave linen.

The yarn (thread) from which the Shroud was woven is fairly heavy and has the distinctive "Z twist" that shows it is a very old type of yarn.

Roman historian Pliny (A.D. 23–79) describes the steps in processing yarn as including a bleaching in alkaline wood-ash, applications of starch, and a softening by washing in a "struthium" solution, which is assumed to be soap weed. This latter step would provide a toxicity to preclude mildew, mold, and decay—thus explaining in part the excellent condition of the Shroud today. This factor also helps to account for the low-grade fluorescence found in the Shroud.

The sticky-tape samples of surface debris lifted from the Shroud were taken by Dr. Max Frei to his Zurich laboratory to examine the pollen fossils adhering to the adhesive. Pollen is microscopic, or nearly so, and imperceptibly it lodges in the fabric of any cloth exposed to air during the pollen season. These pollen grains are almost indestructible, and, under examination through an electron microscope, their type, classification, and other physical characteristics become quite clear. Comparing with pollen grains that are found in specific areas of the world but in no other areas, Dr. Frei was able to determine with absolute certainty that there was a significant quantity of pollen on the Shroud from plants that grew exclusively in Palestine and the Anatolian steppes of Turkey, as well as pollen from France and Italy. He concluded that the cloth at some time in its existence had been exposed to the air of Palestine and Turkey—very strong evidence that goes a long way toward obviating the possibility of a European counterfeit.

After several years of careful study of the Shroud surface debris samples, Dr. Frei delivered a supplemental report to the cardinal of Turin on April 1, 1981, confirming all of his earlier, tentative work on the commission. He had found fifty-six varieties of pollen on the Shroud, including fourteen found only in the eastern Mediterranean, and two-thirds of these varieties come exclusively from plants growing in semi-desert areas from Palestine to Turkey. He also determined that the latter varieties were at least 500 years old, making it most likely that they had become embedded in the Shroud before it was brought to Europe. It is his opinion that the cloth of the Shroud is indeed about 2,000 years old and came from the area of Palestine. Dr. Max Sulser-Frei, criminologist of Zurich, Switzerland, was involved in both the 1973 and 1978 scientific exercises. His book *Pollens of the Shroud of Turin* was scheduled for 1983 publication, but his unexpected death held up publication. Dr. Frei's published scientific papers make abundantly clear, as summarized in *this* book, that the pollen from more than ninety plants found on the Shroud come from four areas only: Near East desert (Dead Sea area); Anatolian steppes of Turkey (Edessa); Bosporus (Istanbul/Constantinople); Western Europe (France and Italy). He has stated flatly that the "spectrum of pollens from Palestine and Turkey could not be explained by storms and accidental contamination" carrying the pollen to Western Europe. Frei's pollen samples and research files were delivered to ASSIST in 1988 by the Frei heirs.

Dr. Professor Werner Bulst, S.J., of Darmstadt, West Germany (as well as other scientists in Europe, Israel, and the United States) has extended and validated the Shroud pollen work of the late Dr. Frei, and it is reported in Nos. 10, 19, and 27 of *Shroud Spectrum International* (Nashville, Indiana) and in *Biblische Zeitschrift*. Notably, Bulst has obtained written reinforcement from Professor Avinoam Danin of Hebrew University and Professor Aaron Horowitz of Tel Aviv University, who find Frei's work to be without flaw. (Frei had been one of the world's most esteemed criminologists and had been president of the United Nations Commission on Criminology; in his Shroud studies, Frei made seven expeditions to the Near East to identify *all* of the pollens found in the Shroud.)

Bulst points out that although the Shroud was exposed to the air at least twenty-seven times in the West since the fourteenth century, only seventeen species of European plants are represented on the Shroud. Danin and Horowitz are satisfied that indeed the Shroud of Turin was fabricated in Jerusalem to account for the high pollen count of species from that area. They point out that the prevailing winds in Palestine blow *from* the north and west. Bulst comments: "The spectrum of non-European species is highly astonishing."

Frei also reported that he found traces of aloe ointment made from the variety of aloe plant that grows only on the island Socotra off the coast of South Yemen (Oman). Dr. Frei has often used pollen data (collected from clothing, for instance) in testifying in court in the course of his forty years' work as a criminologist. Such testimony, by an expert like Frei, is regularly accepted as evidence in court.

Many varieties of the pollen grains from the air that were embedded in the weave of the Shroud (see also chapter 7), were found to have originated in Palestine and nowhere else, and some of those varieties have been extinct for several centuries. This data does not *prove* that the Shroud was in Palestine in Jesus' time and not later, but it is evidence that leads us toward that conclusion.

Similarly, development of the three-to-one herringbone twill weave of which the Shroud cloth was made occurred in the Middle or Near East (India-Mesopotamia-Syria) in the millennium preceding Jesus' birth, and it was available in Palestine in Jesus' time. This piece of cloth was probably made in adjoining Syria (chapter 7 describes the findings of Dr. Raes on this point). Linen with such a weave would not have been available in France until considerably after the crucial date of 1357. So, again, this piece of cloth *could* have been in Palestine in Jesus' time and probably was.

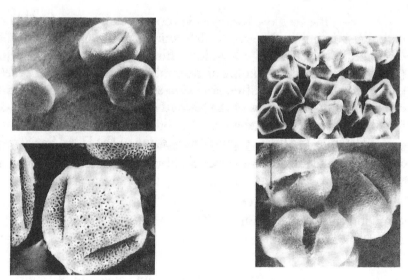

Figure 1.
Pollen grains magnified. The *Roemeria hydrida* in the upper left are from the Anatolia (Turkey) steppes, especially near Edessa; *Haplophyllum tuberculatum*, upper right, are from Eastern Mediterranean desert areas, specifically near the Dead Sea; *Epinedium pubigerum*, lower left, are from the Bosporus, near Constantinople (Istanbul); *Cistus creticus*, lower right, are from the entire Mediterranean basin, including Palestine as well as Italy and France. *(Courtesy C C Pollen Co.)*

Even more impressive is the coin-on-the-eye work of Professor Francis L. Filas of Loyola University, Chicago, which seems to give us a verified date for the Shroud image that is far more precise than carbon-dating can ever be.[1]

Three-dimensional enlargements of the Face of the Shroud are like relief maps, and there are some objects on the eyelids that stand up like thick buttons. During their early 3-D work, Drs. Jackson and Jumper noted these definite protuberances and tentatively concluded that they *might* be coins placed on each eyelid to keep them closed, as was a common burial practice in the first half of the first century in Judea.[2] Thereafter, tentative validation came by happenstance in August 1979 when Professor Filas was enlarging his slides of the Shroud image to fill a twelve foot, closed-circuit television screen. He was startled to see what appeared to be Greek letters on the right *eye* of the Shroud Face. With better enlargements and the technical assistance of coin expert Michael Marx, he discovered a 15mm (5/8 inch) disc inscribed with four recognizable Greek letters and an astrologer's staff, a *lituus*. After research on historic coins, the size of the coin, the size and shape and position of the inscriptions, and the sequence of the four letters, were all found to be exactly correct for a small bronze coin known as the Pontius Pilate coin, minted in Palestine from 29 to 32. (Pilate was procurator of Judea from A.D. 26 to 36). The astrologer's staff was used as an independent symbol on no other coin in the Roman world at any time (it occasionally appeared as a small side decoration). The odds in favor of the identification of the coin and its date are in the range of millions to one against any other interpretation.

Although the coin is very rare, copies of it are available and have been compared with the Shroud by Filas. However, the coin of the Shroud has a misspelling: magnification shows the Greek letters "Y CAI" but should read, "TIBEPIOY KAICAPOC" (meaning, "Of Tiberius Caesar"). Some variations of the coin show only IOY instead of the full name of Tiberius (language specialists use different letters for transliteration of the Greek characters; IOY, end of first word, is rendered IOU by some). All coin experts know that coins of that period and coinage did sometimes contain spelling errors, and now, even more spectacularly, Filas has found three actual Pontius Pilate coins that do have that error, a C instead of K. In fact, numismatists admonish that Pontius Pilate coins, as a class, are of wretched technical quality, poorly pressed, off-center, and contain misspellings.

Some critics claim that all this is just Filas's imagination, because better and later photographs of the Shroud Face show no hint of such coin details (Filas used the 1931 Enrie photos). There are two answers to this: first, that *something is* there, because the 3-D projections of Jackson and Jumper have been replicated by Italian scientists; second, Filas explains that it is not necessarily desirable to get "better" photographs. Enrie took two pictures of the Shroud Face. One is a close-up that provides a life-size face (about nine inches wide). For the second, he backed off a few feet and used a telescopic lens, with a resulting two-thirds-size face (six and nine-sixteenths inches wide). If the eye areas on the close-up are magnified, the letters on the coin are poorly defined and the weave of the cloth interferes. But when the two-thirds-size picture is magnified, all details of the coin become sharper and the background weave is barely noticed. Why? The answer is very simple— when Enrie backed up, he stood in the six-to-ten-foot range, where viewing of the Shroud with the naked eye is best. So, not only his eye but also his camera got maximum clarity.

Filas has not only examined the eye area of all of the Giuseppi Enrie photographs, but also those of Secondo Pia in 1898, of Judica Cordiglia in 1973, and of Vernon Miller in 1978. He suggests that another reason Enrie's views are best for this purpose is that he tacked the Shroud onto a backboard to stretch it to maximum tautness. Conversely, the scientists in 1973 and 1978 were especially careful that no one should think they were mistreating the Shroud. In 1978 they attached it to a frame with magnets, which may have permitted some wrinkles and sags to affect the image. It should also be remembered that the image on the Shroud is made by oxidation of the topmost fibrils of certain spots on certain threads; it cannot be the same as a continuous pattern on a hard, smooth surface.

Considering the Filas claim of four letters in proper sequence, and the twenty-three letters of the Greek alphabet, mathematically there are odds of one in 8 million that such a juxtaposition of letters could have happened by chance.

Figure 2.
(top left) A 3-D enlargement of the right eye of the Shroud. *(Courtesy Francis L. Filas, S. J.)*

(top right) The Shroud Face, right eye circled. *(Courtesy Francis L. Filas, S. J.)*

(left) A Pontius Pilate coin (left) and the Shroud cloth magnified over the eyelid. *(Courtesy Francis L. Filas, S. J.)*

The very strong evidence presented by Filas in dating the Shroud was supported in spring 1982 by the independent research of Professor Alan Whanger of Duke University. Whanger developed a photographic technique (described earlier in this chapter) using polarized light and computer enhancement. Using one of Filas's actual Pontius Pilate coins to superimpose over a right-eye enlargement of the Shroud face, he states that he has found seventy-four points of congruence between the two. He finds the actual coin to be almost a perfect match for the markings on the Shroud face, so that the only reasonable conclusion he can come to is that they were coins struck from the same die. Whanger was able to extend the findings of Filas by identifying six Greek letters (IOY CAI) on the Shroud, whereas Filas had been able to discern only four.

Whanger's technique identifies the coin on the left eye as another Pontius Pilate lepton, known as the Julia coin, struck only in the year 29, in honor of Caesar's mother, who died that year. Sheaves of grain and parts of eleven (out of a total of fourteen) letters that appear on the coin are identified by Whanger. This is not as certain an identification as the coin on the right eye, but no other coin of the period will fit at all.

In order to obtain maximum clarity, Filas had three-dimensional digitized photographic projections of the Shroud eyes made by Log E/Interpretation Systems in Overland Park, Kansas, using Standard Earthview equipment. He shared these materials with Whanger. Filas found that in making twenty-five-times enlargements, the photographs of his coins had far better shades and contrasts when photographed in black-and-white than in color.

Of course, as every courtroom habitué knows, there is always an expert with a contrary opinion. Mr. Mel Wacks, editor of the journal of the Biblical Numismatic Society, disagrees with Professors Filas and Whanger on the identity of the coin. He agrees that the letters CA are present but says they are in the wrong sector of the coin's edge for the letters Y CAI to be correct. With the *lituus* upright in the middle of the coin, the letters CA are at ten-thirty and eleven o'clock, respectively, according to Filas. Wacks says they should be at about two to three o'clock, because the entire legend begins at about seven-thirty and ends at six o'clock.

Wacks is supported by another numismatist, W. K. Yarbrough. But some numismatists report that these coins sometimes abbreviate Tiberius, using IOY, so this would swing all of the lettering to the left (to balance it), and then Filas's report about location of the letters on the Shroud coin could be exactly right. Wacks has agreed that misspellings were not uncommon on Judean coins (about 103 B.C. to A.D. 59) and that they generally were crudely struck. Wacks then seemingly tries to give Filas an "out" by proposing that the Shroud right-eye inscription could readily fit coins from Procurator Coponius (A.D. 6–9) or Procurator Ambibulus (A.D. 9–12), which do have a barley sheaf in the middle.

Filas now owns two Pontius Pilate coins with the C for K misspelling and knows of a third one owned by a collector in Texas. These actual coins not only validate details of the Shroud image, but are different from what numismatists said was possible. The experts had never heard of a C for K misspelling on these coins. Also, numismatists said the second word, KAISAROS, would begin at the same place every time. Yet these three known coins are each different from the other. Additionally, the authoritative book *History of Jewish Coinage* by Frederic W. Madden, first published in 1864, clearly shows some Pontius Pilate coins with the K at ten-thirty o'clock and others with the K at one o'clock.

Considering the poor quality and errors regularly found in the Judean coins, as all agree, and especially in view of the specific, careful, detailed techniques used by Filas and Whanger, I feel that the clear preponderance of evidence supports their conclusions. The work of Dr. Whanger is particularly impressive in recording seventy-four points of congruence when he superimposed photographs of the coin of the Shroud right eye and the coin owned by Filas.

Even the critics do not say the 3-D protuberances over the Shroud eyes are not coins; the disagreement is whether a particular coin is proven. It is an interesting sidelight that we really do not know which side of the coin is imaged onto the cloth! Is it the "down side" that was next to the skin or the "up side" that was next to the cloth that appears on the image?

In any event, the Filas/Whanger coin identification work would seem to completely eliminate the possibility of forgery of the Shroud.

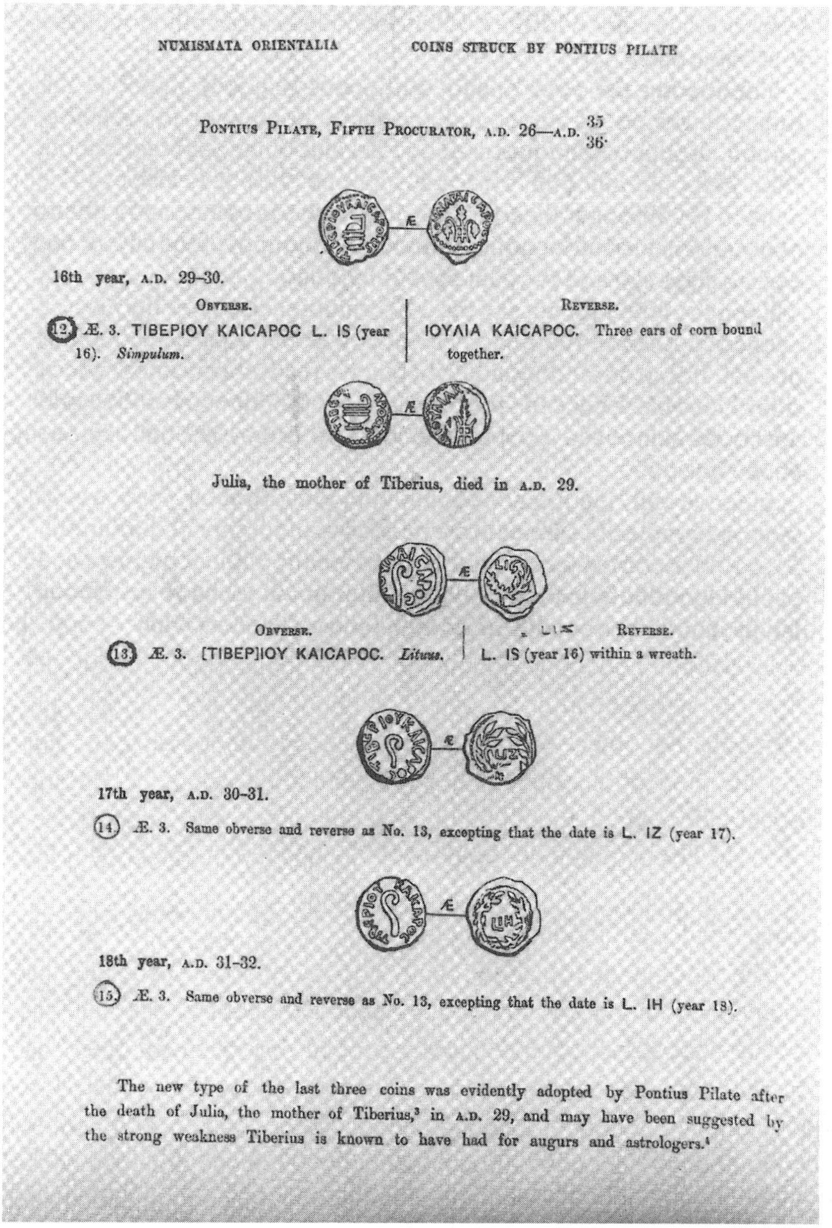

NUMISMATA ORIENTALIA   COINS STRUCK BY PONTIUS PILATE

PONTIUS PILATE, FIFTH PROCURATOR, A.D. 26—A.D. $\frac{35}{36}$.

16th year, A.D. 29–30.

OBVERSE.	REVERSE.
⑫ Æ. 3. TIBEPIOY KAICAPOC L. IϚ (year 16). *Simpulum.*	IOYΛIA KAICAPOC. Three ears of corn bound together.

Julia, the mother of Tiberius, died in A.D. 29.

OBVERSE.	REVERSE.
⑬ Æ. 3. [TIBEP]IOY KAICAPOC. *Lituus.*	L. IϚ (year 16) within a wreath.

17th year, A.D. 30–31.

⑭ Æ. 3. Same obverse and reverse as No. 13, excepting that the date is L. IZ (year 17).

18th year, A.D. 31–32.

⑮ Æ. 3. Same obverse and reverse as No. 13, excepting that the date is L. IH (year 18).

The new type of the last three coins was evidently adopted by Pontius Pilate after the death of Julia, the mother of Tiberius,[3] in A.D. 29, and may have been suggested by the strong weakness Tiberius is known to have had for augurs and astrologers.[4]

Figure 3.
Pontius Pilate coin illustrations from Madden's catalog, *Coins of the Jews,* 1903.

Such a forger/artist would have had to execute, without pigment and in photographic negativity, tiny coin imprints on each eye containing letters one-thirty-second of an inch (one millimeter) high.

The three scientific techniques, by Professor Francis L. Filas of Loyola University, Chicago, by Log E/Interpretation Systems in Overland Park, Kansas, and by Dr. Alan D. Whanger of Duke University and wife Mary, identifying the Pontius Pilate coins of A.D. 29–31 on the eyes of the Man in the Shroud, have been further validated and extended by Dr. Robert M. Haralick of the Spatial Data Analysis Laboratory at Virginia Polytechnic Institute (four different techniques). Haralick's use of computer-enhanced digital image analysis now gives strong evidence for nine Greek letters in sequence on the perimeter of the coin appearing over the right eye, expanding the four-letter sequence found initially by Filas, who died February 15, 1985. This work would seem to historically pinpoint the death of Jesus to the seven-year period from A.D. 29, when these coins were first minted in Judea, to A.D. 36, when Pilate left office (since his coins then would no longer be legal tender)—*if* this was the burial shroud of Jesus! Subsequently, in 1985, Italian numismatist Mario Maroni announced confirmation of these findings.

The Turin Commission discussed the possibility of carbon 14 dating of the cloth of the Shroud, but recommended against such testing. The state of the art in 1973 being such that excessively large pieces of cloth would have to be destroyed, three or four repeated tests would be desirable, and accuracy could not be guaranteed (this type of testing is discussed at length in chapter 11).

Coinciding with the closing days of the exposition of September–October 1978, a Sindonological Congress was held on October 7 and 8 by the International Center. It was held in one of Turin's finest halls with an instant translation system so that attendees could use earphones and select one of several languages for listening. Nearly four hundred people (sindonologists, scientists, historians, clergy, and other specialists) were in attendance. Twenty-five papers were presented and discussed. Drs. Jackson and Jumper on behalf of the American team were there to report on their computer enhancement and 3-D studies, using the Enrie photographs of 1931. Their work is discussed in chapters 8 and 9.

EIGHT

AMERICAN SCIENTISTS AND THE SHROUD OF TURIN RESEARCH PROJECT

IF AMERICAN scientific interest and activity on this subject can be credited to any one person, it must be Dr. John P. Jackson, a major in the Air Force Reserve and a physicist, who now teaches in the Electrical Engineering Department of the University of Colorado at Colorado Springs. Presently, with his wife Rebecca, he operates the Turin Shroud Center of Colorado in Colorado Springs. Raised in a Roman Catholic home, he first became interested in the Shroud at about age fourteen when his mother showed him a picture of it. That interest was reinforced in the late 1960s by John Walsh's book *The Shroud* (Random House, 1963). The field of image-processing was then just opening up, the Mars fly-by was being planned, computer enhancement of images had become a reality, and he knew then that he wanted someday to apply these techniques to the Shroud pictures. Six years later he met and interested Donald Devan (of Information Science, Inc., Santa Barbara) in the problem, and then Eric J. Jumper (a major on active duty at the Air Force Institute of Technology in Dayton in 1983). At this point, Jackson says, "the whole project took off." Jackson obtained a set of the Shroud photographs made by Giuseppi Enrie in 1931 and began three-dimensional (3-D) experimentation with them.

The Albuquerque Conference of 1977

In 1975, Drs. Jackson, Jumper, and Ray N. Rogers (a physical chemist at the Los Alamos Laboratory) met with Father Adam J. Otterbein (president of the Holy Shroud Guild) at the Kirkland Air Force Base to discuss their plans. Other scientists, many with space probe skills from NASA-related and nuclear science activities, became interested, and an American conference of research on the Shroud was planned for March 1977 and ultimately held at Albuquerque. By this time, Jackson and Jumper had joined the faculty of the U.S. Air Force Academy in Colorado Springs. Nine historically and religiously oriented papers and fifteen scientific research papers were presented at the two-day conference, which was attended by some twenty highly qualified American scientists plus other researchers and guests. The result was a significant breakthrough along lines that were revolutionary in sindonology.

With a total attendance of about forty, the conference included six specialized scientists and technicians from the Air Force Academy. Other facilities unofficially "represented" were the Air Force Weapons Laboratory, Information Science, Los Alamos Laboratory, Jet Propulsion Laboratory, and Sandia Laboratory. Specialties among the attendees included image analysis, chemistry, physics, electrical engineering, aerodynamics, photography, and computer science. Other participants were from the fields of history, medicine, archaeology, and theology, including several clergy. The papers presented focused on four basic areas: the three-dimensional aspects of the body image; fluorescence, radiation, and thermography; chemistry and color; and, image analysis.

The Frenchman Paul Vignon was perhaps the first to utilize science in a study of the Shroud, and he was the first to report[1] that the intensity of the body image seemed to vary inversely with the distance from the cloth to body—thus, on the Shroud itself, the eyebrows and the ridge of the nose were dark-colored, since their distance from the cloth was zero, while the adjacent eyelids (perhaps a quarter to a half inch from the cloth) were very lightly colored. Vignon, however, had no way to demonstrate this and prove his theory. Jackson and his associates have, for the first time, been able to do so by using computers, and the results are most dramatic. The *Proceedings* of the Albuquerque conference[2] includes four papers on this 3-D aspect of the body image; they are authored by Drs. Jackson and Jumper, Bill Mottern,

Figure 1.
Drs. John Jackson (left) and Eric Jumper examine an actual-size photograph of the Shroud image (front view), preparatory to making three-dimensional reliefs of the Shroud image by computer projection. *(Courtesy National Catholic News Service)*

Figure 2.
Three-dimensional reliefs of (above) a full frontal view of the body and the Face, (below left) showing the "buttons" on the eyes, and (right) as computer enhanced. *(Courtesy Giovanni Tamburelli, CSELT)*

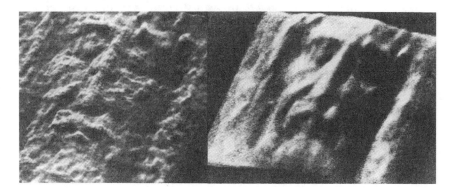

Lt. Thomas M. McCown, and Maj. John D. German Jr. Using a live model, they were able to determine the cloth-to-body distances over the image. A microdensitometer measures and records numerically the values of image intensity, ranging from the very light (barely discernible) to the very dark. Using a microdensitometer, they scanned a photograph of the body image of the Shroud to measure image intensity over the image. Then the computer compared the data, established the relationships, and proved the hypothesis that the body image on the Shroud is "equivalent" to a three-dimensional surface of the body of the Man on the Shroud. From this data a 3-D relief projection (like a relief map) can be constructed by using an Interpretation System, VP-8 Image Analyzer (which is a digital computer) that converts shades of light and dark to vertical relief, and thus give depth to NASA photos of deep space.

Although ordinary photographs, like artists' paintings, involve a shading from light to dark, they do so primarily on the basis of angle of perspective, the lighting on the subject, and sometimes by "retouching" by the artist. They are called "albedo" images. The shading does not depend on planes and depths of the structure of the subject, as does the image of the Man on the Shroud.

The Shroud's uniqueness and its enigma are evidenced by noting that ordinary photographic images cannot significantly or accurately be converted to true 3-D reliefs.

A VP-8 Image Analyzer *will* make a three-dimensional projection from any two-dimensional (flat) picture, because it will simply read the degree of darkness and lightness and project accordingly. *But,* because ordinary images, whether photographed, drawn, painted, or created in any other way, are "albedo" images where the shading from light to dark is based on perspective, the 3-D result will *always* be distorted and unrealistic—unless it is the Shroud image! The Shroud image is unique in that the body-to-cloth distance is *precisely* related to image density. Such is possible only when the degree of illumination received *from an object* depends only on its distance to the camera—which is true, though irrelevant, in regard to photographs of a star, since star images are only *point* images. There are other intrinsic characteristics of the

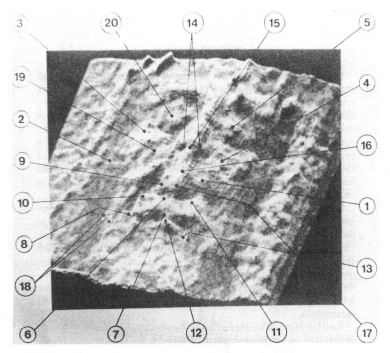

Figure 3.
A 3-D view of the Shroud Face, annotated. Shroud scientist Giovanni Tamburelli, the University of Turin and CSELT (Centro Telecomunicazioni of the IRI-STET Group), has been one of the foremost researchers using computers for three-dimensional projection of the Shroud body images. On this 3-D face he identifies twenty features that were not discernible prior to the use of this technique. (Note that blood is white, since this is a negative). *(Courtesy Giovanni Tamburelli)*

1. A clot of blood on the left cheek near the side of the nose
2. Blood clot on the right cheek
3. Blood and swelling at the point of the left cheekbone
4. Bloody cuts on the point of the left cheekbone
5. Clot of blood at the edge of the left eyelid
6. Streams of blood flowing from each nostril
7. Blood under a split upper lip
8. Blood at the right edge of the upper lip, strongly three-dimensional
9. A pointed drop of blood emerging from the right nostril
10. A clot of blood on the right side of upper lip
11. A clot of blood higher on the left side of the upper lip

12. A clot of blood on a possibly burst lower lip
13. Flowing blood from the left corner of the mouth
14. Depressions on each side of the bridge of the nose, possibly indicating a crushed cartilage
15. A deep cut across the bridge of the nose
16. Abrasion of the skin of the nose
17. The tip of the nose is out of alignment (a deviated septum?)
18. The beard is drenched with blood on the right side
19. Blood and possible depression on the right cheek
20. Circle on the middle of the right eyelid, which may be a coin

Shroud image. For instance, the back image is as "faithful" as the front and is totally compatible, with one exception: The hair on the front of the body stands out in natural relief, but on the back it appears compressed, as would be true of a body lying on a hard surface. Also important is the conclusion that the Shroud image could not have been created by direct total contact of the body with the Shroud; the 3-D data and image-intensity/body-cloth distance completely preclude such a suggestion. On the contrary, it is firmly concluded that the image has been formed *through* space.

The Jackson/Jumper 3-D work on the Shroud images was summarized by STURP in the statement, "The unique three-dimensional quality of the Shroud image proves beyond doubt that the linen cloth must have wrapped around a human corpse whose volume contours were encoded in the varying intensity levels of the image."[3]

One of the most exciting developments presented by Jackson et al. at that 1977 conference was a 3-D close-up of the Face on the Shroud, converted from an Enrie photograph of the Shroud, which very clearly shows what appears to be a "button" sitting high on each eyelid. After considering and rejecting five alternative theories, they conclude that a real, physical object is on each eyelid and that it probably is a coin, which historians verify as a custom among Jews of the Near East in the first century to keep the eyelids closed. (The further work of Father F. L. Filas and others on these "buttons" is in chapter 11.)

Some interpreters of the New Testament Gospels (see the comments of Dr. John A. T. Robinson in chapter 15) construe the language there as describing a "chin strap" of cloth that would keep the mouth closed. Initially, the 3-D data was thought to show the hair on the left side of the face as if draped over the edge of some invisible object—possibly the chin strap. Some scientists still adhere to this interpretation. However, a contrary view is reported in chapter 10 in connection with the paper presented in 1982 to the American Chemical Society symposium.

Another facet of the three-dimensional reconstruction of the body of the Man on the Shroud is that, if upright, the reconstructed body replica seems to assume a "forward lean," which would be consistent with the rigor mortis of a corpse after *hanging* on a cross until dead.

Chemical and color analyses were covered by two papers presented by Drs. Rogers and Jackson, respectively. Chemically, three hypotheses were considered: that the body image was painted on the cloth; that it was produced naturally by reactions between volatile products from the cellulose of the Shroud and from the spices and vapors or fluids produced by the body, or any combination of them; and, that it was produced by rapid heating. The fire of 1532 would have altered all organic colors on a painted image, but since the fire altered no coloration, the colors could not have been organic. Shading is accomplished by variation of density, not by variation of color;[4] since inks, stains, and dyes were not found, it was concluded that if painted, the image would have to be of a "stable, particulate inorganic pigment in a water base," determinable by x-ray fluorescence. This test was later performed, in October 1978, with a negative result—no paint residue was found.

As to the second hypothesis, it is observed that the parts of the body image in contact with the charred/burned/scorched areas have identical color tone and density as the parts of the image at maximum distance from those discolored areas. But, if natural product molecules were responsible for the image, they should have decomposed, changed color, or volatilized at different rates depending on their distance from the fire-damaged areas.

The facts fit the third hypothesis: an image formed by thermal discoloration (caused by a form of heat or some form of intense radiation, for example, a nuclear flash) because such an image would not change the relative color or density with additional heating.

When color photographs were taken of the Shroud for the first time by the Turin Commission during the 1973 examinations, an original color transparency of the Face was obtained and later scanned with a microdensitometer probe beam, by the American team. The scans failed to find any difference "between the color composition and variation with neutral density" of the body image, the hair images, the blood images, and the burn patterns, thus confirming an image formed by something akin to thermal discoloration and not by paint. (The word "thermal" is qualified and is used here advisedly rather than dogmatically—descriptively, rather than technically—since with our present knowledge and present vocabulary we can do no better.) As of late 1982, both the Adler/Heller data and the Pellicori data exclude a "scorch image process" as such. Although the Shroud body image has many physical and chemical properties of a light scorch, it definitely is not a true scorch—it was not made with heat.

Fluorescence, thermography, and radiation examinations were considered in three papers by Capt. Joseph S. Accetta and Dr. Jumper. Accetta describes x-ray fluorescence analysis[5] as a subset of spectroscopy,[6] that involves excitation of the sample being examined (the Shroud) so that identification of its constituent elements is possible from the characteristic emission spectra resulting from the excitation. For proposed use in the infrared band of the spectrum, he describes the operation of a thermograph,[7] which, while scanning the Shroud, will convert the radiant emission (in the infrared band) to a visual image. Acceta recommended that both x-ray fluorescence analysis and thermography be used if examination of the Shroud was to be permitted in 1978 (both were used as described in the following chapters).

Jumper discussed the theory of radiation as an image-forming process, after first evaluating the molecular (vapor) theory. He points out that an organic stain mechanism (such as Vignon's proposed vapor-graph process) acting alone can hardly form images of inert objects such as the coins on the eyes. He emphasizes that the Shroud image was made by an image-forming process that acted *through space,* not by contact, and notes that the hair images follow the same "law" of intensity versus distance as does the body image, even though they are different substances. And most important, he cites the 1969 Turin Commission's certain finding that the image was only a *surface* phenomenon. The image was formed only on the top of the crowns of the threads of the cloth (from experimentation he concludes that either a dry or moist vapor staining either a dry or wet cloth will penetrate *fully* every fiber or thread it touches). Finally, he finds as very significant the absence of "saturation" as to intensity of the back body image of the Shroud, and that the image was not "pressure sensitive"—that is, the image of the Man's back has the same shading characteristics and lack of saturation as the image of his front.

Experiments convinced Jumper that a forger could not, for instance, use a bronze statue that was heated glowing hot (just less than melt temperature), throw a linen cloth over it, and quickly remove it. A scorch image would result, but the heat would be of too high an intensity to form *a surface* image only—it would also burn through and be present on the back of the cloth.

Jumper became convinced, by the above evaluations and by experiments conducted by Jackson and himself, that images comparable to those on the Shroud *could* be created by radiation.

Image analysis was considered in four papers presented by Don Devan, Donald Janney, Jean J. Lorre, Donald J. Lynn, and by Drs. Jackson and Jumper. Basically, these four papers consider what computers and other specialized equipment can do with Shroud photographs (especially, the better photographs), and what photographic techniques should be used in making future photographs of the Shroud. Two of the papers do report some preliminary work with existing photographs. Specifically, these papers proposed that future photographs of the Shroud should be precisely oriented to scientific use—that is, for subsequent study of the photographs using image analysis and evaluation and enhancement techniques, including the use of digital computer technology. Image enhancement of a photograph is a computer process that involves the creation of a "better" image. Operations on the original photograph will include the removal of distracting, noninformative features (called "noise"), the sharpening of blurred or indistinct edges, and the exaggeration of subtle differences in gray shade or color value. The result may in some respects also be more suitable for human visualization—but not necessarily so.

These proposals do not denigrate the quality of previous photographs, but recognize that for the most part they were concerned with aesthetic portrayal and enhancement, which may not necessarily be what is desired in photographs taken for scientific use. Typically, new photography would have to be planned so that the weave pattern of the cloth would minimally interfere and distort the data when magnified by enlargement.

Even using the then (1977) existing photographs (of 1931 and

1973), computer enhancement presented some new possibilities. One is the possibility that Barbet's speculation, that the thumbs remained drawn into the palms at the time of burial, may not be valid. Computer enhancement *seems* to show thumbs that were (naturally) about three centimeters from the Shroud and therefore so indistinct on the image that they are not discernible with the eye alone. Also enhanced by the computer are the side-images.

On To Turin

About twenty scientists were present at the Albuquerque Conference in March 1977. In September, seven of them went to Turin with Fathers Otterbein and Rinaldi, and scientific testing of the Shroud was requested in connection with its planned fall 1978 exposition. In April 1978 the Turin authorities approved in principle the testing that had been requested by the American scientists, to immediately follow the public exposition in October.

Also in 1978, Drs. Jackson and Jumper (for the American group) presented a paper at a scientific congress in Turin (note 1, item 15, chapter 9) that reported considerable success, based on the 1931 Enrie photographs, in the use of computer techniques, as had been initially discussed at Albuquerque the previous year. They were able to affirm that these efforts resulted in better images; enhancement with the discovery of features previously unseen; eliminating "noise" (such as wrinkles in the cloth, water stains, etc.); and removing weave pattern interference. Using the Fourier analysis technique it was shown that the Shroud body image possessed no "directionality" whatever, proving that the image could not have been produced by an artist using conventional brush-stroke painting, which would show the stroke directions.

They also reported their preliminary work on the three-dimensional (3-D) characteristics of the Shroud, confirming Paul Vignon's early claims that the Shroud body image varies inversely with the cloth-to-body distance; that is, the closer the body was to the cloth at any one point, the darker the image at that point. With a 3-D projection of the image (having thickness or depth), they were able to rotate the image as if it were a statue, and thereby view it from various angles. This resulting 3-D portrait shows a body that is naturally proportioned and lacking any distortion.

The Jackson/Jumper 3-D findings of 1977–78 were later replicated in every particular by Italian telecommunications scientist Giovanni Tamburelli, whose paper was published in late 1981 (note 1, item 1, chapter 9). His work, with illustrations, specifically confirmed the Jackson/Jumper claim that photographs of the Shroud were unique in having innate 3-D information. In contrast, he used a photograph of a dead soldier whose face had been noticeably injured; a 3-D effort on that photo was disproportionate and a meaningful "relief" depiction was not possible.

In June 1978, at a meeting in Colorado Springs, detailed plans for the Turin tests were made and the Shroud of Turin Research Project (STURP) was formally organized.

All of the scientists associated with the project (STURP) did the Shroud work on their own time and at their own expense. Nor was their Shroud activity supported, sponsored, or endorsed by any of their several employers, nor by NASA or the air force. Once the special examination and testing of the Shroud was approved in April 1978, a most difficult period ensued. The STURP members had to borrow, rent, or buy the several million dollars' worth of highly sophisticated equipment they would use in Turin, and they also had to solicit funds to acquire, crate, and ship the equipment as well as cover travel costs for the scientists who could not finance their own trips to Turin.

They succeeded, and in September 1978, STURP members brought all the special equipment to Connecticut, where they held a precisely arranged dry run to simulate everything they would do the following month in Turin. Then the equipment was shipped to Turin. Father Rinaldi, vice president of the Holy Shroud Guild, reported that even while the public exposition was in progress, in early September, the tests had been approved only in principle. When the Americans arrived on September 30, the approvals were still more implicit than explicit. On October 4 their seventy-two crates of equipment weighing eight tons were still being held by the Italian Customs Office. The equipment arrived just hours before it was to be used, thanks to the influence of Cardinal Ballestrero of the Customs Office.

As soon as the public exposition closed on Sunday, October 8, 1978, Church authorities quickly moved the Shroud from the cathedral into a hall of the adjoining palace of Umberto II, the deposed king of Italy and titular head of the House of Savoy. There, in a once-festive hall of the palace, the scientific equipment had been hurriedly set up in readiness for the concentrated study of the Shroud, which began immediately and was the first full-scale multidisciplinary study of the Shroud ever made. Work continued around the clock for five days, to conclude on Friday night, October 13.

The Shroud was quickly removed from its exposition stand and was fastened by magnets onto a specially built, rotating aluminum frame, so that both sides and all angles of the Shroud could be examined. The reverse of the Shroud had not even been seen for 470 years, as when the nuns of St. Clare repaired the 1532 fire damage they strengthened it by stitching a solid linen backing onto it.

Church authorities and palace staff were most cooperative and helpful to the scientists. The fifteenth-century royal palace in which they worked was something else. They doubtless had thought one of their hosts might have been speaking with tongue-in-cheek when he told them that the hall where they would work was "probably more artistic than functional"—a gross understatement, they soon found. Samuel Pellicori who, with Mark S. Evans, was assigned to do color photomicroscopy (comparing the various parts of the Shroud with each other: the clear background, body image, suspected blood stains, water marks, scorches, burns, and charred spots), says that the wooden floors fairly "heaved" at the slightest footfall. For him this meant that it would be possible to work with magnification only up to 20 times, instead of a preferred magnification of 100 times. Also, "mysterious drafts" that periodically coursed through the medieval palace tended to make a "virtual sail" of the fourteen-foot-long cloth. Supplemental lighting and wartime blackout curtains were a big help in shutting out glare and obliterating shadows, but with dark walls and twenty-foot-high ceilings, lighting for their work was far from perfect.

All STURP scientists and operational associates had been given, in advance, a copy of the *Operations Test Plan,* a guidebook of sixty-plus pages written by Jackson and Jumper. The plan apportioned every minute of their five days on the various experiments and activities. (It also provided cogent comments as to team members' attitudes and actions vis-à-vis the Italians.)

Tests, examinations, and recording of data ranged over many types of activity, including x-ray fluorescence analysis, photographs in several wavelengths, radiographic analysis, microchemical analysis, optical microscopy, ion microprobe analysis, electron spectroscopy, infrared and ultraviolet analysis, multispectral narrowband photography, microphotography, x-ray radiography, and extensive high-resolution photographic coverage, using a variety of films and filters to get pictures ideally suited to computer analysis. More than thirty-thousand photographs were taken, including photographs of the back of the Shroud cloth for the first time and use of a fiber-optic fluoroscope projected through from the back.

A fiber-optic fluoroscope is especially designed for projection through fibrous substances such as linen cloth. Along with x-ray penetration, such "fluorescing" permits observation that gives data respecting the internal structure and condition of the cloth and its threads. Many of the techniques of examination and testing used on the Shroud were designed in the previous months specifically for this job, but some had been used successfully for years in art forgery detection, criminal investigation, space probe photographic analysis, and the like.

On Saturday, October 14, 1978, the American scientists' equipment was crated for return shipment, and STURP members began flying back to the U.S. with their film and voluminous data, to begin their evaluations.

NINE

ADDITIONAL FINDINGS OF STURP

F OR THE balance of 1978 through 1982, in the aftermath of Turin, STURP members and associates devoted their spare time to developing and evaluating data, consulting with each other, and drafting reports. Some papers were published in professional periodicals as they became ready.[1] STURP has also projected five broad reports that will be the consensus of all STURP members. The first of these is the Heller-Adler report on the *Chemical Aspects* (item #3 of note 1), which is also available as a Holy Shroud Guild booklet. This report was presented before a meeting of the Canadian Society for Forensic Science, August 24–28, 1981, as the formal STURP response to a critic's claim of paint traces on the Shroud. The second was tentatively called the "Official Summary" because it was delivered to Umberto II and to Pope John Paul II in the fall of 1981; it is authored by L. Schwalbe and R. N. Rogers, and is listed as item 14 of note 1.

Three more official reports were projected by STURP: One, tentatively titled "Theories about the Shroud," was a proceedings of the STURP Connecticut Symposium of October 10–11, 1981, combined in a STURP omnibus volume in 1984 that also reprints the major papers listed in note 1 of this chapter.[2] The chemical aspects, authored by E. J. Jumper et al., appeared in *A.S.C. Advances in Chemistry,* vol. 3, 1983,[3] and a final report on the "Three Dimensional Characteristic of the Shroud Image" was available in 1983.[4]

Personnel of the Brooks Photographic Institute in Santa Barbara were the official photographers for STURP. On April 17, 1981, they displayed more than one hundred photographs of and about the Shroud, many of them lifesize, in the Hall of Fame in Santa Barbara. The exhibit remained there until September and was visited by thousands. On the occasion of the Connecticut Symposium of STURP, the Brooks Institute in cooperation with the Holy Shroud Guild moved the exhibit to the University of Connecticut campus at Avery Point. Over a period of six weeks it was viewed by more than thirty thousand persons.

Since 1959 the International Center of Sindonology in Turin has published its journal, *Sindon*,[5] on an occasional basis, with articles predominantly in French and Italian. Also, on an occasional basis, STURP and the Holy Shroud Guild have issued newsletters for researchers. A new journal, *Shroud Spectrum International* (in English), was inaugurated in January 1982 under the editorship of historian-sindonologist Dorothy Crispino.[6]

Note 1 of this chapter lists the scientific journal articles written by STURP members. In addition, there have been a few good periodical articles for the general reader.[7] Also, some have appeared in religious periodicals.[8] A Selected Bibliography of books in print is included at the end of this book.

Some phases of the work of the American scientists at Turin in October 1978 were completed then and there. For the most part, however, it was a matter of observing, measuring, gathering information, and recording, with the bulk of their work to follow in the months to come. Their work falls naturally into four broad categories: the tests, examinations, and evaluations that were performed directly on the Shroud; the computations and evaluations later made from some of that data; tests later made on the "surface material lifted" from the Shroud; and the later processing and study made of the several thousand photographs of different kinds that were taken of the Shroud. Control experiments were performed in the laboratory to simulate possible Shroud conditions and special factors. Both modern and ancient control pieces of linen were tested in various ways for comparison with the Shroud.

Chemical and Spectroscopic Tests: Was There Blood? Was There Paint?

One paper, "Blood on the Shroud of Turin," that appeared in *Applied Optics* (19/16) for August 15, 1980, was authored by Dr. John H. Heller of the New England Institute at Ridgefield, Connecticut, and Dr. Alan D. Adler of the Department of Chemistry, Western Connecticut State College. This paper was based on spectroscopic and chemical tests that they conducted on samples of surface materials that had been carefully lifted from the Shroud by Ray Rogers and Robert Dinegar.

The lifting from selected locations on the Shroud was done by pressing strips of special "sticky tape" onto the Shroud, and then preserving for laboratory examination all of the surface materials that adhered to the tape. (Surface materials were also lifted, by vacuuming, by Italian scientist G. Riggi, but these were not available to these researchers.) These surface materials were described as fibrils (small fibers from the linen cloth), particulates (minute separate solid particles), shards (thread coating fragments), globs (lumps), and incidental debris (fragments of insects, pollen, spores, etc.). These materials were studied through microscopes, by photographs, by chemical tests, and spectroscopically.

While in Turin, an x-ray fluorescence study directly on the full Shroud established that significantly high concentrations of iron residue appear only in the bloodstain areas. As a control against which to check studies of the Shroud, Heller and Adler obtained a piece of roughly woven, undyed Spanish linen known to be three hundred years old, which they then impregnated with twelve-month-old blood from Heller. Under microscopic examination the appearance of the stained control was very similar to the Shroud's "bloodstains" except that the former appeared slightly more garnet-colored and less brown than the Shroud, which would be expected considering the ages of the blood that stained each.

Linen fibrils lifted from each by sticky-tape were examined by microspectrophotometry. "Micro" denotes the use of a microscope for localization of the object; "spectro" refers to utilization of the color bands of the spectrum; "photometry" is the measurement of the intensity of the light focused through the linen fibrils. This equipment and technique is used for spectral analysis within the dimensions of microscopic objects. This examination helps evaluate the chemical state of any hemoglobin in the suspected blood, since there is no one specific spectrum band for whole blood itself. Also, in Turin, reflection-spectroscopy was carried out directly on the bloodstain areas of the Shroud. In this type of spectroscopy (also see chapter 8) the light is beamed at an angle to the cloth, for evaluation by reflection of the beam. This helped to identify the presence of blood hemoglobin in those areas of the Shroud. (Hemoglobin is a compound, containing iron, found in red blood cells.)

Using various chemical reagents and irradiation processes to test the Shroud fibrils and the control (Spanish) fibrils, Heller and Adler then made spectroscopic examination of the materials at each stage of the tests. They were able, without qualification, to conclude that the Shroud's "bloodstains" do in fact contain blood.

Subsequently, a critic who was not a participant at Turin, Dr. Walter McCrone of Chicago, made some microscopic evaluations of surface material samples from the Shroud and, largely utilizing the public press, claimed to find paint traces on the Shroud and labeled it a medieval fake painted by an artist.[9] He claimed that the body image is due to an iron oxide earth pigment bound with an age-yellowed animal protein binder that had been painted onto the cloth, and that the blood marks are attributable to a mixture of iron oxide pigments and vermilion (mercuric sulfide) in this same binder. That critic's views are not consistent with the conclusions of the STURP scientists, and the Heller/Adler team has categorically disagreed with him. Spectrochemical and other tests (such as microphotography, x-ray fluorimetery, ultraviolet fluorescence photos, and direct microscopy on the Shroud at several hundred magnification) of both the Shroud and control pieces of linen by S. F. Pellicori have convinced him that this critic's claims of iron oxide as a causal factor for the Shroud's body image are unsound (see note 1, item 2).

After conducting wide-ranging and exhaustive additional tests with the same and additional materials, and using standard microchemical techniques, Heller and Adler (along with Drs. John P. Jackson and Robert Bucklin) formally represented STURP on a panel presentation before the Canadian Society for Forensic Science's annual meeting at McMaster University, Hamilton, Ontario, on August 24-28, 1981.[10]

Additional microscopic, spectroscopic, and chemical tests were performed by Heller and Adler. These included: photomicroscope, both transmission and reflection mode; polarizing microscope; phase contrast microscope; stereozoom binocular microscope; tungsten sources, and xenon arcs.

Altogether, they utilized 23 of the 36 sticky-tape samples from different areas of the Shroud; eleven different classes of sample objects were tested. These included: burn area, patch, nonimage water stain, image water stain, lance wound, body image, bloodstain, water stain, and blood, nonimage, backing cloth, scourge mark, blood, and burn area. Twelve different tests have been performed confirming the presence of whole blood on the Shroud. Tests were run seeking to detect sixteen different metallic substances thought possibly to be present on the Shroud; for half of them two different tests were run. Tests were run to detect sixteen different types of organic materials thought possibly to be present on the Shroud. Twenty-one different solvents were used in dye extraction tests.

In these tests the three-hundred-year-old Spanish linen sample was again used for control comparison, as additionally were samples of a Coptic burial linen dated to about A.D. 350, and of a Pharonic burial linen dated to about 1500 B.C.

The claim of Walter McCrone—for the presence of "an iron oxide earth pigment bound with an age-yellowed animal protein binder"— was conclusively disproven in every particular. For one thing, protein was found *only* in the bloodstain areas of the Shroud, and definitely is not present as a pigment binder in the body image areas. Moreover, Heller/Adler found blood residues, other than hemoglobin and protein (that is, bile pigments), in the bloodstain areas of the Shroud. Conversely, they found no significant levels of any substance that could have been the residue of organic or inorganic paint pigments, or of stains or dyes.

Perhaps the most conclusive finding in their extended study relates to the presence of iron residues: The only heavy concentration of iron is in the bloodstain areas, where it should be if the stains indeed are blood. Significant concentrations of iron are in the water stain margin areas—again, where it should be expected. Throughout the entire

Shroud, and for all three of the control samples of old linen, a significant but uniform deposit of "covalently bound" iron is found. Again, this is not surprising: Since antiquity, the technique in Mediterranean countries for making linen from flax included an extended period of soaking and fermenting (called "retting") while the flax is submerged in large outdoor vats of water. (This practice, and the strong odor associated with it, will be retained indelibly in the memory of every Allied soldier who served in Italy during World War II, because of the omnipresence of the vats of soaking flax.) And the clincher of the Heller/Adler study of iron concentrations is the strong and clear conclusion that no iron, in any form or combination, was found in the body image areas of the Shroud except at the same levels as found in the nonimage areas, and specifically, that no iron oxide residues are found in the image areas.

Traces of other metals were equally nonsignificant as concerns the authenticity of the Shroud. For example, particles of silver were found on the Shroud, but only in the scorch areas, from the molten silver of the casket coming in contact with the Shroud during the fire of 1532.

Comparative study of the different areas of the Shroud was totally neglected by the critic in his reported evaluations. Specifically, protein and other materials, which he thought to be paint ingredients, came from bloodstain areas of the Shroud and not from the body image areas. Moreover, by the use of chemical and spectroscopic testing techniques (in addition to microscopic examinations), Heller and Adler demonstrated that McCrone's specific claims for the presence of paint residue were prematurely and erroneously made with insufficient data—that *no* materials on the Shroud can scientifically be claimed as paint, dye, or stain residues.

Thus, on the basis of these very extensive tests, Heller and Adler are able, without qualification, to fully reaffirm their previous conclusion that the bloodstain marks on the Shroud are in fact composed of blood. Subsequent reports covered in chapter 10 consider whether it is human blood. Their meticulous work has also provided collateral validation in other areas: Pierre Barbet, in his book *A Doctor at Calvary* (Doubleday, 1953), concluded that the blood images represented clotted blood (as from a corpse) and were not "free blood flows" as would be true if the body were still living when wrapped in the Shroud. The Heller/Adler findings confirm this, since they found "non-heme serum" proteins at the borders of the bloodstains.

The work of Vernon D. Miller and S. F. Pellicori was reported in their article "Ultraviolet Fluorescence Photography of the Turin Shroud," *Journal of Biological Photography* (item 9 of note 1 of this chapter).

They also validate this phenomena through their ultraviolet photographic studies (and fluorescence photography), which show a "serum halo effect" at the margin of blood clots and around the scourge marks; these effects are so precisely correct, both chemically and anatomically, that direct contact of the corpse with the cloth is the only conceivable cause. To Heller and Adler, *applied* pigment would be incapable of rendering all of these amazing image characteristics that are found on the Shroud.

With negligible notice in the news media, Walter McCrone later accepted the refutations of the STURP scientists and in a press release dated September 20, 1980, he retracted his adversary position and acknowledged that the presence of microscopic particles of iron oxide on certain portions of the Shroud "does not prove the Shroud to be a fake."[11]

In December 1981, S. F. Pellicori published a paper entitled "Spectrochemical Results of the 1978 Investigation."[12] Control pieces of modern linen were aged with heat using a standard technique, with a variety of bake-times and temperatures in an attempt to match the various areas of the Shroud. Environmental variables were utilized also, such as pre-exposure to sunlight and the introduction of moisture. Similarly, control linen was artificially aged after the application of light coatings of various substances, including skin secretions (perspiration plus body oils), olive oil, and burial spices such as myrrh. These pieces of artificially aged control linen were then examined by the use of spectral reflectance so that data could be developed for comparison with that observed when the Shroud was examined in Turin. This involved the metering of the amount of light reflected from the cloth (sometimes at right angles to the line of light) and of splitting it into the basic colors (red, orange, yellow, green, blue, indigo, violet) of the spectrum of visible white light.

Fluorescence findings, when the subject material is stimulated by ultraviolet energy, again demonstrated that simple scorching of itself did not create the body image or the bloodstains, because those areas of the Shroud would not fluoresce—and yet even the faintest scorches (near the burn marks) fluoresced a reddish brown. Laboratory simulation with control linen behaved the same way.

Pellicori ends this paper with the conclusion that although science can understand the chemistry of the Shroud's body image, we have a few clues but no real explanation as to how the image transferred from body to cloth. He does find it certain, however, that the blood on the body was transferred to the cloth by direct contact and considers it probable that skin oils, perspiration, and spices also transferred by direct contact and were a factor in the forming of the body image. He is sure that these extremely minute quantities (having left no trace today) were not a determining factor in the creation of the body image and especially the "distortionless face image."

Pellicori and his associate R. A. Chandos at the Santa Barbara Research Center designed and constructed a portable spectrophotometer the size of a shoe box for use in Turin; this miniature, battery-powered, photoelectric instrument gave them spectral reflectance data directly from the Shroud features. [13]

Pellicori's spectral work was very closely related to that of Roger and Mazrion Gilbert of the Oriel Corporation, who built a special reflectometer/fluorimeter for continuous, higher-resolution measurements. [14] Both the Pellicori and the Gilbert instruments permitted ultraviolet-visible reflectance and fluorescence study of the Shroud. Testing by the Gilberts involved the utilization of electromagnetic energy ranging from the ultraviolet through the infrared region of the spectrum.

Some of Pellicori's most effective work was with the bloodstains of the Shroud, which were found to have penetrated through to the reverse side of the cloth. In the area of the apparent lance wound, he found evidence of a soaking with other than blood—a viscous fluid and a liquid less dense than whole blood, such as the blood serum that separates from whole blood at death (reminding us of the Gospel's reference to a flow of "blood and water" from Jesus' side). Pellicori has no hesitation in saying that his findings produce at least one certain conclusion—that the Shroud was not the product of human chicanery or of a clever thirteenth- or fourteenth-century artist. As to the "bloodstains," the most that he and the others of the Project can say is that there is hemoglobin there, and none of their tests has shown it not to be blood.

The three-dimensional work of American researchers was first reported in March 1977 in Albuquerque. This work his been paralleled in Italy by Professor Giovanni Tamburelli of the University of Turin and CSELT-IRI (Centro Studi e Laboratori Telecomunicazioni), who was named "Turinese of the Year" in 1979 for his outstanding 3-D work on the Shroud. His publications on the subject have included a paper presented in Turin in October 1978 in the International Congress on Sindonology, one in *Sindon* no. 29 of December 1980, and the lead article in issue number 2 of *Shroud Spectrum International.* In the latter, he points out that the 3-D data must be interpreted cautiously in terms of hypotheses or probabilities, but, nevertheless, the three-dimensional images of the Shroud obtained with the computer reveal many details that were undetectable or doubtful while viewed only in our conventional two-dimensional images. Tamburelli identifies twenty specific features on the 3-D image of the Shroud Face that were not discernible on two-dimensional images of it. For example, he finds that the 3-D Shroud Face image discloses a drop of blood from the right nostril that has a pointed form, indicating with fair certainty that the Man of the Shroud died while on the cross, before that drop could fully form and fill.

After four years of study of the data gleaned at Turin in 1978, the American scientists are succinctly positive on a number of points. Raymond Rogers: "The burden of proof is now on the skeptic." Donald Lynn: "It would be miraculous if it were a forgery." Samuel Pellicori: "We can conclude for now that the Shroud image is that of a real human being (and) is not the product of an artist." Robert Dinegar: "We have absolutely no indication that the image was produced by the hand of man." For many of the European and American scientists the work will go on, including the hope of an early return to Turin for another direct examination of the Shroud, because they now have more ideas and many more questions. Informal negotiations with Turin authorities continue intermittently, especially on the possibility of carbon 14 testing to establish the age of the Shroud cloth.

Bias in favor of the Shroud's authenticity has often been charged against STURP. However, one member of the 1978 STURP team who went to Turin and examined the Shroud was Barrie Schwortz, the documentary photographer for the project. Schwortz says he was

Figure 1.
Leo Vala, a London photographer-artist, with a sculptured clay head (above) that he made by projection from the Shroud Face. On the next page he is holding a photograph of the sculpture next to a photograph of the Shroud's Face. The projection process, which Vala invented in the 1960s and calls "Valaform," enabled him to convert a two-dimensional image (a flat picture) into a full three-dimensional image (a statue). Vala was convinced that the Face of the image on the Shroud of Turin would be an ideal subject for Valaform because of its excellent photographic quality. He concluded that the Shroud has a precisely full-face image that is absolutely symmetrical and in perfect perspective. Transparency slides of the Shroud Face and of the back of the head were separately projected onto two sides of a lump of sculptor's clay. From this "pattern" Vala shaped the clay to conform with the projected images, which, in effect, wrapped themselves around the lump of clay. This resulted in a clay head complete from all angles and completely responsive to the Shroud images, frontal and dorsal. *(Courtesy Leo Vala)*

"raised as an Orthodox Jew," and upon completion of the project, he states, "I am still Jewish, yet I believe the Shroud of Turin is the cloth that wrapped the man Jesus after he was crucified."

Carbon-Dating of the Shroud Cloth

In 1988 the Vatican permitted pieces the size of a postage stamp to be cut from one "corner" of the Shroud and given to each of three laboratories for carbon-dating, and their "unanimous" decision was that the cloth was produced between A.D. 1260 and 1390

Not only has that conclusion been totally refuted in subsequent years, but Shroud researcher Joseph Marino reports that independent scientific evaluation later the same year (1988) disclosed that the samples that were cut for laboratory testing were cut from a border area obviously restitched and contaminated, so that the cloth cut out was 40 percent first century and 60 percent sixteenth century origin.

Conservation of the Shroud Cloth

In June and July 2003 the Vatican authorized a team led by a cloth expert, Dr. Mechthild Flury-Lensberg of Switzerland, to remove the Holland-cloth backing and thirty patches from the Shroud, all of which had been added in 1534 to repair damage caused by a fire and to strengthen the cloth. Additionally, they removed organic remains, dust and dirt that had accumulated on the back of the Shroud, and ironed out the crease marks that had been caused over the years by folding the Shroud. In 2003, Dr. Flury-Lensberg published a book detailing that work and responding to criticisms concerning same. As an unexpected side effect from that conservation exercise, Italian scientists have found a dim but accurate matching image of the face of the man of the Shroud on the back side of the cloth (reported by AOL News, April 15, 2004).

And perhaps the most important finding of Dr. Flury-Lensberg was that a very unusual style of stitching on the back side of the cloth was observed that was used in Judea for a brief period in the first century A.D. and was used nowhere else. Examples of the same had been observed in cloth found in the ruins of the citadel of Masada, a fortress destroyed by the Romans in A.D. 74.

TEN

LATER STURP REPORTS

T HE STURP consortium of American scientists, which began informally with three people in California in 1974, was incorporated in 1978. In the fall of that year they carried out the scientific investigation in Turin. STURP has since grown to about forty scientific members and associates. These specialists come from some twenty organizations that train or use the cream of America's technical skills. In addition to the six organizations whose employees were involved at the Albuquerque Conference, as mentioned in chapter 8, STURP's current participants also come from IBM, Oriel Corporation, Santa Barbara Research Center, Brooks Institute of Photography, NUTEK, Colorado University, Lockheed Missiles and Space Corporation, Western Connecticut State College, Nuclear Technology Corporation, New England Institute, Wright-Patterson Air Force Base, Barrie M. Schwortz Photography, E. G. & G. Corporation, and the Los Angeles County Museum of Art.

STURP has provided Church authorities with the results of their studies and also stands ready to give the staff of the Turin Cathedral detailed advice concerning protection and preservation of the Shroud; this advice could cover optimum storage facilities and techniques, including data as to desired atmosphere, temperature, humidity, and other factors.

In addition to reflectance photography (discussed in the preceding chapter), Vernon D. Miller and S. F. Pellicori have reported[1] the use of ultraviolet fluorescence photography on the Shroud. Ultraviolet light is in waves shorter than humans can see. By fluorescing—a chemical process—the ultraviolet light is converted to visible light and is then photographed. This was primarily for the detection of organic and inorganic compounds through their emission spectra—the wavelength, color, and other characteristics unique to, and identification for, the substance in question (see also chapter 8). Filtered light sources were aimed at 45-degree angles to the camera focus plane to ensure that the film would record only radiation (fluorescence) in the visible range. The camera and light-source assembly was moved along a rail parallel to the long dimension of the Shroud; photography and subsequent reconstruction was conducted of 132 square sections (by laying out the Shroud into sections six squares wide and twenty-two squares long). Data were compared for six different areas: clear background, bloodstains, scourge marks, body image, water marks, and fire scorches.

Subsequently, the same equipment was used in simulated laboratory control situations for comparison with the Shroud, using modern linen, some of which was artificially aged, stained with blood, and similarly altered. Contact of linen with a hot statue has been postulated by some critics, especially Joe Nickell, as the likely subterfuge used by a medieval artist to create the Shroud body image. However, whenever laboratory-produced scorches were tested, they fluoresced with reddish emissions, and yet *the Shroud body image does not fluoresce.* Miller/Pellicori conclude that their fluorescence photography results flatly contradict the critic's hypothesis.

The actual scorches (from the 1532 fire) that are on the Shroud fluoresce orange *because* they were produced by scorching. *But,* the Shroud Image does *not* fluoresce orange, so it was not produced by an elevated temperature of any kind–whatever made the Image was of low temperature. Image-making processes can be considered only if they will produce the physics of the Shroud *and* the chemistry of the Shroud *and* the biological characteristics of the Shroud, all at the same time.

Joe Nickell, a stage magician and private detective, has become a Shroud critic with his claim of producing replicas of the Shroud. He first said a cloth could be briefly laid on a heated metal statue. Later he claimed to mold a wet cloth onto a statue, which was then dried and a pigment of myrrh and aloes was applied with a dauber. His second claim is totally refuted by the paper of Schwalbe and Rogers (note 1, item 14, chapter 9) discussed later in this chapter.

Similarly, the bindings of medieval books fluoresced brightly when tested, as did all manner of paint ingredients used by medieval artists, such as proteinaceous materials, seed and nut oils, animal collagen, fish glue, plant gums, honey, sugar, starch, egg white, gelatin (even from a laboratory rat's tail), and human ear wax. Fluorescence testing seems conclusively to eliminate all paints, pigments, stains, dyes, and protein as factors in the creation of the Shroud body image.

Although various characteristics of the bloodstains on the Shroud seem to indicate cloth-body contact, it is clear that *pressure* in connection with that contact was not a significant factor; all data considered, it seems probable that the body lay on its back on the Shroud for some period, and yet the fluorescence testing indicates that detail and contrast is only slightly more prominent on the dorsal Shroud image than on the frontal image.

In a 1980 report,[2] R. A. Morris, L. A. Schwalbe, and J. R. London present results of x-ray fluorescence measurements made on the Shroud. (See note 3 in chapter 8. Other fluorescence and reflectivity measurements were conducted in the infrared, ultraviolet, and visible bands of the spectrum.) Particularly, elements such as calcium, strontium, and iron were identified comparatively in various areas (bloodstains, image areas, scorch, clear linen). After the data collection was completed in Turin, a reassembly of the experimental setup was made at Los Alamos with similar apparatus. Calcium and strontium were found to be uniformly distributed over the cloth in quantities best explained simply as due to the retting process. With reference to the possibility of applied pigments or dyes to explain the images, they report that they found no elemental composition differences between image and off-image areas. Nonuniform, substantial concentrations of iron were found in the heavy "bloodstain" areas (as would be expected if it is blood), especially at the heels (dorsal side) and at the "wound" in the side (frontal). Critics have proposed that jeweler's rouge (iron oxide) may have been used as a coloring agent in the making of an artificial image, but these x-ray fluorescence tests—including extensive laboratory experimentation—could find no support for such a claim.

In the infrared region of light, J. S. Accetta and J. S. Baumgart presented[3] preliminary findings of reflectance spectroscopy,[4] and spectral comparisons between laboratory data and Shroud observation data; they also discussed findings of infrared thermographic imaging.[5] The examination and testing of the Shroud employed as many nondestructive tests as possible, since it was not clear in advance which specific techniques might be the most useful in determining comprehensively the physical characteristics of the Shroud images, and possibly the manner in which the images were formed. Infrared investigation was one such technique used, to contrast with and perhaps go beyond findings possible in the visible range of the spectrum.

On-site difficulties, such as early failure of a minicomputer and the extreme atmospheric moisture fluctuations in the medieval palace where they were set up (caused by precipitation outdoors and high humidity indoors), handicapped the recovery of optimum data on this initial effort with sophisticated equipment. Nevertheless, some fifty spectra were taken in the Shroud areas of body image, bloodstains, scorches, and clear linen. Infrared thermography showed the presumed bloodstains as bright crimson, in contrast with the dullness in visual appearance. In general, they found emissivity differences throughout the Shroud to be too small for meaningful results under the examination conditions.

x-ray radiography at low voltage was used by R. W. Mottern, J. R. London, and R. A. Morris in examination of the Shroud. x-ray radiography (photography) at low voltage is a type of photography in which the x-ray permits depiction of internal features as well as the front and back of the Shroud cloth.

In the course of making x-ray photographs of the entire Shroud,[6] they collected data from the areas of the body image, scorches, water stains, and blood-flow stains. All the film was immediately processed manually in a nearby temporary darkroom. Data from this study is being cataloged to go along with the x-ray photography to give the scientists a comprehensive basic record of the Shroud. Additionally, some of the more important results of these examinations were the production of the x-ray photographs showing much detail such as: clearly seen punched holes, burned holes, patches, stitching, needle holes, creases filled with debris, and so on. Significantly, the *image* is not seen on these x-rays, thereby demonstrating that the image cannot be due to a heavy-metal pigment such as iron oxide, as claimed by some critics.

A companion to the x-ray radiographic photography just described was the color photomicroscopic work (photography through the microscope) of Samuel F. Pellicori and Mark Evans, which provided surface photographs of selected areas of the Shroud, in the visible range, but in greatly expanded detail through the microscope.[7] The visible, or optical, range is 400 to 750 nanometers; when the visible spectrum is "split" into the colors, they range from violet to indigo, blue, green, yellow, orange, and red; thus infrared and ultraviolet are beyond our visible spectrum at the two "ends," respectively. These microscopic color pictures have now been studied extensively. As in other tests, the bloodstains under magnification have the typical brownish color of dried blood, except that a reddish crusted material seems caught in the fibrils nearest the top of the cloth—it appears startlingly like recent blood in color and brightness, as it also contains significant amounts of orange-bile pigments, a known decomposition product of blood. In some areas, particularly at the edge of heavy blood flows, a colored liquid less dense than whole blood is found, which would be correct if it is the blood serum ("water") that separates from whole blood at death.

In this study of the body image, the findings of other members of the STURP team are confirmed as to the lack of depth in the image coloring—only the very top fibrils at the crown of a given thread are colored. And this is true even at the most intense areas, such as the heel and the nose—there is no penetration of the color into the body of the thread. Moreover, differences in the light and dark intensity is a difference in the number of colored fibrils per unit area, not a difference in shade or color. The creation of the body image is very clear and simple from a mere chemical standpoint: The body image is not truly stained, but rather is colored by the oxidation and loss of water in only those fibrils making up the body image. This is a well-understood process about the oxidation of cellulose, the basic component of linen. What can cause oxidation of cellulose? The exposure to heat and light. Yet, what event, by what mechanism or action, did heat and light darken only the topmost fibrils in a precise pattern to make such an accurate and meaningful image of a crucified man and not oxidize the thread to a greater depth? Only the chemical action is clear: Those "selected" fibrils were affected by cellulose oxidation—under dehydrative reaction conditions.

Of course, as other team members found in other tests, if body oils and perspiration, olive oil, myrrh, and aloes were applied to the surface of a piece of linen and it was thereafter artificially aged, cellulose oxidation was accelerated and the body image coloration was matched. But this is irrelevant, as we know from several tests that the body image was imprinted through *space,* and contact between body and Shroud was a minor factor.

Pellicori and Evans hope for another opportunity to examine the Shroud under circumstances where a stable platform for the Shroud can be provided; this would permit magnification five times more powerful than they could use in 1978. However, even better arrangements for repeat examinations (better x-ray fluorescence, for instance) would not likely solve the basic enigma and tell us what process oxidized the cellulose with such amazing detail and permanence.

A wrap-up by L. A. Schwalbe and R. N. Rogers of the work done on the Shroud in the fields of physics and chemistry has now been released by STURP.[8] This is the report that has been called the "official summary" and which was delivered in fall 1981 to Pope John Paul II and King Umberto II.

The conclusions include the primary judgment that no paint, applied pigment, stain, dye, or artificial coloring was responsible for the body image of the Man on the Shroud. It was not made by artist, craftsman, or forger. The areas that appear pictorially as "bloodstains," are in fact stains of blood. Both the body image and bloodstain areas involved some contact between body and cloth, but contact alone does not explain the detail and the permanence of the markings.

At a distance of four to five meters (about fourteen and a half feet) from the cloth, the optimum viewing distance, the image features on the Shroud are easily recognizable. At a closer range the image disappears, which clearly shows the impossibility of the Shroud as a man-made artist's rendering—he couldn't see to paint. The density changes in the image are not shadings of color but are found to be inversely related to the body's distance from the cloth, point to point. That, plus the 3-D "information" contained in the body image photographs and its photographic "negativity," with hidden details that become known only with high magnification and computer analysis, all buttress the chemical evidence that the Shroud images were not made by art or artifice.

Thus the scientists have eliminated all historically known, and all known but technologically feasible, methods of creating the images. As they put it, "If the image were produced by painting, block printing, transfer-rubbing over a bas relief, spray painting, or some unreported photographic-like process, a foreign material would have been added to the cloth. The foreign material would cause changes in relative density, chemical composition, spectral reflectance characteristics, mechanical properties, and/or microstructure." But there were none.

On the contrary, up to the present time no *natural* process ever known has been postulated by the scientists as the technique by which the Shroud images were created. In chapters 16 and 19 other possibilities will be considered.

None of the critics, skeptics, art experts, professional atheists, or pseudo-detectives have been able to offer any evidence or explanation that has stood up to scientific evaluation by STURP. Every claim, supported or not, has been painstakingly considered. The claim that iron oxide (Fe_2O_3), found in some Shroud locations, was in fact evidence of paint[9] was exhaustively considered and totally eliminated as a possibility. Heller and Adler reported[10] that iron oxide used in medieval paints and paint pigments comes from hematite, ochres, and earth pigments, and is therefore invariably contaminated with manganese, nickel, cobalt, or aluminum. However, there were no traces of manganese, nickel, cobalt, aluminum, arsenic, copper, lead, or magnesium on the Shroud—proving that the iron oxide came either of hydrologic (water—the retting process) or biologic (blood) origin. All foreign substances on the Shroud were ultimately satisfactorily resolved. For instance, some of the wrinkles (which show up as lines on Shroud pictures) were found to be creases that contained deposits of debris. Chemical and spectral analysis of those deposits showed concentrations of calcium and strontium—the natural accumulation of dust and lint.

There has been speculation that heat (somehow applied) has been the basic factor creating the body image; but those parts of the image that intersect scorches (from the 1532 fire) were observed to have identical color tone and density as the image areas farthest from the scorches—so that neither heat directly nor heat changes in the cloth can be the explanation of the image. In this regard, the fire of 1532 turns out to be a fortuitous happening. The burns of the cloth were caused by the melting of the silver casket in which it was kept. Pure silver melts at 960 degrees centigrade, but because of alloys put into the silver in making the casket, it may have melted at about 850 degrees C. Neither organic dyes or stains nor inorganic pigments available in the Middle Ages could have withstood such temperatures without considerable change in color, and this would include oxides, ochres, and siennas; in fact, iron oxide would have turned black. Paint made with proteinous plant-gum, or starch-base, would have changed color more rapidly than would the cellulose of the linen (at about 310° C.). Water used to extinguish the fire produced stains on the Shroud, but did not change the color tone of the images.

Magnification should show pigment particles, if any were there. During the 1978 examination, fifty-times magnification was used, and on the surface particles lifted by sticky-tape the later examination was made at 1,000-times magnification. No particles were found in the image areas that could indicate the original presence of dyes, stains, inorganic pigments, protein, starch, or wax-based painting media. Nor were such foreign elements found by x-ray fluorescence, spectrophotometric reflectance, or by ultraviolet fluorescence.

It seems logical to assume that the blood got on the Shroud by contact. If so, the body image could not have been made by any heat process to scorch the cloth, because then the blood would have been burnt wherever it intersected with the body image. But this did *not* happen. Yet wherever the bloodstains were near the burns of the 1532 fire, they were burnt.

The Schwalbe/Rogers conclusion is that we seem to know what the image is chemically, but how it got there remains a mystery. They say: "The dilemma is not one of choosing from among a variety of likely transfer mechanisms, but rather that no technologically credible process has been postulated that satisfies all the characteristics of the existing image."

The chemistry of the various stains and images on the Shroud was reviewed and updated in a broadly based presentation to the American Chemical Society in the fall of 1982 (note 3 of chapter 9) by six of the STURP scientists.

The color of the body-only images of the Shroud has frequently been described as sepia. However, these researchers say that such perception would be true only under low-color-temperature lighting. They find that the true color under white light is yellow (straw yellow).

They report that physical microscopic examination of the Shroud disclosed that the yellowed surface fibrils (body image) were not "cemented" to one another as would have been true if a pigment-binder were present. This finding was visually demonstrated by probing the fibrils with a dissecting needle. Moreover, they found that at magnifications of up to 1,000-times, these fibrils do not appear to have any coating of any sort. And to "paint" a fibril would be impossible, because the thinnest known paintbrush bristles are huge in diameter compared to the size of a single linen fibril.

In nearly all instances, the yellow coloration of the fibril is interrupted as the thread goes beneath a crossing thread in the weave pattern—thus demonstrating again that only the upper surface fibrils are colored. This was also found in physically tracing a single fibril: The fibrils are yellowed only on the portion that is in the uppermost position on the thread, and are not yellowed continuously over their entire length. The fibril loses its coloring in the normal course of following the twist of the fibrils making up the thread, as it leaves the upper portion of the thread and moves to the lower portion of the thread.

Some researchers have noted a possible "mashing" of the beard along the sides of the face and the absence of an image at the crown (topmost portion) of the head—between the frontal and dorsal images. They have interpreted these aspects as tending to establish the presence of a chin band or jaw band, traditionally used to keep the mouth of the corpse closed, knotted at the crown. However, this STURP paper reduces the probability of such an interpretation, since the authors state that a number of these longitudinal stripes of lighter color, including the ones about 2.5cm wide along the sides of the face, are due to the different lots of thread used in the manufacture of the cloth (see also discussion in chapter 8).

Nevertheless, in another paper, Robert H. Dinegar states as a qualification to this point: "An argument can be made, however, from other aspects of the image, that a chin band is indeed around the head." ("The 1978 Scientific Study of the Shroud of Turin," *Shroud Spectrum International,* no. 4, September 1982.)

But what caused the accelerated aging, known as cellulose degradation, of selected portions of some topmost fibrils of the cloth—the yellowing that accounts for the front and back images of a crucified man on the Shroud? Again, the most certain findings are negative ones. The process took place at low temperatures (less than 200 degrees C.), so it could have been caused by "ambient heat" but was not caused by scorching. On the contrary, a very different chemistry is present where actual scorches appear on the cloth because of the 1532 fire; there, a high temperature was present. Additionally, laboratory simulation of accelerated aging confirms that the body-only images were caused by the dehydration and oxidation of the cellulose in the linen; this chemistry is similar to that which causes the natural yellowing of linen with age.

In examining the microscopic characteristics of the blood images on the Shroud, these researchers note that all bloodstains appeared to have had much of the upper portions of the dried stain removed as if abraded by mechanical wear. This could have been caused by the hundreds of times the Shroud was folded and otherwise carelessly (even if reverently) handled over the centuries. The folding has apparently resulted in translocating some of the abraded material (dried blood) to other locations on the Shroud. Therefore, the residue of dried blood is largely absent on the crowns of the threads and is most abundant between the threads, in the interstices of the weave, and between the fibrils of the threads.

From the standpoint of image theory, it is interesting that researchers report the absence of body image on the wound image margins, which suggests to them that *the blood images were present on the cloth before the body images were "placed or developed" on it.* Also, in areas of heavy blood flows, the fluid seems to have followed contours of the cloth, such as folds; this seems clearly to have happened at the small of the back.

At magnifications of 250-times to 1,000-times in the bloodstain areas, it was found that the fibrils clearly were coated and the joints were filled with some substance. Of course, this is just the opposite of the findings for the body-only image areas. Laboratory tests were made by coating three-hundred-year-old Spanish linen with partially clotted blood, which was then allowed to stand for eighteen months. Resulting examination thereafter was completely consistent with the Shroud findings.

The darker portions of the blood images on the Shroud are quite red. There is a considerable range of "blood" color, from brown through red to orange. However, in general it is of a crimson appearance as would be expected for old bloodstains containing some blood decomposition products, such as bilirubins.

Dried blood is usually black or brown. The Shroud blood is *red,* which is chemically possible only if the blood is from a severely beaten person—thus agreeing with the pathological evidence of the Shroud.

The report concludes that the stains are composed of primate blood that is probably human. These researchers have used antialbumin and anti–whole sera tests to confirm the Italian immunochemical tests and findings by Baima Bollone.

When the findings of this paper are coupled with reports of the pathologists, the researchers can say that these blood images are the natural consequences of the linen being in contact with wounds on a human body. Nevertheless, they acknowledge that the body image process must have been *more* than just contact—that there must have been a "kind of projection" through space, because *there often seems to be an image present even where it does not seem possible the cloth was in contact with the body.*

In October 1982, Jackson, Jumper, and Ercoline presented an experimental paper to the Seattle conference of the Institute of Electrical and Electronic Engineers (IEEE) to round-out their 3-D work on the Shroud body images (note 4 of chapter 9). One of their conclusions was that the visible image on the Shroud is not the work of an artist in an eye/brain/hand coordination sense, nor does it appear to be the result of direct contact only, diffusion processes, radiation from a body shape or engraving, dabbing powder on a bas-relief, or electrostatic imaging.

The first 3-D work of Jackson and Jumper confirmed the very early suggestion of Paul Vignon *(Shroud of Christ,* Dutton, 1902) that the density (darkness-lightness) of the Shroud body images varied according to the distance from the body to the cloth (for example, the tip of the nose is dark, the eye sockets are light). Their next step was the discovery that the variance of those distances was so precise that with an Interpretation Systems VP-8 Image Analyzer they could project a relief image in three dimensions. Put in scientific terms, they state that the Shroud's three-dimensional characteristic means "that the image shading can be self-consistently interpreted as being correlated with the distance between a body and an enveloping cloth."

This paper presents a series of laboratory experiments in comparison and contrast with the shading structure of the Shroud face. Their first hypothesis was to consider the Shroud image to possibly be the work of an artist. Certified police artists, with pencil and paper medium, were asked to do a freehand image, shading it in proportion to relief. The experiment was repeated a number of times, using a variety of standards and requirements, though all were based on the same facial shape. Then 3-D reliefs were generated from the artists' sketches. The results were not convincing when compared with the 3-D of the Shroud; in general, they had a masklike quality and possessed relief deformities that were quite significant.

The next series of experiments was based on direct contact, especially by various techniques that have been suggested by Shroud critics. A statue's face covered with printer's ink was covered with a cloth, but much of the area made no contact with the face and left no mark on the cloth. Even when the cloth was gently brought into complete contact with the face, a relief made by the VP-8 resulted in a highly distorted image.

Another series of tests attempted to use a diffusion technique to stain the cloth with vapor from the subject. Although a variety of trials were made, no useful result was evidenced by 3-D projection.

In attempts to transfer facial contours by radiation, the experimenters covered the subject face with phosphorescent paint, which they then optically charged, covering the face with contoured sheets of sensitive photographic film in lieu of a cloth. But again, almost no correlation was found on the 3-D projection. In each series of experiments a number of variations in technique were attempted.

Several critics have suggested some type of transfer from a bas-relief statue. This the experimenters attempted from a bronze cast, using several techniques. Stretching the cloth over the heated statue did produce an image from which the VP-8 could project a 3-D replica. However, if the statue was heated enough to produce an image on cloth, the heat discolored the back of the cloth within a few seconds (linen of the same thickness as the Shroud was used); thus, there seems no way to produce a Shroudlike image that is only two or three fibrils deep. By using wet linen on the heated statue it was possible to largely limit the image to one side of the cloth, but at almost a complete sacrifice of the 3-D projection capability that could be encoded into the image.

A book published in Turin by Claudiana Press in 1982 (*The Shroud: a Mystery Revealed,* by Carlo Papini) carries the subtitle *The American 'Verdict' Does Not Confirm Authenticity* and makes sweeping criticisms of the STURP research. The writer claims the Shroud image was artificially produced by suspending a cloth over a heated bronze relief. One presumes that his book might not have been written if the author had awaited the American research reports.

One of the more persistent critics has been Joe Nickell, whose claims are further discussed in chapter 12. Using a wet cloth molded onto a cold bas-relief statue, he has claimed that a powder could be later "dabbed" onto the dried cloth to bring out a "photographically" reversed image. However, these experimenters found his mechanism unacceptable when attempts were made to project a 3-D relief from such an image; they concluded that the shading of an image made by his procedure seemed to contain *curvature* rather than *distance* information when processed by the VP-8 Analyzer.

Two final tests were conducted, one holding the cloth over a heated engraving, and the other using electrostatic imaging possibly associated with lightning phenomena. Each of these techniques were also found not to be viable.

ELEVEN

DATING THE SHROUD; SURVIVAL OF ANCIENT CLOTH

Rome Symposium 1993

MANY PEOPLE react incredulously to the implicit claim of some two thousand years of age for the flax-linen cloth of the Shroud. (Rather, the truly amazing factor is the sharp, *sometimes subliminal* detail, and the indelibility of the body-image and bloodstains after so long a time.) However, as to the cloth itself, Elizabeth P. Benson, archaeology researcher-administrator for American pre-Columbian history at Dumbarton Oaks Institute, Washington, D.C., says in a private communication: "Certainly there are textile remains of cotton and, I believe, llama-wool that are older than the Turin Shroud should be." She notes that Dumbarton Oaks held an entire conference on the subject of early Andean textiles.[1]

There are many examples of preservation from ancient times. An article in *Archaeology*[2] tells of the numerous textile artifacts found in arid areas of the Andean highlands dating to the era between 3000 and 2000 B.C., known as the Preceramic Period. Both illustrations and text relate to various textiles found with sizable fragments intact; the authors identify both cotton and "coarser plant fibers." The authors of that article say that "Peru is famous for its ancient textiles which comprise one of the best preserved and numerically richest archives of ancient craft." Photographs with the article show numerous samples of four-thousand-year-old cloth in an excellent state of preservation. The text notes, however, that frequently if the dye or paint used to make decorative stripes (for instance) was slightly acid, it would eventually destroy the cloth under those precise stripes, while much of the surrounding fabric survived. Comparably, several thousand feet lower, in deserts of the Peruvian coastal plain where it doesn't rain for several years at a time, grave clothes are found in an amazing state of preservation, even though found in shallow graves. There, at the Paloma village site, coarsely woven textiles were found,[3] carbon 14 dated to seven thousand years ago.

Near the Dal Cataract of the Nile in the Upper Nubia area of Sudan, University of Kentucky archaeologists in 1979 disinterred more than four hundred bodies in Christian cemeteries where the burials had occurred about fourteen hundred years ago.[4] The arid conditions of this fringe of the Sahara, plus burial practices that involved brick tombs in some cases and pottery jars to hold the corpses of young children and fetuses, combined to provide remarkable preservation of the bodies. Surviving in excellent condition were burial shrouds, clothing, hair, skin, and internal organs. It was possible to test the mineral content of the hair and even to extract parasites from bowel and stomach contents. For instance, a young mother had died, as had her child, during a breach-birth delivery. They were buried together, along with the blood-stained matting during the delivery. Reverend Wuenschel has reported that in Egypt the linen mummy wrappings are so well preserved that the Arabs make them over into garments for daily wear.

In July 1980, Chinese archaeologists of the Shanghai Museum excavated a desert site and found the almost perfectly preserved body of a woman thirty-two hundred years old. Photographs they sent to the United States with their report show that, indeed, even her hair is well preserved.[5]

The superintendent of the Museum of Egyptology in Turin, Italy, states that his museum has many pieces of ancient Egyptian linen in excellent condition, some of which date to 2800 B.C.[6]

In these cited instances, the preservation of cloth has probably depended largely on two factors: the exclusion of air, totally or mostly, and an arid climate—because humidity is definitely a destroyer. Now, if the Shroud of Turin is truly the burial cloth of Jesus of Nazareth, then it would be natural that everyone who has possessed it, from that first Easter onward, would have reverence for it and would have treated it with great care—both from the standpoint of preserving it and from the standpoint of protecting it from political and religious enemies. It is our knowledge from 1502 in Chambery onward (and our logical speculation plus knowledge for the entire previous period) that the Shroud was probably kept most of the time in caskets that were airtight or nearly so, or was otherwise sealed from the air, such as by masonry.

As noted in chapter 7, first-century historian Pliny describes the steps of processing yarn to include washing in a "struthium" solution as a softener. Struthium is assumed to be soapweed, and its use would give the treated cloth a toxicity that effectively would preclude mildew, mold, and decay. Such conditioning provides one more possible explanation for the Shroud's excellent condition today, although such has not yet been chemically established.

The contrast of body-image to cloth color is probably less with the passing of centuries as the cloth ages and *its* color deepens—especially if one assumes that the image gets no darker. Dorothy Crispen in *Shroud Spectrum International* no. 2 says the Poor Clare nuns' 1532 report indicates that the image may have been stronger in antiquity.

Dr. Alan D. Whanger, a professor at Duke University Medical Center, is an amateur photographer and a Shroud research buff. He had noted, as had several others previously, the marked similarity between the image on the Shroud and early artistic portrayals of Jesus dating back to the sixth century. After years of comparing these images in many ways, he developed a procedure in December 1981 that he calls the "polarized image overlay technique," by which two different images can be compared in minute detail. This same technique was later used by him and his wife Mary to validate the work of Father Francis Filas regarding the identification of the coins over the eyes of the Man of the Shroud (described later in this chapter). They compared images of Jesus on early icons, mosaics, and Byzantine coins with the image on the Shroud and found marked similarities between them, some in almost microscopic detail. The four faces they used for detailed comparisons and analyses are: the Mosaic of the Transfiguration at St. Catherine's Monastery, Mount Sinai, dated between 527 and 564; an icon of the face of Jesus, St. Catherine's Monastery, Mount Sinai, which was probably painted between 527 and 564 but no later than 590; a gold Byzantine coin, a solidus of Justinian II struck between 692 and 695, about the size of a nickel and having the facial portrait 9mm high; and another gold solidus of Constantine VII struck in 945, with the facial portrait only 6.5mm high.

The comparison technique is relatively simple. Two projectors are used side by side (or one above the other on a special stand), and they project on the same area of the screen. A polarizing filter is put in front *of each* lens, with the planes of polarization of the filters at right angles to each other. When the images are then projected on a lenticular-type screen and viewed through a third polarizing filter, one image can be faded out and the other faded in by rotating the third filter, enabling one to compare fine points in detail. The images must be aligned as exactly as possible according to size and position; this is facilitated by having zoom lenses on the projectors.[7]

In comparing these images, the Whangers devised a method of comparison that they call points of congruence, the presence of a similar or identical feature on each of the two images. These may be described in detail or recorded on a drawing for tabulation. (This method is rather similar to that used in the forensic sciences, such as in fingerprint or tire track identification, wherein fourteen points of congruence are acceptable in a court of law to determine identity.) The presence of large numbers of congruences between these portraits and the image on the Shroud convinced them that all of these images were based on that of the Shroud. They noted 33 points of congruence with the face on the mosaic and 34 points of congruence with the face on the coin of 945. The face on the icon has 46 points of congruence and has such exact and fine detail (for example, seven abnormalities of the left eye that are seen on the Shroud) that they felt the only adequate explanation of these similarities is that the artist producing the icon was looking directly at the Shroud image and copied it as exactly as he could. Even more amazing is the image on the coin of A.D. 692–695 which has over 63 points of congruence with the Shroud image, many of which are too small to be seen with the naked eye. Again, there could be no other reasonable explanation of these similarities except that the die cutter was looking directly at the Shroud image and making measurements to maintain exact proportions.

It is Dr. Whanger's opinion that this technique is as exact as fingerprint comparison, and that any number above 25 congruences should be accepted as conclusive proof of identity of origin.

To watch Dr. Whanger repeatedly demonstrate this technique with these images is an experience that is profoundly moving and beyond adequate description. It is also most impressive to see peripheral anomalies (such as will be discussed in chapter 19, with reference to researchers Vignon et al.) utilized by the artist; for instance, a dirty crease or wrinkle in the cloth that appears where the neck meets the chest is exactly reproduced by some artists, but is worked into a design of a garment or item of adornment.

To the problem of the dating of the Shroud, the importance of the Whanger work looms very large because the minting date of coins is known exactly or within two or three years, and the commissioning of major works of art is recorded by the patron or done with almost as much certitude. For example, the mosaic of the Transfiguration at St. Catherine's Monastery, Mount Sinai, was commissioned by Justinian I and executed under his rule from 527 to 565. This is a magnificent work, covering the entire arc of the dome in the apse of the Church of the Virgin in the monastery. The monks have been so diligent in their custodianship that this mosaic has been untouched since it was completed. The mosaic and the icon probably were executed in the early to middle of the sixth century—the icon no later than 590. The Justinian II coin was struck in the late seventh century, and the Constantine VII coin in the mid-tenth century. Once the Image of Edessa was found above the city gate, that Face immediately became the subject of major art projects all over Byzantium, to make copies of the Face.

Since Dr. Whanger's press conference in early 1982[8] reporting his findings, his work, in one bold step, takes us right back to the Edessa gate, about A.D. 57.

At the same time, Whanger's evidence also represents a strong refutation of persistent claims that the Shroud is a medieval forgery or artist's creation. It will also render unimportant any real need to establish a historical chain of evidence of ownership over these intervening 767 years—and, of course, this brings full authentication much closer to a certainty.

In a related area, Dr. and Mrs. Whanger reported in 1984 that they have been using their polarized image overlay technique to match the Shroud face with the claimed facecloth of Jesus (called by some the Sudarium) that has reposed in the cathedral of Oviedo, Spain, since the ninth century. The Whangers have recorded 130 points of congruence between markings on the Shroud and the Facecloth; the latter has a number of markings and bloodstains that match with those of the Shroud Face, though the facecloth does not show a photographic-like facial image as does the Shroud. The Sudarium of Oviedo is said to date from the first century, and that it was brought from Jerusalem across North Africa. The latter aspect of this claim was validated by Dr. Frei, who found a number of African pollen varieties on it. It was displayed with other relics for King Alfonso VI on March 14, 1075, and a record was made of the event.

Dr. and Mrs. Whanger have verified that the bloodstains on the facecloth coincide exactly with the bloodstains on the face of the Shroud image, and with the shape and form of the face of the Man of the Shroud. Also, they confirm that the Sudarium was in contact with the dead man's face for only a limited time because only fresh blood had stained it, not coagulated or clotted blood. Dr. Whanger concluded that both cloths must have covered the same face at the same time.

Dr. Whanger says that the facecloth—which measures two feet nine inches by one foot nine inches and has the texture of a taffeta weave—was placed on the face shortly after death and before entombment because it is much bloodier than the Shroud. The bloodstains on the facecloth have been matched to the Shroud Face bloodstains with 130 points of congruence by the Whangers. The facecloth is dated with certainty to be no later than the seventh century.

Similar to chemical analysis of the Shroud, Dr. Whanger notes that bilirubin can be spectrally detected on the facecloth as well as yellow serum on the coated fibers. Thus, this new spectral evidence matches and supports the previous chemical, immunological, and forensic work on the Shroud.

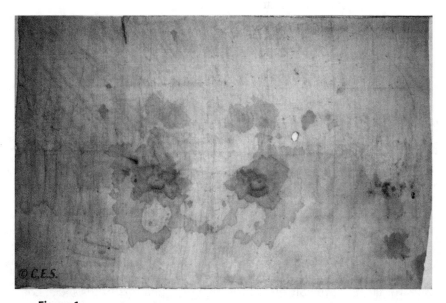

Figure 1.

Facecloth ("Sudarium") of Oviedo, Spain

Our news media have taught us in recent years to speak glibly of carbon 14 dating as the way to determine the age of materials that originate in the vegetable kingdom. But this fairly new technique (utilizing a radioactive isotope of carbon) is not as simple and practical, or as reliable, as we often are led to suppose. All of the scientists researching the mysteries of the Shroud are fully aware of the C-14 tool, but there are problems. On October 8, 1978, as the public exhibition in Turin was closing and the scientific intensive was getting under way, a news conference was held at which a press release from the archbishop's office was read; it included this statement: "The carbon-14 test has not been requested and will not at this time be included among the tests."

Some newsmen felt that this position was unwarranted and protested orally to the spokesman, Father Coero-Borga, secretary of the International Center, who responded with this comment:

> The decision not to include at this time the carbon-14 test was not arbitrary. We simply do not have at this point a consensus from the experts on the unqualified validity and efficacy of this test in the specific case of the Shroud. A prerequisite *is* that only minimal parts of the cloth be used. The moment we will have this assurance, and not just from one source, we will certainly move on this test.

A simple description/definition of "carbon-dating" is provided in the Special Introduction to this Edition.

In the years 1985–88, new developments emerged regarding carbon 14 dating of the Shroud cloth. In 1977, in a fortuitous social conversation, Professor Henry E. Gove of Rochester University conceived of a new method for C-14 measurement, now called the "accelerator technique" or, officially, the AMS (accelerated mass spectrometer) method. The technique of the original C-14 discovery by W. F. Libby in the 1940s is known as the "proportional-counting technique." Until recently, one of its drawbacks was the large size of cloth sample (napkin-size) that would have to be destroyed. Now, there is less difference in quantity required, but the accelerator method will use a piece smaller than a postage stamp.

In August 1985, world experts on radiocarbon dating met at an International Radiocarbon Congress in Trondheim, Norway, and again in September 1986 in Turin, Italy, to agree on a detailed and precise protocol respecting any future carbon-dating of the Shroud and to compare their methodologies and devise uniform procedures. As a result, it was agreed that seven prominent laboratories would each make a "blind" test of a piece of the Shroud cloth along with other control samples of cloth from antiquity whose age was known. It was also arranged that the conservator of the British Museum would monitor and referee the proceedings on behalf of the Church.

In preparation for the ultimate tests, the British Museum set up an intercomparison experiment with six of the laboratories in which they blind-dated pieces from an ancient Egyptian linen cloth; five of the six laboratories produced dates very close to one another, and close to the known First Egyptian Dynasty date of the cloth. Unfortunately, the Zurich AMS laboratory missed by some thousand years—admittedly because of faulty pretreatment.

Church representatives were present at Trondheim and Turin and it was assumed that they accepted the final protocol. However, informally in October 1987, and officially early in 1988, it was announced from Turin that the decision of Cardinal Anastasio Ballestrero, archbishop of Turin, after consultation with his science adviser, Professor Luigi Gonella, was for only three laboratories to participate in the C-14 testing; they were to be the University of Arizona facility at Tucson, the University of Oxford, England, and the Federal Technical Institute at Zurich, Switzerland; all three used the new accelerator method. No formal explanation has been given of the reason for this departure from the Trondheim/Turin protocol, but it is generally assumed that reducing the amount of cloth to be taken was the principal consideration.

Apart from the disappointment of the four rejected laboratories, some experts expressed concern that the results might be neither scientifically viable nor convincing to the public at large or the Shroud critics in particular. That concern proved fully justified, for on October 13, 1988, Ballestrero formally announced that the three laboratories had unanimously found the cloth's age to date between A.D. 1260 and 1390 (midpoint 1325), and that he accepted their conclusions. That report was widely carried by print and broadcast news media. Within three days, press releases from leading sindolologists (Professor William Meachem, senior archaeologist, University of Hong Kong; Rev. Albert R. Dreisbach Jr., director of the Atlanta Shroud Center; Professor Paul C. Maloney, director of the Association of Scientists and Scholars International for the Shroud of Turin; and Dr. Alan D. Whanger of Duke University) protesting the botched carbon-dating exercise and putting the misleading announcement in perspective were issued, but all major news media ignored them with the exception of a fairly balanced presentation by the Canadian Broadcasting Corporation.

The exercise was badly flawed and the result inexcusably misevaluated in several respects:

1) The AMS method of radiocarbon dating had been operational for a period of five years or less, so that experience in its use was very meager. And, most important, it requires a *pure sample;* thus, in order to date a sample from a subject such as the Shroud of Turin, which is known to be extensively contaminated from foreign matter, it is necessary for the sample first to be chemically purified by a procedure called "pretreatment." In the years 1987–88 the technique of pretreatment was still a chancy matter, as indicated by the Zurich laboratory's thousand-year error during the "dry run" as noted above; in other words, no one really could say (in 1988) whether samples of contaminated cloth could be successfully "purified" chemically by AMS pretreatment without jeopardizing the integrity of the process and without risk of throwing out the baby with the bathwater.

2) To have included all seven laboratories, as the scientific protocol of Trondheim/Turin specified, would have necessitated sample cloth aggregating four by seven centimeters—no more than the area of three large postage stamps; on April 21, 1988, the sample cut from the Shroud was one by seven centimeters in size, less than two small postage stamps in area. By using the other four laboratories, the exercise would have been enhanced by the forty-five years of experience in the improved Libby method ("proportional counting"), plus the advantage that that technique does not need an uncontaminated sample.

3) Recorded history of the Shroud of Turin establishes clearly the repeated contamination of this cloth by oil, wax, candle smoke, fungi, insect debris, pollen, dust, soap, paint, molten silver, ointments, open wounds, saliva, sweat, hot water, rain, and direct sunshine.

4) Neither in the sample-taking nor in the drafting of the October 13, 1988, announcement were members of the two scientific groups (STURP and ASSIST) permitted to be present, nor were they consulted. On the contrary, although the exercise was publicized as "blind testing," in fact, such was not the case; representatives of the three laboratories were present at the sample-taking, and were given certificates specifying the identity and known age of the so-called "control" samples.

5) The scientific protocol furnished the Turin authorities specified that samples be taken from five different sites on the Shroud, or at the very least, from three sites. Instead, a single sample was taken from just one site. No explanation has been forthcoming as to why the scientific protocol and recommendations were ignored in this and all other respects; it is known that because of advanced age and poor health Cardinal Ballestrero left all handling of the exercise to his adviser, Luigi Gonella; although there is no basis for questioning the honesty and good intentions of the Turin authorities, the reasons behind the exercise of such poor judgment is a legitimate area of concern.

6) The site on the Shroud from which the sample was taken could hardly have been more controversial and undesirable: The site is on an extreme edge that is so badly contaminated that it is noticeably darker than the balance of the cloth; this area involves a side panel or "filler strip" of cloth some five inches wide that has been discussed for several years by experts, many of whom suspect that the laboratories may have been testing mostly threads used in reweaving to repair the damage.

7) The sample was cut *very* close to a burn area, and the threads given the laboratories *may* have been scorched. One sindonologist queried forty laboratories worldwide and learned that none had ever tested a piece of scorched cloth. The question *must* be raised of what effect scorching might have to alter the cloth's carbon 14 isotopes (by molten silver at 850-plus degrees centigrade heat,

from the 1532 fire). Textile technology specialist John Tyrer, writing in the December 1988 newsletter of the British Society for the Turin Shroud, observes that the Shroud, inside of its silver casket during the Chambery fire of 1532, could have been subjected to "pressure cooker" conditions, causing surface contaminants to be dissolved and transported "into the linen or into the internal molecular structure" of the linen fibers.

8) And finally, evaluation of this carbon-dating exercise must inquire—*if* this was Jesus' shroud, what effect might the power of the Resurrection event have had to alter the ratio of carbon and oxygen isotopes in the cloth? STURP scientists coined the term "flash photolysis" to describe the image-making event for this Shroud's images. Could the Christ presence in action have provided such a flash of light or spiritual power in the moment of the Resurrection? Several scientists have raised the question. One suggested that the Resurrection arguably could have irradiated the cloth; another proposed that it could have altered the proportion of C-14 to C-12. Then in the British *New Scientist* of September 22, 1988, it was noted that in radiocarbon work "there is a fundamental assumption that the Carbon-14 got there by natural processes... [but] if there was any extra Carbon-14 present due to the Resurrection energy release, this would give the appearance that the Shroud was younger than it really is.... if energy release in the Resurrection process activated an extra eighteen percent of Carbon-14 compared to that present naturally in the cloth, the Shroud, although being 2000 years old, would appear [by C-14 measurement] to be only 650 years old [A.D. 1338]; and it is certainly possible to produce that amount of C-14 via a short burst of high energy." Radiocarbon laboratories admit that this explanation is theoretically possible.

If carbon-dating is to be one tool among many, what else can we look to? The many factors that historians and researchers have been pointing to for ten years or more: Some of these point specifically to Jesus; some to the first century and the area of the Holy Lands; some point to an early period in the Near East; some show the *impossibility* of a human artist, a natural causation, a West European creation, or a fourteenth-century creation. Throughout this volume, some two dozen of these factors have been identified. Since late 1988 the combined logical weight of these many factors has been referred to as the "preponderance of evidence" that demonstrates beyond question that the Shroud of Turin *must* be much older than the reported carbon-date.

Do those carbon-dating results of 1988 have any value or significance for us? Yes, they may be speaking to an event or events in the life of the Shroud rather than its origin. The three laboratories may have come up with an "accurate" date, but of what? Most of the sindonologists and scientists involved with Shroud research began 1989 with pleas to Turin and the Vatican to authorize *proper* retesting of the cloth to determine meaningful data. And if such further research is not authorized, then what? Slow and laborious research along other lines will be continued until attitudes change; several decades may be lost to the research progress, much as was true earlier in the twentieth century when Chevalier and Thurston, with flawed data, convinced the world by force of their prestige alone that the Shroud was a fake. Whether sindonology's recovery this time is rapid or slow, there can be no doubt that the Shroud-dating fiasco of 1988 has been cruelly hurtful to sincere religionists of all faiths and grossly misleading to the general public.

First, I will mention two obstacles in carbon-dating the cloth—one is probable and the other certain:

1) In the 1970s, two researchers separately suggested that the 1532 fire at Chambery, France, which caused the silver reliquary to drip molten silver onto the cloth, also may have created a "pressure cooker effect" of driving known contaminants on the cloth *into* the molecules of the cloth, so that the carbon content was skewed. More recently, at the Rome Symposium of 1993 and subsequently, Dimitri Kouznetsov of the Sedov in Moscow has asserted that during the 1532 fire the molten silver acted as a catalyst for carboxylation of the cellulose, so that subsequently the cloth became enriched with carbon, making the cloth younger.

2) However, much more certain is the work of Dr. Leoncio Garza-Valdes and associates at the University of Texas in San Antonio, which he reported in 1993 at Rome and subsequently at five symposia in Canada, the U.S., and in Mexico. Garza-Valdes reports that a natural microbe, the "isodiametric," which is often found on ancient cloth and is definitely on threads of the Shroud, exudes a gel known as *lichenothelia varnish,* which is high in carbon content; the relevance for us is that every century the Shroud of Turin gets *younger* with our present carbon-dating techniques. The laboratories in 1988 did no testing for this microbe and its gel and used no treatment that could eliminate it. Garza-Valdes is presently working on a technique that will cleanse the Shroud cloth safely and make carbon dating accurate.

On April 21, 1988, when Professor Giovanni Riggi of Turin took the cloth sample for the carbon tests, he also took several blood samples from the Shroud—from the occipital (back) of the skull and from the side of the Man of the Shroud. The cloth sample from the Shroud he cut in half (the strip 8cm long); the half (4cm) he cut into thirds, giving a third to each laboratory. The other 4cm of cloth he put in a bank vault with the blood samples.

In 1992, Riggi took both cloth and blood samples from the bank vault and then delivered them by hand to Dr. Garza and associates of the University of Texas (San Antonio campus). The blood samples were readily found to be human blood containing both X and Y chromosomes, which indicates male sex. The cloth sample was found to be coated with gel from the microbe just noted. Moreover, the microbes on the Shroud cloth were *still alive* and producing more gel.

TWELVE

FORGERY AND THE CRITICS

COPYING ALONE does not necessarily amount to fakery. Many relics, including the Shroud, were copied[1] openly and exhibited as such in the early centuries and the Middle Ages. There was no fraud in that, in and of itself; it was done because often travel and security were major problems precluding a traveling exhibit with a true relic. Moreover, there was a tradition that if a copy was touched to the original religious relic, the copy would also have mystical powers for the sincere believer. For this discussion it is not important whether healing, protection, or other mystical power could adhere to a piece of cloth; the point is that many people then believed so. Also, all forty-two copies of the Shroud of Turin (or of Constantinople, or of Besancon, or of Lirey, as the case may be) that have been identified by researchers were clearly copies.

The genuineness of the Shroud of Turin is what the STURP research is all about. Thanks to that work, we can be sure the Shroud is no copy of anything, and we can now be virtually certain that it was "not made by human hands." No other religious relic has been so exhaustively examined and tested. The provenance and bona fides of most other relics may have to be taken almost entirely on faith. For instance, Lady Helena, mother of Constantine I, engaged in a series of archaeological digs in Jerusalem and environs in the early fourth century. She labeled one of her finds the "True Cross." Without an early-day STURP to evaluate her find, one is perhaps entitled to some skepticism. But she was reportedly a genuine psychic-sensitive with demonstrated paranormal abilities that might well be credited in principle by modern anthropologists such as the late Dr. Norman Emerson, known as "the father of Canadian archaeology" and developer of reliable techniques for archaeological exploration that exactly parallel the pioneer efforts of Lady Helena.[2]

One thing is now virtually certain, regardless of who was wrapped in the Shroud of Turin, or when, or of how the images came to be made on the Shroud: This is not a fake or a counterfeit in any respect. The images were not painted or otherwise *put* on the cloth by a medieval (or earlier) artist, technician, or hoaxer. Such a medieval forger could not have known that the nails must go through the wrists, not through the hands as Bible translators have erroneously stated; he could not have known about arterial versus venous blood flow; he could not have known about the specifics of postmortem rigidity of crucifixion victims; he could not have known of the crucifixion reactions of such victims, such as the need to elevate the body to permit exhaling—the list could go on. Historical data had been largely lost for a thousand years, and scientific data would not be known for another five hundred.

And yet, Dietrick E. Thomsen, senior editor of *Science News,* wrote in the October 3, 1981, issue:

> The resurrection was not a circus trick…. [but] We may never know for sure what the Shroud of Turin is. *Why not let it rest in peace in its reliquary?* [emphasis added]

One wonders, "What is he afraid of?" It is doubtful that his "let it rest" suggestion would satisfy either curious scientists or searching religionists.

What can modern science do on the issue of possible forgery? Images on cloth, accomplished by art or artifice by any method ever known, would leave a foreign substance residue as long as the image remains, even if visible material such as hardened paint had fallen off in time. Scientists can identify any microscopic presence, or residue, or past presence, of physical agents that would have been put on the cloth in order to make the image; these include paints, paint pigment, spices, preservatives, stains, dyes, inks, acids, natural coloring substances, or gases. The many sophisticated methods of examination (such as by x-ray, by fluorescence, and by spectroscopic viewing) would have disclosed the residue, but they have found no such additive or evidence that any such was ever on the cloth. They included tests for all possibilities known today as well as substances available in the crucial first through fourteenth centuries. Moreover, they find no evidence of any technique or medium for applying any additive, such as a brush, a tool, or hand application.

The fire of 1532 would have discolored the images in *varying* degrees if there had been a residue, but it did not. Since the image is still there, the substance in at least some residue form would have to be still there, if any substance was used to make the Shroud's images.

Science can determine, and has determined, why the images are there. They have found that the reason for the body images is the slight discoloration (yellowing) of the uppermost fibrils of certain of the linen threads through the process of oxidation, caused by excessive light or heat. As to the "bloodstains" they have found that actual blood was and still is present. As to how such images could have been made on the cloth with such detailed accuracy and with such permanence, they have no explanation—only a long list of negatives, that is, ways it did not happen.

The Shroud did make its Western historical debut in highly equivocal circumstances, in a century (the fourteenth) notorious for devout chicanery and pious relic-mongering. However, as to fakery, Professor Philip McNair of Birmingham University, England, points out that the occasional cotton fibers in the Shroud were of the *Gossypium herbaceum* variety of cotton, which was cultivated in the Middle East during the first century, but was not known in Europe during the period when possible faking of the Shroud could have occurred. The few cotton fibers in the Shroud's cloth show that cotton could have been previously woven on the same loom. Moreover, he cites Jewish law (Leviticus 19:19) that expressly forbids the blending of vegetable (flax) fiber with animal (wool), and thus the presence of even one wool thread in the cloth would have "contaminated" it and precluded its use as a Jewish burial shroud. Analysis reveals a total absence of wool in the composition of the cloth of the Shroud.[3]

A few critics have claimed that Jesus did not die on the cross and that the Shroud proves this. Professor J. Malcolm Cameron, Home Office pathologist of the British government, would seem to squelch for all time these allegations. Cameron concludes that the image on the Shroud is consistent with that of a crucified body in a state of post-mortem rigor, in the position into which the body would naturally slip after death. He also considers that the arms of the Man on the Shroud had been forcibly bent across the abdomen to break the rigor of the shoulder-girdle—not an unusual burial problem in order to get the body into a straight position for burial, regardless of the cause of death. Cameron's credentials are beyond question, in sharp contrast to the so-called experts sometimes cited by the critics.[4]

The potential truth of the Shroud, when one soberly reflects upon it, is so tremendous and so provocative that the full realization staggers and shocks one upon initial impact. The result for some can be abject fear and even hysteria; the reaction for some is to attack—and the attack is frequently irrational.

One of those who claimed Jesus did not die on the cross is the German writer who variously calls himself John Reban, Kurt Berna, and Hans Naber—with the last names using the same five letters. Reban says that the Shroud proves his claim. However, a most exhaustive medical evaluation and exposé of Reban's claims was written by the late British physician-sindonologist, Dr. David Willis.[5] The work of Willis and Cameron totally demolished the position of Reban, and, if there could longer be any doubt, the microscope and computer brought into play in the recent years have eliminated it now.

The Shroud of Turin has never lacked for critics—even in high places. Assuming (as I do) that the Image of Edessa was the Mandylion was the Shroud of Turin, we can find critics right from the first century. When Ma'nu VI, the second son of Abgar V, came into power in A.D. 57, he was so critical of the Shroud and what it had done to (or for?) his family and nation that he immediately abolished Christianity, so that the Shroud had to be hidden.

The Byzantine emperor's sons were doubters also. Bishop Henri de Poitiers of Troyes vacillated by praising the de Charnys' exhibition in Lirey and then trying to stop them. His successor, Bishop Pierre

D'Arcis, tried to stop later exhibitions there, but the pope told him to back off or face excommunication. Researchers of the twentieth century have found a D'Arcis memorandum of 1389 (presumably intended for the pope) stating that Bishop Henri knew a painter who admitted to painting the Shroud image. French scholar Ulysee Chevalier believed it, and so did the English Jesuit Herbert Thurston. The late Dr. John A. T. Robinson also believed it at first, but he kept on reading and convinced himself that the Shroud and its images were genuine. Just in the last decade, Parisian researchers have determined that the so-called D'Arcis memorandum was no memorandum at all, but just a clerk's draft in poor Latin, never dated nor signed nor sent to the Vatican, and with no official copy either in Troyes or in the Vatican.

The sixteenth through nineteenth centuries were relatively quiescent years for the Shroud, while it lay in its vault in Turin. But, as the twentieth century was ushered in, on the heels of the discovery that there was photographic negativity inherent in the Shroud image, controversy arose at once. The critic this time was the august French Academy of Sciences. And ammunition for the academy's attack on member Yves Delage for his support of sindonologist Paul Vignon was provided mainly from the literary research by Shroud critic Canon Ulysse Chevalier. He published a scholarly critique[6] that resurrected the D'Arcis protest to Pope Clement, along with thirty-two lesser documents (that might largely be termed gossip against the Shroud and its owners).

One truism our civilization seems slow to learn is that critical claims and attacks should themselves be taken critically, because the critic and the skeptic have just as great an obligation to the public for careful research and careful allegation as does the proponent whom they attack. So often, alleged exposé is believed without question, and the higher the person or thing attacked and the more shocking the charge, the more quickly it is reported, repeated, and believed. Subsequent retraction or correction never gets the same circulation.

Prominent and respected British Church leaders Thurston and Robinson were among those who accepted, uncritically, the attacks on the Shroud by de Poitiers and D'Arcis, the bishops of Troyes. Thurston died much earlier in the twentieth century, and apparently had no occasion to revise his negative opinion. Dr. Robinson, however, read the scientific data favorable to the Shroud as it came out in recent years, and has now reversed himself and has made a significant contribution to modern sindonology (see chapter 5).

Defectors seem always able to find a forum. Informally associated with the early American scientific research in 1977, Dr. Walter McCrone of Chicago did not participate in the Turin exercise of 1978, but he was loaned some of the samples of Shroud "surface debris" on sticky-tape for microscopic examination. After hurried and superficial evaluation, he rushed into print a charge that the Shroud was a painted fake (see chapter 9). When he was subsequently shown his errors, McCrone did call a press conference and withdrew his negative charges;[7] however, negligible reporting was made of his retraction, and the damage was done. In a scientific and orderly manner, scientists Adler and Heller and others proceeded to totally demolish the McCrone charges (note 1, item 3 in chapter 9), but little notice, comparatively, was taken of their reports on the positive side of the Shroud's ledger.

Shroud critic McCrone, in his own journal *The Microscope*, and in newspaper interviews, has claimed that the surface debris lifted from the Shroud blood images was composed of iron oxide, and was paint residue, not real blood. At the March 3–9, 1986, Hong Kong Symposium for Shroud Studies, Dr. Alan D. Adler of Western Connecticut State College again totally rebutted McCrone's charges for which there appears to be no scientific basis (see also chapter 9).

McCrone had first received national publicity three decades ago when he announced that Yale University's Vinland Map with the Tartar Relation was a forgery that couldn't have been drafted as early as Yale believed. The questionable quality of McCrone's Shroud research, noted by Adler and Heller, stimulated review of the Vinland Map controversy and validated the map (*New York Times*, March 2, 1996).

One group, headed by Michigan sociologist Paul Kurtz (who, wearing different hats, produces *The Humanist* and *The Skeptical Inquirer*), appears to feel that scientific method is for "the other guys." One label used by the group is the Committee for the Scientific Investigation of Claims of the Paranormal. Having used the tar-brush attack on astrology[8] and parapsychology,[9] they have now turned their attentions to the Shroud of Turin and, predictably, see the STURP reports as "replete with misinformation," and propose artifice as "the most tenable explanation" for the Shroud's images. Moreover, the thousands of man-hours of meticulous research and documented reporting by STURP scientists stand in marked contrast with the bare, unsupported, and implausible charges and arguments presented by these critics.

Joe Nickell is a stage magician and a private detective, and is a darling of *The Humanist* and *The Skeptical Inquirer* because he says he can duplicate the Shroud of Turin *very easily*. He says that all he, or a fourteenth-century artist, needed to do was carve a wooden bas-relief figure, mold wet linen onto it, let it dry, and rub onto the cloth a mixture of myrrh and aloes with a dauber. This, he says, will create a negative image; later, vermilion mixed with powdered iron-earth pigment is painted onto the cloth with a brush to represent "blood."

The Nickell technique may be simple, but there is simply no possibility of duplicating the detail of the Shroud. Nickell's gross technique would not, for instance, reflect on coarse cloth the letters of a coin laid on the statue's eyelids; his technique would not distinguish between arterial blood surge and sluggish venous flow, nor give the halo effect of dried blood when the watery part has separated; nor would it explain the presence of pollen grains from Near East locations embedded in the Shroud. Most important of all, if Nickell has honestly described his process, his Nickell image would not duplicate the Shroud images; the latter are caused by oxidation (brought on by excessive light or heat). This oxidation of the Shroud fibrils is readily observable in the laboratory; it would not be present on the Nickell cloth.

The shroud that Nickell has made contains none of the hidden properties found subliminally in the Shroud of Turin, such as the three-dimensional coding embedded in photographs of it. The Holy Shroud Guild's president, Father Adam Otterbein, reported that when Nickell's photographs were computer-projected on the VP-8 Image Analyzer by STURP scientists, the results were flat and distorted like ordinary photographs; they do not contain true 3-D data and thus do not produce natural and lifelike 3-D projections. Moreover, one doubts that Nickell will ever submit the Nickell shroud to STURP for examination and testing.

Even if a forger of the Middle Ages had procured (at great cost and trouble) a linen cloth from the Near East that contained microscopic cotton fibers and non-European pollen, he would have had no real motive to do so because the science of his age could not have identified these factors nor could they have determined the origin of the cloth.

Why would a medieval artist want to paint or somehow create a "negative," even if he had the skill to do so, since his achievement could not be understood or admired by his contemporaries? It would be more than half a millennium before anyone would recognize what he had done and could compliment him on his abilities. If, with a flash of inspiration or by accident, an artist were to lay a wet cloth onto a bas-relief statue, rub it afterward with myrrh and aloes, and thus obtain a Nickell negative, what would he do? He would doubtless throw it away in disgust, for he would not know that in five or six hundred years it could be photographed so that his bizarre image would look natural.

If, half a millennium ahead of his time, an artist or technician-forger did produce a photographic negative on cloth, he would surely be dissatisfied with it and want to see it reversed to check its accuracy, but this would be impossible in the Middle Ages, so long before the invention of photographic inversion. Nor could he have retouched or overpainted it, which Nickell suggests is the way the bloodstains were added as a positive image, because of the distance factor. The optimum viewing distance for the Shroud image is six to ten feet; no artist could have painted from such a distance, and close up could not have created such detail because at a distance of less than six feet the image virtually disappears.

It is beyond belief that any artist or technician in the years and ages before 1357 could have successfully "encoded" three-dimensionality into the Shroud images that cannot be seen by the naked eye. How would he know he had done so, since such an effect could not have been detected without modern photography and subsequent computer enhancement and manipulation? How would he know he had created something worth saving? It would not have been attractive, much less natural-looking.

Much ado has been made by Nickell over a small anomaly: There is a blank space of perhaps four or five inches between the frontal and dorsal images on the Shroud. The distance is about right for the top of the head but there is no image of the crown. This situation seems to imply that an object at the top of the head interfered with the "image-making action," whatever that was. One of the more likely explanations is that the sudarium (the jaw-band, Robinson calls it) was knotted at the crown of the head. Also, it is possible that the miscellaneous cloths (the *keiriai*) intended for use on Sunday were laid there in a bundle, and/or there might have been a small bundle of spices for future use. Technically, the explanation given is that the Shroud image is not an isotropic projection nor a contact image.

In 1980, Professor Averil Cameron, in her inaugural lecture as professor of ancient history at King's College, London, attacked the Ian Wilson hypothesis that the first-millennium Face of Edessa, the Mandylion, was in fact the Shroud of Turin, folded. At the March 3–9, 1986, Hong Kong Symposium for Shroud Studies, Wilson responded. He repeated the arguments in his book (*The Shroud of Turin,* Doubleday 1978) keyed to the unique Greek words used to describe the Face in antiquity: *tetradiplon,* meaning "doubled four," and *ektypoma,* meaning "not made by human hands." He also cited ancient records that would appear to indicate that some few persons knew that the Edessa relic was a *full* image of a man (Ordericus Vitalis in *Historia Ecclesia,* part II, book IX, 8; Gervase of Tibury in *Otia Imperialia III;* the "Latin Abgar Legend" found in Dobschutz's *Christusbilder*). His argument seems overwhelming. In a critique of that lecture, patriarch sindonologist Werner Bulst[10] of Darmstadt, Germany, says: "I had come to the opposite opinion—there must be relations between the Shroud and the Mandylion of Edessa. Now, after many new findings, I believe the identity between them is very probable…. The [Ian] Wilson hypothesis, I believe, is not improbable."[11]

Although critics' alternative suggestions as to the making of the images have often been made in bad faith, the STURP scientists have meticulously tested all and found all of them to be seriously wanting. This is not an image that modern scientists cannot explain.

The bottom line as to forgery, fakery, great art, or chance creation of a photographically negative image is that the data of modern scientific findings involve so much *subliminal* detail. This data precludes the possibility of such a creation by craftsmen, even today, much less in the Middle Ages or earlier. Beyond all doubt, the Shroud of Turin is a genuine artifact, and its inexplicable character seems to compel us to add, "not made by human hands."

THIRTEEN

SOME ANSWERS, EVALUATIONS, AND OPINIONS

HE TERRIBLE risk of making a single relic an article of supreme religious faith and, indeed, the ultimate evidence for the historicity of the existence and crucifixion-death of Jesus of Nazareth was so obvious, and the implications for fraud so awesome, that many ecclesiastics have wanted no part of the Shroud of Turin from the beginning. That attitude is understandable. The stakes of the sindon-scientists are considerably different but in some ways potentially as great. Nevertheless, about forty scientists of considerable stature, with slight possibility of personal gain, have entered into this research because of the unique challenge and of the enigmatic nature of the Shroud. Like a great mountain, "it is there" and dares one to understand it.

The little-known French biology professor Paul Vignon was so impressed in 1898 with Secondo Pia's discovery of the Shroud's character as a photographic negative that he embarked on a lifetime of activity in Shroud research. In 1902, just four years later, he published the first scientific book on the subject. Yves Delage, a Sorbonne professor of comparative anatomy and member of the French Academy, was well known for his agnosticism and his aversion to anything savoring of the miraculous or supernatural. However, he was a friend of young Vignon and was so impressed by the biologist's work that he decided to present it on April 21, 1902, to the august French Academy of Sciences.

One report said that a "secret committee" of the academy took but fifteen minutes to consider and vote a rebuff of Delage. He was ridiculed and ostracized by his colleagues and by the public press. The secretary of the academy weakened Delage's paper in the academy's journal by not reporting the heart of his presentation; he was told that the rest of his paper had been "lost." Delage thereafter restated his points in a letter that was printed in the *Revue Scientifique*. It included this statement:

> A religious question has been needlessly injected into a problem that in itself is purely scientific, with the result that feelings have run high, and reason has been led astray. If, instead of Christ, there were a question of some person like a Sargon, an Achilles, or one of the Pharaohs, no one would have thought of making any objection.... I have been faithful to the true spirit of science in treating this question, intent only on the truth, not concerned in the least with whether it would affect the interests of any religious party.... I recognize Christ as a historical personage and I see no reason why anyone should be scandalized that there still exist material traces of his earthly life.

In a similar vein, William F. Buckley later wrote in his Notes and Asides column in *National Review* (July 7, 1978, p. 821):

> We fail to understand the manifest hostility toward the Shroud on the part of some Christians. Would they be equally interested, or ostensibly uninterested, in a possible or probable portrait of Xerxes? of Alexander the Great? Is it possible that the details of the Shroud are just too *literal* for an enlightened liberal sensibility? Is it somehow *bad manners* to suggest that Christian claims about what happened to Jesus are, in fact, true?

By the fall of 1981, the Holy Shroud Guild announced that the following preliminary results had been established:

On the basis of the 1978 scientific investigation, no pigments, paints, dyes, or stains have been found on the fibrils. x-ray fluorescence and microchemistry on the fibrils preclude the possibility of paint being used as a method for creating the image. Ultraviolet and infrared evaluations confirm these studies. Computer image enhancement and analysis by a device called a VP-8 Image Analyzer show that the image has unique, three-dimensional information encoded in it.

How was the image formed? Microchemical evaluation has indicated no evidence of any spices, oils, or any biochemicals known to be produced by the body in life or in death. It is clear that there has been a direct contact of the Shroud with the body, which explains certain features such as the scourge marks as well as the blood. However, while this type of contact might explain some of the features of the torso, it is totally incapable of explaining the image of the face with the high resolution that has been amply demonstrated by photography. The basic problem from a scientific point of view is that some explanations that might be tenable from a chemical point of view are precluded by physics. Contrariwise, certain physical explanations that may be attractive are completely precluded by chemistry. For an adequate explanation for the image of the Shroud, one must have an explanation that is scientifically sound, from a physical, chemical, biological, and medical viewpoint. At present this type of solution does not appear to be obtainable by the best efforts of the members of the Shroud team. Furthermore, experiments in physics and chemistry with old linen have failed to reproduce adequately the phenomenon presented by the Shroud of Turin. The scientific consensus is that the image was produced by something that resulted in oxidation, dehydration, and conjugation of the polysaccharide structure of the microfibrils of the linen itself. Such changes can be duplicated in the laboratory by certain chemical and physical processes. A similar type of change in linen can be obtained by sulfuric acid or heat. However, there are no chemical or physical methods known that can account for the totality of the image, nor can any combination of physical, chemical, biological, or medical circumstances explain the image adequately—much less its accurate detail.

Summary. Thus, the answer to the question of how the image was produced or what produced the image remains, now, as it has in the past, a mystery. We can conclude for now that the Shroud image is that of a real human form of a scourged, crucified man. It is not the product of an artist. The bloodstains are composed of hemoglobin and also give a positive test for serum albumin. The image is an ongoing mystery.

The analyzers and computers for image enhancement used by the scientists show that the Shroud image is of a tallish man (5'10" to 6'2") who had been crucified. His wrists and feet had bloody wounds from the nails of crucifixion, the right side of his chest was pierced, his back was lacerated by scourging, and the right shoulder appeared chafed as from bearing a heavy burden. There were multiple puncture wounds on the head as from a cap of thorns mashed into the flesh, a pronounced bruise on one cheek, and the chest cavity has been overexpanded (asphyxiation is a common cause of death during crucifixion). Further study has determined the exact number of lashes administered from the right side and from the left side, and identified the scourge as the "Roman flagrum," which has barbell-shaped metal tips on each lash.

Profile projections made possible by the three-dimensional data inherent in the Shroud photographs have in turn made ethnological evaluation possible, "a physical type found among Sephardic Jews and noble Arabs," according to Dr. Carlton S. Coon, ethnology curator at the University of Pennsylvania and a specialist in racial classifications.[1]

Leo Vala, brilliant British inventor, developer of a 3-D photographic process of his own,[2] and a fashion photographer, puts his reputation on the line with these words, although he claims to be an agnostic: "I can prove conclusively that claims calling the Shroud a fake are completely untrue. Even with today's highly advanced photographic resources nobody alive could produce the image—a photographic negative—embodied in the Shroud."[3]

British writer and scholar Geoffrey Ashe says: "The Shroud is explicable if it once enwrapped a human body to which something extraordinary happened. It is not explicable otherwise."

King Philip IV of France, with some possible basis in fact but not necessarily in good faith, charged Templar masters Jacques de Molay and Geoffrey de Charnay with idolatry (for they probably used Shroud Face copies in orientation exercises and other ceremonies; see the Templecombe data in chapter 3).

There is a risk that the Shroud of Turin, or any religious relic, can become an idol. For that matter, the risk may be just as great respecting a Protestant church building (the "edifice complex" so called), or a church title or office, or almost anything. Many provocative sermons have been preached on the scope of the First Commandment ("Thou shalt have no other gods before me"). However, idols are made not by manufacturing but by the attitudes of individuals.

Doubtless it is with such thoughts in mind that the Roman Catholic Church has often clearly stated that the Church does not wish the Shroud itself to be revered or for it to be made an object of faith. Father Rinaldi explained[4] that the Church has always surrounded the Shroud with much veneration, but its authenticity is not within the scope of the Church's doctrinal definitions; that is left to archaeology and related sciences. He says that the authenticity of the Shroud was never an issue per se with the Holy See; it was rather taken for granted. Veneration, he explains, should be intended for the person of the Christ, and only indirectly for the relic itself.

Over the years thirty-three popes have spoken in favor of the Shroud of Turin, including Pope John Paul II. In 1973, Pope Paul VI made a statement for Italian television that gave the full weight of papal authority for the Shroud's authenticity. Some of his words were most provocative, as when he described the Shroud image as "so human and so divine." He called it "the most important relic in the history of Christianity." As to the Shroud's value to the Christian, he expressed the wish that the relic of Jesus the Christ might "introduce them to a more penetrating vision of his inmost and fascinating mystery."

On September 7, 1936, Pope Pius XI said: "The Holy Shroud of Turin is still mysterious, but it is certainly not the work of any human hand. This, one can now say, is demonstrated. We said mysterious, because the sacred object still involves many problems, but certainly it is more sacred than perhaps any other; and, as is now established in the most positive way, even apart from any idea of faith or Christian piety, it is certainly not a human work." Of course, he *was* a scientist, and he once said, "We speak now as a scientist, not as pope. We have personally investigated the Shroud and we are convinced of its authenticity."

All the popes who have spoken in favor of the Shroud have always based their opinions in part on an actual examination of the relic. On the other hand, these public statements of the popes cannot be decisive, for they speak from then-available evidence and on personal conviction.

While the Shroud was still in Constantinople, folded and known to most as the Face, the Mandylion, its full length and its images certainly came to be known to an inner circle after a time. In about 1130, Pope Stephen III wrote that Jesus "stretched his whole body on a cloth, white as snow, on which the glorious image of the Lord's face and the length of his whole body was so divinely transformed that it was sufficient for those who could not see the Lord bodily in the flesh, to see the transfiguration made on the cloth."

Since the exposition of 1898, when the first photographs were taken, every pope has expressed his belief in the Shroud's authenticity. Pope

Figure 1.
Rev. Peter Weyland's crucifixion statue in bronze. *(Courtesy Holy Shroud Guild)*

John XXIII said it succinctly: "This can only be the Lord's doing."

Professor Werner Bulst has said: "The fact, that *a bloody shroud* with an image *so strange* was preserved through such a long time, can only be explained if the unknown possessors of it had an overwhelming motive: the certainty of its authenticity.... Many things in history are hypothetical. It is impossible to discuss historical problems without hypotheses. Many things in history, accepted by all, are proved not in the least so well as the authenticity of the Shroud."

One man, the late Reverend Peter Weyland, sculptor-clergyman, took it upon himself to validate both the Shroud and the Shroud researchers by a novel experiment with himself as subject, in which he could feel and see the meaning of the crucifixion. In the process, he created what many critics regard as one of the most striking works of sculpture based upon the Shroud of Turin.

He set up a heavy cross and placed a large mirror on the opposite wall. He hung from the cross for short intervals and observed his own body while thus suspended: He said he did this nearly eight hundred times. Students assisted him by making plaster casts of portions of his body while Weyland hung for twenty to twenty-five minutes each time to ensure realistic reaction by his body. He performed thirty-one of these lengthy suspensions, and the students were able to make two complete sets of casts covering Weyland's whole body. They also took many photographs of him while he was suspended. From these casts and photographs, Weyland then completed his crucifixion statues.

Weyland said, "I was anxious to find out where the greatest pain and strain would occur.... [for instance] the more horizontal the arms are, the greater the strain on the arms and chest." He utilized the face and head of the Shroud, mounted above the casts of his own body. Some of his artistic insights are most interesting: The Shroud, he said, "is the face of one who is dead, that is obvious; and yet, it is by no means the face of a corpse.... It shows a clear-cut Jewish racial character, but it claims kinship with all races.... The width of the face on the Shroud must be felt, rather than traced, because there exists no outline."

Almost all skeptics and critics of the Shroud of Turin image claim or assume that it was a medieval painting. At several of the scientific symposia on the Shroud during the past two decades, including one at Rome in 1993, Isabel H. Piczek of Los Angeles has presented highly impressive papers on this subject. Piczek is a professional monumental-artist with a degree in physics and has won international awards for painting and figurative draftsmanship. She has executed artworks in every ancient and modern technique known, including nearly five hundred gaint-size items in public buildings throughout the world. Piczek, in her professional papers respecting the Shroud image, has analyzed every artistic aspect of the image and has concluded that *it is not and cannot be* a painting of any sort, technique, or medium. This conclusion is doubly important because, she cautions, the Shroud image *must not* be conserved *as a painting would be*, "or else we may destroy the only object on earth which is the blueprint of the future of our cosmos."

Ms. Piczek observes that in art anatomy there is no room for personal opinion. It is based on strict rules of proportion, structure, and rules foreshortening. Every highly trained figurative artist would read these rules exactly the same way. The man of the Shroud is leaning forward, his head is at a gentle angle, his knees pulled up. The head is not small (as some claim), one just does not see the sides of the cheeks.

In the late 1980s and the early 1990s, the most active and productive area of Shroud research has been that of the historians (see second half of the Special Introduction of this edition). This work not only establishes the reality and continuity of the Shroud's existence from the first through the twentieth centuries, and that the "Face of Edessa" and the "Mandylion of Costantinople" were indeed the self-same cloth and image known to us today as the "Shroud of Turin," but most important, this work clearly demonstrates the impossibility—and indeed the ludicrousness—of the carbon-dating proponents' claim that the Shroud cloth dates only from the mid-fourteenth century on the basis of the highly controversial C-14 data of 1988.

In the crucial decade of the mid-1970s to mid-1980s, the writings of English historian Ian Wilson dominated this area of sindonology and provided the Edessa Face/Constantinople Mandylion/Turin Shroud identity thesis; but because of his broad interests in other fields, his later writings on Shroud matters have not significantly broken new ground. Conversely, American historian Dr. Daniel C. Scavone of the University of Southern Indiana has brilliantly clarified the heretofore murky periods of Shroud history, that is, 944 to 1204 and 1204 to 1355, and thereby has almost single-handedly shown the impossibility of a late and European origin of the Shroud. Although a few French, Italian, and German researchers, notably Dr. Bruno Bonnet-Eymard, have been credited by Scavone with basic discoveries, it has been mainly Scavone who has retranslated, fitted the pieces, and interpreted them for a plausible scenario focused for us in sindonology.

One of the more serious puzzlements of the 944–1204 period has been the question of *what* arrived in Constantinople from Edessa on August 15, 944—because it is manifestly clear that the full Shroud with full image was what was displayed its last week in Constantinople before its disappearance, probably within the hour of the breaching of the city walls on April 13, 1204. In our Special Introduction to this edition, Scavone credits the Italian scholar Gino Zaninotto with discovery of the ceremonial sermon of the archdeacon Gregory in Constantinople upon arrival on April 15, 944, of the Face of Edessa; Gregory clearly was describing a full-bodied image including blood-flow from the side-wound.

In a 1992 paper, Scavone exhaustively examined more than a dozen documents written by Greek-Constantinople luminary Nicholas Mesarites (see chapter 3 in our text), who was the Constantinople curator circa 1201–4, of the sacred relics in the Pharos Church of the Virgin within the Great Palace complex of the Bouche de Leon (Bucoleon); he later became archbishop of Ephesus and eparch of all Asia, within the Greek church. In describing Jesus' burial shroud among the relics under his responsibility, Mesarites wrote that the cloth was "still smelling of myrrh" and which had wrapped the "uncircumscribed, naked, anointed corpse after the passion." The strange adjective, "uncircumscribed" would be literally translated as *without outline*—and today we might say "vague, as would be true of a photographic negative"— quite descriptive for eight centuries ago! By using the word "naked," Mesarites is describing what he *saw*, which would be untypical of the work of medieval artists of Western Europe, circa 1300–1800, who always covered human loins with unnatural swirls of cloth.

Perhaps Scavone's most important contribution to date is the Besancon scenario (see chapter 4) for the Shroud's "missing years" 1204–1355, as replacement for Wilson's "Knights Templar connection" (see Chapter 3) which, though having the virtue of plausibility, was never more than bare theory unsupported by any historical data. In December 1991, Scavone formalized a paper to present new data, and to elaborate upon and synthesize the theories of himself and others concerning the Shroud's movements in the 1204–1355 period, the Besancon sojourn being at the heart of same.

Scavone's present thesis builds first on Othon de La Roche, who emerged as a leading figure of the Fourth Crusade and acquired the Shroud in Constantinople during the siege of 1201–4. Othon was one of four counselors to Boniface de Montferrat who, as matters turned out, became runner-up to Baldwin of Flanders, the first Latin emperor of Byzantium. The consolation prize for Boniface was Thessalonika and most of mainland Greece, with the Grecian islands falling to him quickly by military conquest. Boniface's position there was strengthened by prior marriage ties. Thus, Othon in late 1204 became lord of Athens, with his castle, the Acropolis, and his position was further enhanced in 1206 by marriage of his daughter to the second Latin emperor, Henri, brother of Baldwin I. So, the Shroud could have come to Othon in 1204–5 during the friendly politicing for the emperorship, or from Henri in connection with his marriage to Othon's daughter. Close relations between Othon and Henri *did* follow.

Whatever the machinations by which title devolved, the fact seems fairly clear that Othon, between 1204 and 1208, did ship to his father in the Burgundian capital, Besancon, France, the alleged Shroud and other relics for keeping by Archbishop Amadeus de Tramelay at the St. Etienne Cathedral. Also, it seems fairly certain that the Shroud's sojourn there ended with its disappearance shortly before the time of the fire of 1349 (caused by lightning) that destroyed the cathedral; the cathedral did claim to have the true Shroud during those years.

But what is the connection between Othon/Besancon and de Charny/Lirey? Probably not Geoffrey himself, but Geoffrey's second wife, Jeanne de Vergy. She was the great-great-granddaughter of Othon de La Roche. The de Vergy family was very prominent and powerful in Besancon for some centuries, and exclusively filled the post *seneschal* of Besancon from 1191 to 1310. And it may be very significant that for the years 1371–91, Guillaume de Vergy was bishop of Besancon and had no comment at all about the eight-foot cloth with the obviously painted image that "turned up" in Besancon in 1353–55 at the probable time of Jeanne's marriage to Geoffrey. Geofffrey died in battle in 1356, but Jeanne commenced the public exhibition of the Shroud in 1357, and the visitor medallions carried the coat of arms of both Geoffrey and Jeanne.

Are these just foibles of family and diocese squabbles? Maybe more. Bishop D'Arcis was having extreme financial problems and delays in construction of the cathedral at Troyes. From 1309 to 1377 the papacy was at Avignon and the popes were French, pursuing a French foreign policy, with the "great western schism" to follow in 1378. The Hundred Years' War between England and France raged over France throughout most of the fourteenth and half of the fifteenth century. And, if the Shroud moved from Besancon to Lirey in the 1349–55 period, the effect would be of removing it from Germany and securing it for France, the way national boundaries were then drawn. And, if all that wasn't upsetting enough, the bubonic plague of 1348–58 practically cut the population in half. The "times were out of joint," but Scavone makes a good case for the Greece-Besancon itinerary of the Shroud, in lieu of Wilson's "Knights Templar connection."

FOURTEEN

DO MIRACLES HAPPEN THROUGH THE SHROUD?

N THE simplest of terms, the Shroud of Turin is either a scientific wonder, a fraud, or a miracle; there can be no in-between possibility. If it is a miracle, it is a breathtakingly spectacular miracle at that.

What is a miracle? A miracle is an occurrence in prima facie contradiction to the known laws of nature. Saint Augustine wrote: "There is no such thing as a miracle that violates natural law; there are only occurrences that violate our limited knowledge of natural law." It is important to note that the Shroud, like all miracles, is a sign that points to a greater and deeper reality, beyond the miracle itself.

The scientific data reported in this book make it abundantly clear that the Shroud is not a fraud. And I hope it is obvious that I am taking a "practical" stance on miracles—that is, I use a standard definition (above) and apply it to the facts; this is true as concerns both my characterization of the Shroud as a miracle and also respecting possible miracles through the Shroud, as well as parallel occurrences that could be termed miracles. No doubt we will learn more and more about the laws of nature, but to date, scientific evaluation of the Shroud has had the effect of deepening its mystery rather than explaining it.

But whether a wonder, fraud, or miracle, a secondary question has arisen from time to time in its history: Can the Shroud be a continuing *channel* for miracles, including healings? (I do not consider here the more remote possibility that the Shroud is *itself* the "cause" of healing—only that miraculous happenings have occurred *through* it or in its presence.)

There can be healings of spirit and peace of mind as well as healing of the physical body. In the fall of 1978, as Father Peter Rinaldi observed the pilgrims who viewed the Shroud during the Quatro-Centennial Exposition, he heard many express the great feeling of joy the experience had given them. "That," said Rinaldi, "is the miracle!" And it certainly may have been. To untold numbers of observers, perhaps that miracle involved a permanent change in themselves. We will never know for certain, of course.

But we do know this: From its earliest years, legends surrounding the Shroud have persistently spoken or hinted of miracles and physical healings that occurred in the presence of that venerated cloth.

The Image of Edessa is thought to have been the Shroud that now reposes in Turin. The tradition of that area of Asia Minor holds that Abgar V, king of Edessa, was mortally ill and sent a request that Jesus come and heal him (as reported by Eusebius). As discussed in chapter 2, Thaddaeus (one of "the seventy") went to Abgar after the crucifixion, showed him the face on the cloth, and he was healed. This is the first recorded healing effected through the Shroud.

Four credible writers report that in 544, when Edessa was threatened with siege by a Persian army, the image was rushed to the top of the city wall and prominently displayed; the army turned and abandoned the siege.

In 944, while the Mandylion (Shroud) was being carried from Edessa to Constantinople, it was said that a man possessed of demons was healed when he touched it.

Very few such happenings have been heard of in modern times, probably for two reasons: First, because public exhibitions of the Shroud have been so rare, sometimes forty and fifty years apart; and second, because the Roman Catholic Church has purposefully played down any expectation of, or reporting of, healing miracles surrounding the Shroud. In fact, the status of the Shroud itself has been carefully and very modestly stated by Church spokesmen. The Church has never officially proclaimed the authenticity of the relic, and Church spokesmen say that such a statement will never be made. The Church honors and reveres the Shroud and all sacred relics directly as objects of faith and worship, but in veneration of the persons whom the relics represent. In the case of the Shroud, the spokesmen say it is the Christ who is to be worshiped. It is said that the point of any exhibition of the Shroud is to bring worshipers to a clearer and deeper realization of the mystery of the Christ—of his sufferings, death, and Resurrection.

The Church is very careful about matters that might involve the miraculous or supernatural. This is one reason for the very lengthy, circumscribed procedures in beatification and canonization cases that include provision for validation of possibly miraculous incidents. Consequently, my use of the word "miracle" in these various contexts should *not* be taken in that more restricted sense, implying a Church position.

Under the dogmatic theology of the Roman Catholic Church in the 1950s, a miracle was defined as a *sensible* fact, *extraordinary* and *divine.*

1) "sensible," in that it is perceived by the senses;

2) "extraordinary," in that it is completely beyond the power of nature to accomplish;

3) "divine," in that the sensible, extraordinary fact must have been caused by God.

For example, respecting canonization, forty-two years after his death in the Auschwitz concentration camp, the Reverend Maximilian Kolbe was declared a saint by Pope John Paul II at a Vatican ceremony on October 10, 1982. Kolbe had been beatified by Pope Paul VI in 1971, following a twenty-three-year study of his life. News accounts stated that ordinarily a minimum of two miracles must be validated before canonization. Kolbe did not qualify in that respect, but the pope granted dispensation to waive the requirement.

More typical perhaps is the case of the Capuchin friar Padre Pio, who died in 1968 and whose cause was to be submitted to the Vatican for beatification in the fall of 1982. Pio was world famous for scores of claimed "miracle cures" by spiritual healing (at least one of which occurred after his death) and for other striking spiritual and paranormal events that occurred in his ministry. These matters began to be widely publicized by stories coming out of World War II. (As a long-time friend of Pope John Paul II it is reported that Pio once predicted that "John Paul" would become pope at a time when such an occurrence seemed highly improbable.)

The Lourdes shrine of Saint Bernadette in the Pyrenees of south-western France is perhaps the world's most famous healing shrine, and it is visited each year by thousands of supplicants seeking healing. Scores of claims of miraculous healing at Lourdes are carefully investigated each year by the International Medical Committee of Lourdes, composed of sixteen lay doctors from six countries. Cases that the committee certifies as medically unexplainable are then reviewed exhaustively by the Roman Catholic Church. In the twentieth century, the Church has recognized only sixty-four healings as miracles attributable to powers manifest at Saint Bernadette's shrine.

Referring to the Roman Catholic Church procedure for investigating and validating miracles, premier American sindonologist Rev. Edward Wuenschel (who later was named director of the Redemptorist Institute of Higher Studies, Rome) wrote: "This [the Shroud] is not strictly a miracle and yet who can deny that the finger of God is here."

Significant physical healings through the Shroud appear to have happened repeatedly. The idea of such an occurrence should not be too surprising, if in the abstract we accept the possibility of spiritual healing. Three of the Gospels clearly report the story of Jesus' healing of the woman who had an issue of blood that had persisted for twelve years (Matthew 9:20–22; Mark 5:25–34; Luke 8:43–48). They all report that while he was in the midst of a large crowd, the woman came up behind him and touched the hem of his cloak and was instantly healed. Her action seems clearly intentional on her part but was unobserved by him. Matthew and Mark state that "she said, 'If I may touch but his clothes, I shall be whole.'" Nor was such healing technique limited to the powers of Jesus. Acts 19:11–12 reads: "God did extraordinary miracles through Paul. Handkerchiefs and aprons that had touched him were taken to the sick, and their illnesses were cured and the evil spirits left them."

The use of handkerchiefs blessed by prayer continues to be a method favored by some present-day spiritual healers for the conveyance of healing at a distance. It is a practice, for instance, used in the healing ministry of Herb Beyer of Cleveland, Ohio.

In A.D. 544 the city of Edessa was threatened with siege by a Persian army. The Image of Edessa was rushed to the city wall and prominently displayed; its appearance was credited with miraculously protecting the city from attack, according to contemporary writer Evagrius. This supernatural intervention on behalf of the city was also attested by Job of Alexandria, Christopher of Antioch, and Basil of Jerusalem.

During much of the sixth through the sixteenth centuries, copies of the Face (and later the entire body image) were painted and then touched to the true Shroud. This action, with an appropriate ceremony, not only consecrated the copy but was thought to imbue the copy with the miraculous powers of protection and healing assumed to be in the true Shroud.

In Chambery, France, when the chapel of the Shroud was a fiery inferno in 1532, four men raced into the burning building, probably by way of a rear corridor, to save the Shroud. Its silver casket was locked behind a metal grille already glowing with intense heat by the time the rescuers reached it. Breaking the grille, they carried the casket to safety even though it had started to melt (silver melts at 900 degrees centigrade). It is recorded that neither the men nor their clothes were affected by the flames or the heat.

For at least the first two hundred years that the House of Savoy owned the Shroud, it was reported that they regularly used it to safeguard them from danger, even to the point of having it carried on a staff to flutter above them wherever they rode or walked.

Citizens of Turin in the late seventeenth century had no doubts about the potential power available through the Shroud. In 1692, when the black plague was ravishing Europe and began making inroads among the neighboring cities in Lombardy and Piedmont in north Italy, the people of Turin prayed before the Shroud that their city be spared—and it was. A bronze plaque on a city wall still today commemorates this "miracle."

Modern skepticism automatically rejects the idea of miracles of protection or of healing as implausible and ridiculous. With regard to happenings in past centuries we can hardly argue with such skepticism. However, there are miraculous events associated with the Shroud in the last half of the twentieth century.

One documented modern account deserves detailed mention. In 1955, in a small village of Gloucestershire, England, eleven-year-old Josephine Woollam was in the hospital dying of a severe bone disease, osteomyelitis in the hip and leg, plus lung abscesses. In spite of continuous great pain, Josie always had a smile for everyone. Her doctor had advised the family that there was no hope for Josie, and she received the last rites of the Church. Josie learned of the lectures about the Shroud by retired RAF group captain Leonard Cheshire, and told her mother that if she could only see the Shroud she was sure she would be able to walk again.

The letter that her mother, Mrs. Veronica Woollam, wrote to Captain Cheshire in early May 1955 was so touching that an assistant answered it in the captain's absence, saying that the Shroud was in Turin, Italy, and only rarely shown to the public. A photograph of the Face on the Shroud was enclosed with the reply.

Josie was given the last rites of the Catholic Church, after doctors told her mother that Josie might not live until morning. That evening the eleven-year-old held the photograph of the Face on the Shroud. By morning the osteomyelitis was apparently in remission.

Five days later Mrs. Woollam wrote Cheshire that Josie was out of bed and moving around the hospital ward in a wheelchair. In another two weeks another letter reported that Josie was home in her wheelchair and still hoping to see the Shroud. Cheshire then visited Josie and saw her deformed and scarred legs that had been covered with open, suppurating sores until the arrival of the Shroud photograph, which seemingly had been the turning point for the start of her recovery.

He was so impressed by Josie and her case that, in July, Cheshire took Josie to Portugal to see former King Umberto II, whose permission was then obtained for a rare private session with the Shroud. The archdiocese in Turin was authorized to grant any reasonable request made by Josie. In July a special mass was said for her, and then the Shroud was taken from its casket so that Josie in her wheelchair could

Figure 1.
Josie Woollam at Turin in 1955, with Leonard Cheshire *(Courtesy Leonard Cheshire)* (top), and in 1978 in Turin with Father Peter Rinaldi. *(Courtesy Peter M. Rinaldi, SDB)*

hold it (still rolled and sealed) on her lap. At that moment her personal needs seemed to her unimportant, and Josie later said, "All I wanted was for people all over the world to come close to the Shroud so they can come close to the Lord." Josie left the cathedral still in her wheelchair—that, apparently, was the last that was known of her in Turin.

But in September 1978 Josie, now Mrs. Jones, *walked* into the cathedral for a public viewing of the Shroud, accompanied again by her "guardian angel," Captain Cheshire. Josie told the press: "It's the Lord I came to thank in Turin. The miracle I asked for as a little girl turned out to be many miracles. I am well, as you see. I have a wonderful husband and a dream of a child." As she sat with Father Peter Rinaldi viewing the Shroud a little later, her eyes brimming with tears, she said, "Can heaven be more beautiful, Father?"

For twenty-six years thereafter Josie thrived, worked, married and bore children. She died May 31, 1981, at age thirty-six, without any return of the osteomyelitiss that she had contracted at age 5 and a half as a side effect of double pneumonia. At age seven, she contracted bronchiectasis, a chronic and degenerative inflammation of the bronchi leading to the lungs; it is marked by dilation and loss of elasticity of the bronchi walls. This condition recurred numerous times throughout Josie's life and, oddly, it was not cured when she was in the presence of the Shroud. It was the bronchiectasis from which she died in 1981, after catching a simple cold.

During the fall exposition of the Shroud in 1978, every Wednesday afternoon the cathedral was closed to the general public while the sick and handicapped were brought by buses for a special viewing by themselves. Most, perhaps, were satisfied with just the viewing, the same as able-bodied worshipers. But, in all likelihood, a number of them did hope for a healing, and perhaps some of them, like Josie, received it.

Josie's healing began when she merely saw and held the photograph of the Face of the Shroud. John Campbell-Best of Portsmouth, England, has a full-sized photograph of the Shroud, and he is satisfied that absent healings take place—some at great distances—when he makes intercessory prayer before his replica of the Shroud. Testimonials from people with all manner of problems seem to validate his claims.

Figure 2.
The line of pilgrims at the Turin cathedral in 1978. *(Courtesy Peter M. Rinaldi, SDB)*

Faith healer Ron Halteri in North Weymouth, Massachusetts, has a photographic replica of the Shroud of Turin in his home, before which he prays a "petition for healing" for persons who come or write him for help. He says, "The people's faith in the Shroud is the power that heals them; it's supernatural, but not magic—it's faith and God."

A modern, full-color painting of the face of Jesus of Nazareth by artist Ris Phillips, based on the Shroud-face contours and coloring suggested by apocryphal accounts from the first century, is described in chapter 19. Col. Frank O. Adams, who commissioned the painting of the Face, says that many reports have come to him of unusual occurrences, including healings that have been experienced by persons who have bought prints of the painting. Many claim to feel heat from the Face, even though the framed print may be glass-covered.

Of course, it is not feasible here to validate the claims of Campbell-Best and Halteri, or the reports of Adams. Even assuming that many of these healing testimonials are factual, there is no way realistically that the Shroud can be credited. This is especially true because numerous dedicated Christian healers later, like Brother Mandus in England and Olga Worrall in the United States, without invoking any claim on the powers of the Shroud, repeatedly demonstrate the power of the healing touch and of intercessory prayer. Scientists in a number of laboratories have solidly established the dramatic extent to which Olga Worrall's prayer-healing can effect such changes. Using water, she can change the hydrogen-bonding, the surface-tension, and the spectroscopic values. With enzymes (from the human gastrointestinal system) in a test tube, her magnetic power can be measured as she heals the enzymes and accelerates their growth. The mysterious excitation of electrons in a nuclear cloud-chamber can be observed as she sends them her healing energy.

The reality of spiritual healing can hardly be doubted today because investigation using scientific method has verified it. The first Templeton Award in Religion in 1973 went to Mother Teresa of Calcutta, whose miracle healings were well attested before Templeton, a hardheaded investment counselor, would give her his two-hundred-thousand-dollar award.[2]

Without discussing the reality of God, naturalistic versus theistic worldviews, or arguments of the naturalism versus supernaturalism debate, it will be obvious that I believe miracles can and do happen—even though today's miracle *may* be tomorrow's science.[3]

FIFTEEN

THE RELIGIOUS PERSPECTIVE

G OD IS mystery!—this is the most accurate statement we can make about the nature of God. Nevertheless, each of us has a personal "picture of God" that we make and modify throughout our lives. We fashion these pictures from the inspired scriptures of the world, commentary on the scriptures, the lives of Jesus, the saints, and others, and, especially the insights and inspirational disclosures that God gives to each of us.

The Shroud has the most value for those who recognize that basic reality—the mystery of God—and who yearn to know God more fully. To such, these words by Paul and Peter were especially addressed:

> Study to show thyself approved unto God, a workman that needeth not to be ashamed, rightly dividing the word of truth. (II Timothy 2:15)
>
> Add to your faith virtue, and to virtue, knowledge. (II Peter 1:5)

Study, increase your knowledge. Building on those admonitions, the Reverend G. Vale Owen (Church of England) wrote: "Be it always in the mind of those who are sincere that they can do no irreverence to Him who himself is Truth in inquiring what the Truth is as He revealed it."

And in the same vein, the archbishop of Canterbury in 1976 said: "Each generation needs men who, in honesty and devotion, are prepared to undertake 'exploration into God,' to press beyond the confines of what hitherto we have grasped, and to move away from places that have become too narrow for us in the light of modern knowledge and experience."

But admittedly, a study of the Shroud of Turin is not for everyone. Some Christians feel they need no proof of Jesus' life and death, that their faith and the Bible are enough. Some go further, and are critical of the scientific examinations of the Shroud and call it meddling. Longtime Shroud proponent Father Peter M. Rinaldi, S.D.B., has said: "Sindonologists are persistent and simply will not 'let go' of the Shroud problem. Some of them are quite convinced that the mystery of the Shroud will never be solved, but this belief in no way lessens their fascination for it. If anything, it makes the challenge greater. I personally like to see science 'meddle' with the Shroud, but I hope—in fact, I am quite sure—that science will never be able to solve its mystery. Like the Man of Nazareth, the Man of the Shroud will continue to disturb men's minds and trouble their hearts. And that is the way it should be."[1]

Conversely, for many other Christians the question of the Shroud's sacredness and venerability is directly connected with its authenticity, and they welcome scientific validation of it, even though that validation can never amount to total proof.

One can presume that most Christians of every persuasion find their faith sufficient in their religion but will always welcome something that supports their faith, assuming it also to be compatible with sound reason. The Shroud fits in this category; both scientific and forensic (logical) evidence tend very strongly toward authentication of the Shroud—toward proof that it is the Shroud on which Jesus of Nazareth lay. Never mind that science can never prove that absolutely. This additional support of our faith is a comfort. (Incidentally, this is one area of religion that, for instance, can be a legitimate topic of conversation in any company.)

Religious relics present a difficult area to handle, especially for the Protestant—to say nothing of the agnostic. The Shroud does teach a sound approach—that a relic deserves respectful attention, and possible ultimate veneration, only when it harmonizes reasonably and practically with history, legend, scripture, apocryphal accounts, inspired and mystical accounts of obvious quality, and finally with sound common sense and science.

In just the past decades, the mystical, the meditative, and the contemplative modes of the spiritual dimension of humankind have been brought to our attention by the media, by lectures, and by books for the general reader as facets of our being that can and should be experienced by everyone (and in fact are being experienced by many) to heighten our consciousness and develop our potential for enlightenment. In past years it was assumed that only true mystics, and perhaps those pursuing monastic lives, might have a valid mystical experience. Even more negatively, it was assumed that the visions of a mystic had no veridical components or qualities. The Shroud now provides another way of putting the lie to this latter assumption.

Four well-known mystics, Saint Bridget of Sweden (1303–73), María de Agreda of Spain (1602–65), Catherine Emmerich of Westphalia (1774–1824), and Teresa Neumann of Bavaria (1898–1962) have had repeated, detailed visions in which they watched Jesus' passion, and all have provided extensive written accounts of these visions. But those accounts are rarely quoted by scripture commentators, and when they are, the commentators usually dismiss them as pious contemplations representing the mystic's own preconceived notions, being therefore of no value.

But the accounts of these four mystics agree with each other and with the Shroud data in meticulous detail and with very little discrepancy.[2] This is all the more remarkable when we realize that much of what we now know by analysis of Shroud data was not known at all a few decades ago—except for some first given by the mystics!

Teresa Neumann describes the crown of thorns as "like a helmet; it is not just a crown as we see it depicted in our pictures." As for nailing the feet with a single nail, Catherine Emmerich explains that she watched as the executioners cut a "cavity in the upright beam for the heel and then fixed a small piece of wood on the upright beam for the instep of the foot." This is most amazing because the block of wood for the instep would never have been imagined until the burial ossuary of crucified Jehohanan was opened in Jerusalem in 1968 and the nail through his feet was found to still impale a small block of acacia wood (see chapter 5). The cutting of the cavity in the upright to accommodate the heel could explain why the knee was not bent on the right leg of the Man of the Shroud (the leg that was against the cross). Teresa Neumann also saw that a "small piece of wood for the feet is fixed to the cross."

María de Agreda makes a point that cannot be validated but which makes eminent good sense: She saw the executioners first stretch Jesus on the cross and mark the places for the nails. Thereafter, they bored holes in the cross to accommodate the nails. They later drove the nails through his body into the holes. Another interesting observation made by both Catherine Emmerich and Teresa Neumann was that they saw the officer thrust his lance into Jesus' right side near the front, and that it went completely through his body with the tip coming out on the left side. Although Shroud researchers have not deemed it significant, there is a small wound on the left side of the dorsal (back) image that would correspond with the point where the two mystics saw the tip emerge.

British theologian Dr. John A. T. Robinson, onetime Shroud skeptic, found that the biblical accounts at the tomb on Easter morning do square with the data of the Shroud. The largest inconsistency, he finds, is between the various Bible versions, but the New Testament Greek is internally fairly consistent as well as compatible with the Shroud data. Luke and John use the Greek *othonia,* which Robinson believes should be translated as sindon or shroud. *Sudarion* should be translated as a jaw-band; it could be described as "over his head," not "about his head." He finds consistence with John's earlier account of the raising of Lazarus, in which was added the item of the *keiriai*—something that he feels was a "tie" to hold the feet together, the hands together, and possibly to hold the shroud snugly to the body. These final steps had not been taken with Jesus. He finds John consistent in describing Lazarus coming forth with the *sudarion* "bound round the face" *(periededeto),* while in Jesus' empty tomb was the *sudarion* that had been "over the head" *(epi tes kephales).* Both fit the burial custom of a folded napkin or kerchief "tied across the top of the head, round the face and under the chin." Looking at Jackson's 3-D pictures of the Shroud, Robinson sees clearly where the jaw-band has mashed down the beard, and perhaps has been knotted at the top of the head. As to how the jaw-band was seen, says Robinson, "lies more in the eye of the beholder than in the Greek." He feels that the Gospel writer intends us to infer that the jaw-band was "still in its twisted oval shape" as if Jesus' head had somehow vanished from within it without the tight knot at his crown being untied.[3]

Dr. Robinson, Shroud scholar, Bible scholar, formerly dean of Trinity College, Cambridge, and Anglican bishop of Woolrich, England, died December 6, 1983. He appeared in the television film *Silent Witness,* and had written many authoritative papers on the Shroud. He was especially respected as one of the leading Greek scholars of our time in the field of New Testament exegesis.

The Shroud does speak strongly to us in terms of the historical accuracy of the Bible and of the historicity of Jesus of Nazareth. Most scholars and historians today do agree, however, that Jesus lived and was crucified. Further, they do acknowledge also that upon the death of Jesus his followers were a very despondent, dejected, and dispirited group who secreted themselves or slunk away. Then, within a week or so there was an inexplicable renaissance, and their public posture had an exuberance and boldness without parallel. The only explanation that fits is the Resurrection of Jesus the Christ. Only his later appearances can make sense of the turnabout actions of the probable skeptic James (brother of Jesus) and of Saul of Tarsus, the Sanhedrin's hit man turned evangelizer.

The empty tomb, which had been sealed and guarded, was itself a powerful witness to the Resurrection, which was the very heart of early Christianity. Jewish leaders would certainly have exploded the empty tomb claim if they could, and therefore it is obvious that the body could not have been stolen by them. There were no lukewarm Christians in that initial group: Most of them willingly gave up all physical advantages, took beatings, and accepted martyrs' deaths. This certainly was not the role of a group of deceivers who had hidden Jesus' body to make an effective story.

The concept of Resurrection is a very difficult one that is also very complex, to say the least. Both the inadequacy of words in modern languages and the inadequacy of theology in modern religions handicap a meaningful consideration of the subject. But, if there was one thing Jesus' ministry said over and over it was that the kingdom of God is within, that Jesus' kingdom is of the spirit, that we are spiritual beings, that we will survive death. Saint Paul's writings in the New Testament repeatedly echo the reality of this spiritual aspect of man; he talks often of our spirit body and once tells of how he went out of his physical body to view a heavenly scene (II Cor. 12:1–6).

It is irrelevant to a discussion of Jesus' Shroud, and inappropriate to the concept of spirituality, to ask "where" Jesus' spirit was from his death on the cross at 3 P.M. on Friday until his first appearance to Mary Magdalene in the garden near the tomb on Sunday morning. However, if, with reference to spirit survival of bodily death, we speak of that instantaneous transition from physical life to spiritual life as "resurrection"—for want of a better word—then the moment of physical death would have been Jesus' *first resurrection.* If we could reeducate the clergy of the world, Protestants especially, to not use the word "resurrection" in connection with the death of our own physical bodies, the subject would be more clear (we merely drop our first-stage rocket as our spirit lifts off!). Certainly the Resurrection of Jesus the Christ, occurring perhaps about sunup on Easter Sunday, was a unique and very different kind of event.

Many believe that, unassisted, the Christ-spirit dematerialized Jesus' physical body and burst through the Shroud, marking it indelibly in the process. During the following forty days, his ministry, which was so crucial to the establishing of The Way—Christianity—was conducted through what Saint Paul would call a spirit body. He could appear and disappear at will, seeming to pass through stone walls on occasion. He could affect the minds of men and women so that they recognized him when he wished and failed to recognize him when he wished. He could make himself totally solid, including memory-marks such as the stigmata. He could do physical things such as cooking a meal and eating food. He could do practical things, such as effectively directing fishing operations. All the while, he lived *only* in his spiritual body, materializing it to visibility and to firmness as and when he chose. The Ascension was merely the final act in his spirit body as he phased out its visibility. Anecdotal accounts make it seem very likely that he continues through the ages to make himself visible to individuals when it serves his purpose to do so, as well as to appear in dreams and visions.

Many ministers and scholars of the mainline Protestant denominations of Christianity are beginning to recognize some of these precepts, never totally lost from the Roman and Orthodox branches of Catholicism and embraced in more variety among esoteric and metaphysical traditions. As we come full-circle to the understandings of the early Church, it is in part state-of-the-art science, including parapsychology, that is leading us, with many extrareligious organizations in the vanguard.

The Easter Resurrection of Jesus the Christ was a most dramatic event, and it deserves a dramatic modern telling. Such is the imaginative, sound, provocative, lyrical story provided by Robert K. Wilcox:[4]

At some moment in the dead of night, the air in the tomb becomes electric.

Minute vibrations at first, the sort that could be detected by sensitive twentieth century instruments; then they dramatically increase until they shake the ground and blow the boulder from the door.

A glow, faint at first, emanating from the shroud suddenly intensifies until rays of light shoot through the threads, star-filled golden rays, filling the tomb and pouring out the door.

For thirty seconds—no more—the blinding, pulsating movement continues.

The source of the activity is the corpse, the body, somehow being revitalized, dematerialized, its mass being converted into energy, pure energy, which in the material world is radiant white light.

The body rises from the slab through the cloth, hovers for a moment in midair, then disappears.

The cocoon collapses. Darkness returns. Shouts of "Earthquake! Earthquake!" diminish as the two guards run for their lives. And in the air, the distinct odor of scorched linen.

And behold, there was a great earthquake; for the angel of the Lord descended from heaven, and came and rolled back the stone from the door, and sat upon it. (Matthew 28:2)

SIXTEEN

HOW WAS THE IMAGE MADE?

THE MOST conclusive answers that scientists can give to this question are negatives. They know the Shroud was not made by art or artifice, not by paint or stain or coloring, not by heating or scorching, not by a natural or accidental process, and not by trickery or fraud. Although there are superficial similarities to the Shroud images when linen is stained by myrrh and aloes—either when, in powdered form, it is rubbed on the linen as Nickell claims (see chapter 12), or when projected as vapor against the linen as proposed by Vignon—still, science finds conclusively that the myrrh-and-aloes approach alone will not duplicate the Shroud. The subliminal factors found in the Shroud images cannot be duplicated by those methods.

In the year 1902, Paul Vignon's "vaporograph theory" was presented to the French Academy of Sciences by his friend, Yves Delage. This was his reasoning: Funeral ointments used in Palestine in the first century included olive oil and aloes. The aloes break down into aloin and aloetin, and the later oxidizes with alkalies. Dying in great agony results in febrile sweat containing urea. Urea ferments into carbonate of ammonia, giving off ammonical vapor, which is an alkali. When the aloetin vapor oxidizes, as when it combines with ammonical vapor, with an optimum timespan of 24 to 36 hours, those combined vapors will cause light brown stains on linen that match perfectly in color with the images on the Shroud. The time frame is right—from the burial late Friday afternoon until the empty tomb is discovered at Sunday dawn—if the Shroud did wrap Jesus of Nazareth.

One of the early presenters of the vaporograph theory in the United States was researcher Col. Frank O. Adams. In 1970–72 his lectures, pictures, and book helped spread knowledge of the Shroud.

In 1972, I talked and corresponded with Adams about this exciting data. However, I suggested to him that the vaporograph theory seemed to have two weaknesses. One, the Man's likeness on the Shroud was too detailed for vapor alone to account for the result, and two, picture fidelity lasting for two thousand years was too indelible for vapor alone to account for the result. I suggested that the vapor must have been guided and enhanced by some tremendous paranormal charge—call it spiritual or psychic, for want of a better term.

Robert Wilcox's book *Shroud* was based in part on his consultations with the European scientists who worked under the Turin Commission aegis in 1969–76 and with the American scientists who met in Albuquerque in early 1977. By the latter, particularly, he was told, "vapors don't travel in straight lines—radiation does." The scientists seem agreed that the action that created the images came from *within* the Shroud. But if the body within the Shroud was that of Jesus of Nazareth, it had been dead more than thirty-six hours. Could it *then* produce such radiation?

STURP scientist Eric Jumper has observed that an organic-stain mechanism, such as Vignon's proposed vaporograph process, acting alone, cannot form images of inert objects such as the coins that have been found on the eyes of the Man of the Shroud. Jumper says it was an "image-forming process" that acted *through space,* not by contact. Also, he notes that the hair images follow the same "law" of "intensity versus distance" as does the body image. Jumper and other STURP members agree with the Turin Commission in the certain finding that the body images on the Shroud are only a *surface* phenomenon. Therefore, from his experiments, Jumper concludes that either dry or moist vapor, staining either a dry or a wet cloth, will penetrate fully every fiber or thread it touches. This is a further negation of the Nickell claim. Further, Jumper considers it very significant that his data on the three-dimensional image, developed with John Jackson, stand in sharp contrast to their parallel finding of an "absence of saturation" as to intensity of the body images, and to their finding that the images were not "pressure sensitive"—that is, that the image of the back of the Man has the same shading characteristics and lack of saturation as the front.

Those precise findings further demonstrate that no simple explanation is conceivable. The images on the Shroud are both subtle and sharply clear. By the use of sophisticated instruments, the images convey data not knowable to the naked eye. Although "photographic negativity" may be demonstrated by other than photography, as Nickell has demonstrated with his wet linen on a bas-relief statue, the subtle details are not there.

Wilcox explained another method, named "Kirlian images" after its Soviet discoverer. These negatives are produced without a camera, using contact of the object on Polaroid photographic stock, usually within a black sleeve, while a very high-frequency, high-voltage electrical charge passes through the device, plus the suggestion of some sort of auric emanation from the object; yet Wilcox found no fidelity to compare with the Shroud.

In the last fifty years the theorizing has shifted from myrrh-aloes and/or vapor theories to flash-of-heat-or-light theories. One of the first of these was proposed by British Lt. Col. P. W. O'Gorman. His views[1] combined four factors: the vapors proposed by Vignon; radioactive substances from either the burial spices or the body parts; some "electrical radiations of an auracal nature"; and "a sudden radiance of our Lord's body at the moment of the resurrection." That fourth point will be discussed again later in this chapter.

In the 1960s, a spiritual dimension was tentatively discussed by British philosopher Geoffrey Ashe. He suggested that Jesus underwent an unparalleled transformation in the tomb. He wrote: "It is at least intelligible that the physical change of the body at the Resurrection may have released a brief and violent burst of radiation, perhaps scientifically identifiable, perhaps not, which 'scorched' the cloth. In this case, the Shroud image is a quasi-photograph of Christ returning [*sic*] to life, produced by a kind of radiance or incandescence analogous to heat in its effects."[2]

In the late 1970s and early 1980s, more specialized terms, which attempt to put the idea of such a special "energy" into words, have been used. Some of them are: radiation "scorch," searing by thermonuclear flash, a brief burst of radiant energy, and flash radiance. Perhaps one

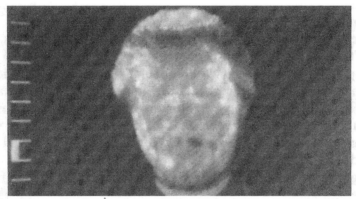

Figure 1.
A thermogram infrared picture of a bearded face. The light areas on the face indicate heat. *(Courtesy John W. White)*

of the best is "flash photolysis" because it describes a great, blinding light rather than heat. Some researchers have suggested that the Shroud images are like a thermogram, which is a diagnostic photograph on Polaroid film, utilizing an infrared flash. However, again, author Wilcox demonstrated in his book that thermograms lack the subtle detail of the Shroud images.

Heat and even light rays will diffuse and spread from the source; they will not travel solely in straight and precise lines. Only laser beams or ionizing radiation will travel in straight lines, and ionizing radiation leaves a definite "signature" that is not found on the Shroud.

Since there obviously is no precise scientific explanation that fits the Shroud images, we must use forensic logic to evaluate the possibilities. Modern physics is moving ever more strongly into basic concepts that embrace the immateriality (the *spirituality*) of all matter and of all life. And hence we should not be surprised that mental and spiritual dimensions do impinge upon and affect solid, material objects.

Because the Shroud's body images are photographic negatives, and since they are best studied by photography, it is worth noting a few examples of possibly relevant oddities in that field. As a basic factor, the manufacturers and purveyors of photographic rawstock of all kinds have known for many years that some people cannot be permitted in the sensitive areas where rawstock is kept, because their very presence will likely cause accidental fogging of even shielded and sealed film, comparable to intentional exposure.

A group of eminent British scientists of the last quarter of the nineteenth century discovered that recognizable persons not physically present sometimes appear as "spirit extras" during normal photography, either in good light or in total darkness. To coordinate their research they created the Society for Psychical Research in 1882.

Dr. Jule Eisenbud, an American psychiatrist and parapsychologist, discovered that an exceptionally gifted person could, by looking into the lens of a Polaroid camera, put recognizable images on the film; sometimes the subject could accurately predict the scene that would appear on the film. Eisenbud called this thoughtography.[3]

Dr. Volkringer of the French Academy of Sciences discovered that certain leaves, which had been left between the pages of a book for over a hundred years, formed a highly detailed negative image on the paper *several pages away.* Dr. Volkringer concluded that some form of life energy had radiated from the leaves, but, he speculated, the energy must have been at a fairly low intensity.

Dr. Marcel Vogel, of IBM in San Jose, took pictures of a tree leaf that lay between pages of the Bible over the Christmas season, because on the leaf was imprinted a clear bust portrait that resembled the conventional "Madonna" picture (see chapter 18).

Many people can hardly doubt any longer that there are subtle currents, rhythms, emanations, and nonphysical forces, which we call "energy" for want of a better word, of which science knows very little. (Present-day science recognizes but four forms of energy: gravity; electromagnetism; weak atomic energy; and strong atomic energy.) These are probably associated with all life forms and certainly with human life. A few brave scientists have spent their lifetimes in such research, with negligible recognition. Dr. Harold Saxton Burr, who died in 1973 as professor of anatomy emeritus at Yale University School of Medicine, spent forty years measuring and researching what he called lLifefields. These L-fields, he found, have some electromagnetic properties and can be measured (in millivolts) on sensitive voltmeters. A person needs only to touch the two index fingertips to the meter connections to get an L-field intensity reading. His "Electro-Dynamic Theory of Life," coauthored with his associate F. S. C. Northrop, was published by the *Quarterly Review o f Biology* in 1935. Some fifty papers on this subject followed in professional journals, culminating with publication of a book in 1972 as a summary overview for the general reader.[4]

In 1981, Rupert Sheldrake, a British plant physiologist, caused a mild sensation with his book about morphogenetic fields (M-fields), which he suggests have neither mass nor energy, yet do the organizing for bodily control (healing and replacement of cells) that Burr claimed to find.[5] All other theorists have postulated an "energy." Without going back to Plato ("ideal forms") and Aristotle ("eternal forms"), there have been at least a dozen researchers in the nineteenth and twentieth centuries who have proposed variously named subtle energies, but none have been explored by conventional science. Could it be that the pursuit of the truth of the Shroud will force science to look seriously at subtle energies, even if it means venturing into the paranormal and flirting with the occult?

A few researchers are now suggesting that the physical body that lay on the Shroud of Turin must have radiated at a very high intensity for a *short* period of time—perhaps for only a few seconds. STURP scientist and chemistry professor Alan D. Adler, Western Connecticut State College, concludes that the Shroud images could have been created only by high-level energy—but he cannot give a name for such an energy. Ray Rogers, a physical chemist of the Los Alamos Laboratory's design engineering division and a STURP member, says, "I am forced to conclude that the image was formed by a burst of radiant energy— light if you like."

But have we ever known of radiant light—a flash photolysis—that formed permanent images by the light and power of itself? Yes. In early 1978, STURP researchers in the Los Alamos Laboratory (operated by the University of California for the U.S. Department of Energy) issued a public statement suggesting that one scientific hypothesis "draws an analogy between the mysterious images on the Shroud and the fact that images were formed on stones by the fireball radiation from the atomic bomb at Hiroshima."

This coincidence of the two phenomena has been noted by historian-sindonologist Ian Wilson[6] and others. The Hiroshima images were reported at the time, both verbally and pictorially, by John R. Hersey in the *New Yorker* magazine and in his book *Hiroshima.*[7] U.S. Army and Air Force photographs provide a variety of these views, as do Japanese photographs.[8]

The light produced by the atomic bomb blast was so brilliant that it cast shadows of upright objects, and the radiant energy of the blast was so powerful that it permanently "etched" those shadows onto both flat, horizontal surfaces such as concrete roadways and vertical surfaces such as the side of a gas storage tank. Many of these images are a half mile to a mile from the blast epicenter. Some subjects, such as formed images of bridge balustrades and large gate-valves, continue to exist. Other subjects, such as a bamboo ladder and a man holding it, were apparently incinerated by the blast. Similarly, the shadow of a man in a cart was posed, as if in a monstrous game, in the act of whipping his horse.

Scientists investigating the effects of the bomb in Hiroshima noticed that it had discolored some concrete to a light reddish tint and had scaled off granite surfaces. It left a permanent shadow of the building's tower on the roof of the chamber of commerce, 220 yards from the epicenter of the blast. Towers on other buildings were similarly immortalized on their roofs, including the Hypothes Bank building a mile and a quarter from the epicenter. Based upon the directions of these "shadows," it was possible by triangulation to fix the exact epicenter, just a few yards from the ruins of the Shima Hospital.

If Jesus of Nazareth was the Man of the Shroud, might not his physical body have been incinerated by the power of the Resurrection blast that Matthew reports as having been accompanied by earthquakes?

The "Resurrection" of the Christ spirit from the Jesus body was more than a transition from physical life to spiritual life; *that* had occurred on the cross. The Resurrection was a tremendous, earthshaking event, and the body was apparently disintegrated and consumed without a trace as the boulder was blown from the door of the tomb.

Such a suggestion may seem too far-fetched. Yet, how else does one explain the bloodstains on the Shroud? Here is an even greater

Figure 2.
Shadows cast from the Hiroshima atom bomb. The roadway of a bridge bal-
ustrade (top). Notice that the sun's shadows (triangular) on the posts are in
the opposite direction from the bomb blast shadows. (Courtesy U.S. Defense
Nuclear Agency). A bamboo ladder (above left) on a gas storage tank one and
a quarter miles from the blast epicenter. The ladder itself apparently was incinerated by the blast. (Courtesy Hiroshima-Nagasaki Publishing Committee). A
valve wheel on a gas storage tank. *(Courtesy U.S. Air Force)*

enigma than the body images. On the one hand, the bloodstains are photographically positive (not negative like the body images), do penetrate to the back of the cloth, and do amount to stains of real blood (obviously, by contact). These facts are solidly reported by the STURP scientists. Nevertheless, just as strongly, those scientists tell us that flows and oozings of arterial and venous blood, each characteristically clear and unique, reflect postburial flows at the side and at the feet, plus postmortem flows while on the cross, plus premortem flows (from the wrists) as he (presumably Jesus) hung *and moved* on the cross, plus flogging wounds an hour or more before the crucifixion. *All* of these various bloodstains, the scientists tell us, are sharp and clear and *unsmudged*—they even show the "halo effect" where blood and water have separated as is typical after death. How can this have happened? What an anomaly! How can the handling of Jesus' body (if it was his) by the soldiers and by Joseph and Nicodemus *not* have smeared and smudged the blood-flows?

Of course, blood from the morning's beatings and scourging as well as pre-mortem flows of blood from the nails and cap of thorns would have partly dried by the time Joseph and Nicodemus got the body. But crusted blood, even if dried for six to ten hours, would have broken or smeared in the handling of the body. Flows from the side and from the nail wounds, at least, would have been still wet with fresh postmortem flows of blood. Yet, none of the blood images on the Shroud were smeared.

Obviously, more than physical explanations must be given for these phenomena. The permanence and sharp detail of the bloodstains logically must be attributed to the *same* paranormal, spiritual event that "photographically" imprinted the negative body images (front and back) with such meticulous and reliable detail upon the Shroud.

How can a dead and cold body produce a flash radiance to mirror and etch its image upon the cloth, creating a perfect and permanent picture of itself? No *other* dead body has ever been known to mark a burial cloth in any respect, except with its own putrefaction.

Sometimes spiritual sources answer spiritual questions best. Charles C. Wise Jr. has for three-score years experienced a mystical, inspirational gift of attunement when he quiets his body and mind in a receptive state of prayer-meditation. At such times he seems able to blend his mind with the mind of different persons who have passed from mortal life and to experience or know their thoughts. These thoughts he can then put into his own words. *Windows on the Passion* and *Windows on the Master* record a series of such stories that focus on the earthly life of Jesus of Nazareth.[9] Subsequently, he published an omnibus volume[10] of such stories, that included an explanation of the Resurrection of Jesus the Christ by an allegedly contemporary personality. The "explanation," which also elucidates the forty days of Jesus' Resurrection ministry, is worth pondering; for many readers it may "ring true":

> The envelope of vitality is called by some the 'astral body'.... It is this material—not truly a separate body in itself—which forms the basis of manifestations by physical mediums and which sometimes can be lent to or borrowed by spirits desiring to materialize.... Most ghosts seem not to have this capability of themselves—except for a brief period at the time of death—and are not able to manifest at will. In this—as in other ways—Jesus was different.... Jesus had a control of his spirit appearances after death never displayed by any other. He was not dependent upon borrowed life-force, but had his own supply of vitality. Some have done similar things, using their own ectoplasm or vitality, but never for so long a period after their bodies were dead. He had a powerful force not available to any other of whom I have heard. This is the answer to the mystery of his body's disappearance: after death, Jesus converted the atoms of his physical body entirely into astral vitality, storing and using it at will, and converting it into pure spirit in the process of drawing upon it for his materialization.... I now know *what* he did, but even today, I cannot imagine *how* he did it. As his envelope of vitality was reduced, his appearances became fewer, shorter, and less definite. They were more spiritual and less clearly physical. But he had ample vitality to achieve his objectives and to depart dramatically on his own schedule.

At the time Wise recorded that inspirational insight (received in 1973), he had no access to or interest in the more recent scientific evaluations that liken the Shroud images to the result of a flash photolysis or the atomic bomb.

Are such stories worth noticing? Consciousness researchers and philosophers are beginning to realize that inspiration, intuition, and creativity are merely specific labels for a broad spectrum of spiritual/mental enlightenment that comes to man in a variety of ways, and which his mind/spirit develops or mediates and channels. They come especially during "altered states of consciousness" such as dreamtime, reverie, meditation, prayer, hypnosis, psychic trance, and benign possession, to name but a few. The admixture in this broad field where the physical, mental, and spiritual blur together, and the vein of gold it conceals, were perhaps first clearly perceived by the late Gardner Murphy. His many writings on the close relationship between creativity and psychic sensitivities were published in journal articles from 1963 on.[11] We also have a mass of anecdotal evidence from creative people who claim that their creations were given them by spiritual sources, and it would be hard to conceive of any reason why they should all fabricate such stories. In modern times there have been scores of writers, from Robert Louis Stevenson to Richard Bach, and numerous inventors, notably Thomas Edison, who have candidly disclosed such "sources."

For some, the Shroud images have another parallel: At the "transfiguration" on the mountaintop with Peter, James, and John, Jesus' face appeared in brilliant light, his clothing dazzlingly white and as lightning (as reported by Matthew, Mark, and Luke). Might this have been a foretaste of powers to come?

Truly, this must be recognized as *spiritual* image-making. The Shroud image has elements or characteristics of x-ray, of photography, and of 3-dimensionality—*but*, it is *not* the result of any of these techniques.

SEVENTEEN

LOGICAL INFERENCE, CIRCUMSTANTIAL EVIDENCE, AND FORENSIC EVALUATION

T IS important, occasionally, to check one's perspective. Today, scientists tell us that the Shroud of Turin is authentic—that is, it is not a fake or a copy, not made by art or artifice or a natural process, not a man-made creation by any process known or conceivable. But what is the significance of such a statement? If the Shroud is authentic, do we need its history prior to 1357 in order to validate it, to *prove* it? From the historian's point of view, the answer is, "yes"; there must be proof.

However, to a logician or a pragmatist, the answer is "no"; authenticity is authenticity, whether we have historical data to prove it or not. Many a work of art or historical or archaeological artifact or relic (religious or otherwise) is discovered fortuitously. Once its authenticity, based upon intrinsic factors, is established beyond reasonable doubt, it should be, and usually is, accepted as genuine. Its authenticity is not altered by the fact that it may be impossible to establish its precise provenance, much less its detailed and complete history.

This is the category into which the Shroud of Turin must properly fall. Since it is not a fake, it is certainly a marvel of reality, and its authenticity should be accepted on the basis of the existing scientific validation, plus the logic of all circumstances that are involved. As to the circumstantial evidence relating to the Shroud, there is no inconsistency, there are no unexplained facts, no facts that do not fit, and there is no alternative explanation that is anywhere near as appropriate to the facts as that of the biblical Gospels.

Trial lawyers know that when an incident is thoroughly investigated, the circumstantial evidence is by far the most reliable basis for telling us what happened in a particular incident. They know, as do psychologists and historians, that personal testimony of so-called eyewitnesses is notoriously more unreliable. Even assuming the greatest honesty and goodwill on the part of the witness, the convolutions of the mind and of memory recall can mislead the witness and his audience.

Scattered throughout the preceding chapters are findings and conclusions from which we can draw logical inferences, the sum of which, because of the internal consistency, should be overwhelmingly convincing. These major findings are now summarized.

In chapter 2 inferences were drawn from tradition and from the religious milieu, favoring the probability that the Shroud *was* saved and *was* secreted by a few disciples. Tradition also tells us that Thomas was responsible for Christian missions to Parthia, and that he sent Thaddaeus to carry the "good news" to Edessa and to take the Shroud to Abgar for safekeeping. This would be a logical move, since Edessa was outside the Roman Empire and beyond the reach of the Jewish Sanhedrin as well.

It must be considered a near certainty that disciples Thomas and Thaddaeus knew that the image delivered to Abgar was the true Shroud of Jesus; it seems likely that Aggai of Edessa also knew this. In all likelihood no one subsequently knew that this was a full sindon, bearing a crucified man's full image, until in the tenth century when it was probably discovered by accident—perhaps when placing the Mandylion Face in a new frame in Constantinople.

Certain faces of Jesus in art, which Vignon and Whanger (by separate techniques) have found to be a very close match for the Shroud Face (chapter 19), are also in some cases distinctively identified by the trelliswork surrounding the face (see chapter 2). This trellis pattern was typically used in the ornamental dress of Parthian royalty at the time Edessa was host to the image. There is also the further "coincidence" that Aggai had been a special craftsman for the making of ceremonial dress for the king, Abgar.

The Vignon comparison of faces and the Whanger comparison of faces seem effectively to establish that the Face of the Shroud of Turin, the Face of the Constantinople Mandylion, and the Face of the Image of Edessa are all one. About a dozen famous portraits of Jesus executed during the first millennium of the Christian era contain most (15 to 20) of the same nonartistic and unnatural oddities that are traceable to a copying from the Shroud (or the Image of Edessa, or the Mandylion).

Standard police practice in fingerprint identification considers 14 points of congruence sufficient to declare fingerprints identical, and 35 points of congruence for a match of face photos, and the courts regularly uphold these standards. Dr. Whanger of Duke University recorded 74 points of congruence when he superimposed photographs of the coin from the Shroud right eye with Father Filas's Pontius Pilate coin of A.D. 29. Whanger also found that the Shroud Face had 46 points of congruence with an icon face of Jesus dated to A.D. 550 and 63 points of congruence with a Justinian coin of 692.

Today the image is faint and hard to see. Considering the very close comparison of many early artists' faces of Jesus with the photographic negative of the face of the Shroud of Turin, one may wonder if the face-on-cloth of those early years might not have been more sharply and clearly visible to the copying artists than it is today for an observer. Might not the early practice (until perhaps the nineteenth century) of carrying the Shroud (or Face) in parades in the hot sun, or the practice of consecrating water by contact with the Shroud (or Face) so that it could be sprinkled across an audience for their blessing, and other similar practices, have weathered and aged and dimmed the Shroud images?

Whoever had possession of the Shroud during the "missing" years of 1204 and 1357 must have known the Shroud for what it truly was, and they possessed and protected it because of their reverence for it—regardless of any other reasons they might have had. Is it the Shroud of Jesus? No other explanation is consistent with the conduct of each possessor of the Shroud—and each must have had a basis for believing that it was so.

The Athens/Besancon/Knights Templar connection is not an indispensable historical link in the Shroud's continuity, but it is well validated now. Because of the intrinsic factors involved, no one today can reasonably doubt that the Savoy shroud, which came from the de Charnys, is of early Christian era provenance that came through Edessa, Constantinople, Athens, and Besancon, to Lirey and Turin.

How did the de Charnys obtain the Shroud? People of the thirteenth and fourteenth centuries doubtless would have considered that the seizure of valuables as spoils of war would effect a "legitimate" transfer of ownership to Othon de La Roche. Conversely, breach of trust or theft might have tainted a transfer in the minds of most contemporaries, and we would expect that such a taint might well have been anathema to de Charny because of his reputed high moral and religious principles. No one ever suggested that the de Charnys did not rightfully own the Shroud—*not even their enemies or critics made such a claim*—not even the Lirey bishops (of Troyes) who protested the expositions of the Shroud.

Current research by Indiana historian Dr. Daniel C. Scavone, which has included discovery of several contemporary supporting documents, now seems to demonstrate with certainty that the Shroud left Constantinople (1204) in the hands of Othon de La Roche, who became the Duke of Athens—it became his as a "spoil of war," his share of the loot of Constantinople. In 1208 he sent it to his father, Ponce de La Roche of Besancon, Burgundy Province, France, who deposited it for safekeeping in the local church of St. Etienne, where it remained and attracted moderate attention as the Face of Besancon. After the church was destroyed by fire in 1349, the face was replaced by a poor copy (apparently without comment from the parishioners), which was later destroyed in the French Revolution.

No record has yet been found of Othon's instructions to his father or to the church of Besancon, but there is no reason to suppose that he relinquished his ownership in the Shroud. In about 1343, Othon's great-great-granddaughter Jeanne de Vergy left Besancon for Lirey, where she married Geoffrey de Charny in 1352. Beginning in 1357, she and Geoffrey began extensive public exhibitions of the *full* Shroud. Dr. Scavone's conclusion is that she brought the Shroud from Besancon as her dowry.

Who was Geoffrey de Charny? He was a very prominent and peripatetic knight during France's Hundred Years' War with England, and the last twenty years of his life were fully packed: His military service (1337) was in southern France in the Guyenne and Languedoc areas, near the Rhone delta and near the town of Beaucaire on the west bank of the Rhone. In 1338 he served in northern France near Calais. From 1339 to 1343 he fought in Flanders, Artois, and Brittany. In 1345 he went with Crown Prince Humber II to the Orient to fight the Turks, until June 1346, when he participated in the Battle of Smyrna. That summer, back in France, at Port Ste. Marie near Toulouse, he took part in the siege of Aiguillon, and later was in the north at Ste. Omer. He received the *oriflamme* (royal banner) four times: in 1347, 1351, 1355, and 1356.

In 1347 he helped negotiate treaties with the count of Savoy in May, and with the king of England in July and September. The same year he was nominated to sit on Philippe's royal council. In 1349 he led a military force in Flanders, and in Calais, and there on December 31 was captured by the English. Just previously, in lieu of pay, the king gave him property rights to collect rents from the seneschalties of Toulouse and Carcassone (near the Pyrenees) and the town of Beaucaire on the west bank of the Rhone near its delta. In 1351 he was ransomed to King John II. Late that year he was negotiating treaties and inspecting outposts in northern France. In 1356 he stepped into a lance thrust intended for the king and died instantly—at the battlefield of Poitiers. *But,* it is the best fit of the facts that the Shroud came to Geoffrey as dowry from Jeanne.

The facts of the Shroud and the statements of the Gospels match completely, and yet both are based on a series of anomalies. Jesus was executed as a heinous criminal, but was given an expensive, although incomplete, burial. The body was separated from the Shroud before decomposition. The bloodstains came from four different time periods, ranging from very early morning to night, yet appear on the Shroud clear and unsmeared. He had scalp punctures indicating a cap of thorns typical in style to oriental crowns but unknown to European royalty. His legs were unbroken, yet he died quickly on the cross.

Medical data reported earlier show the explicit and characteristic accuracy of the Shroud bloodstains as concerns venous blood flow and arterial blood flow, plus the fact that medical knowledge as about the circulation of human blood was only discovered in 1593, nearly 250 years after the Shroud of Lirey (of Chambery, and of Turin) had been historically and publicly established.

Logically, we are forced to assume two separate actions that made the bloodstains on the Shroud. The scientists find the residue of actual blood, so there must have been actual contact between the bloody body and the Shroud. But there are stains on the Shroud of blood flows from four different time periods—(1) blood from the flogging, beatings, and crowning; for Jesus, this occurred very early on Friday morning; (2) blood from premortem flows (from the wrists and feet) as he was nailed and then hung *and moved* on the cross through midday; (3) blood from postmortem flows (side) in the afternoon before being removed from the cross; (4) blood from postburial flows at the side and at the feet, in the evening while lying in the tomb. All of these bloodstains are sharply defined on the Shroud, unsmeared; thus, the permanent, precise bloodstains must have been created paranormally just as the body images were.

Some researchers have hypothesized that natural skin substances plus burial ointments (that might have vaporized) acted as catalysts in degradation of the cellulose in the linen upon contact, and thus, with the passage of considerable time, an image was formed. Yet, the Edessa legend would indicate that the image was already on the cloth shortly after the crucifixion, and no other corpse has ever marked an image on burial cloths. In any event, the images were *not* made by an artist's paints; microchemical tests directly on the Shroud disclosed no pigment or pigment binder to a level of less than millionths of a gram.

Now, if the Shroud is a fake, then whoever fabricated it before 1357, by whatever unknown methods, had command of knowledge and abilities quite incredible for his time. He must have: known the precise methods of crucifixion of the first century; possessed the medical knowledge of a modern expert surgeon; utilized an art process unknown to any great master, never duplicated before or since; been able to foresee and approximate principles of photographic negativity not otherwise discovered for centuries; imported a piece of old cloth of

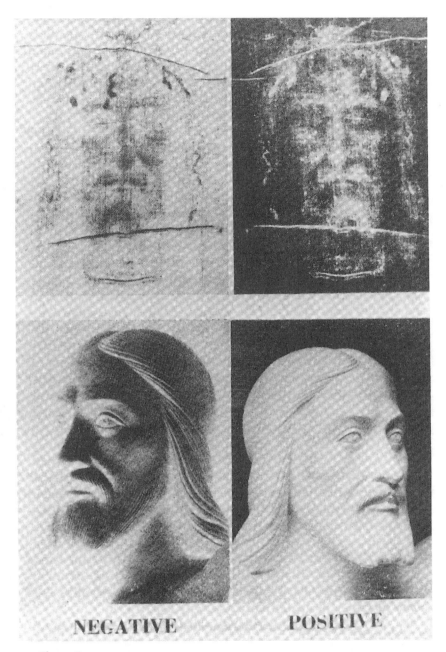

Figure 1.
The Shroud Face and the Weyland plaster statue, in positive and negative views, illustrate photographic negativity. *(Courtesy Holy Shroud Guild)*

Near East manufacture; used a coloring agent that would be unaffected by intense heat; been able to incorporate into his work details (that we have only recently discovered) that the human eye cannot see and that are visible only with the most advanced computer-scanning devices; been able to reproduce flawlessly, on a nearly flat linen surface, in a single color, undistorted three-dimensional characteristics of a human body in "negative format" on the tops of the threads, while conversely showing the "blood" as positive and soaking all the way through. All of this had to have been done prior to 1357, for since that date the Shroud has a clearly documented and uninterrupted history. And even now, with all the scientific knowledge and technical skills at our command, our scientists and artists cannot duplicate the Shroud.

But, forgery of the Shroud image would have been completely illogical. Why would a forger of the Middle Ages have procured a piece of thousand-year-old linen of Near East manufacture on which to put his clever image? Scientists of his day could not have identified it as such. Why would he want to create a photographic negative? His contemporaries could not have understood and admired it. If he created a "Nickell negative" by accident, what would he do with it? Probably throw it away, since he could not know that in five or six hundred years a camera would be invented to make his bizarre image look natural. Even if he knew what he had done, wouldn't he want to see it reversed to check its accuracy? Unable to do so, he wouldn't be able to improve it by retouching. If he was confident of the image, could he add the "bloodstains" by overpainting? No, because he would have to stand ten feet or more away in order to see it (and with light and dark areas reversed at that)!

Sometimes anomalies tell us much more than straightforward information. Before the Crusades there was a Christian tradition in the eastern churches that Jesus was lame, and a few ancient images of Jesus show this, and this tradition is said to be embodied in the Byzantine Cross. We now have a meaningful explanation of that tradition because of our scientific knowledge of the Shroud images. We know that Jesus' left foot was nailed on top of the right and that rigor mortis set in while he was still on the cross, causing the left leg to be bent more than the right. For this reason, on the Shroud the left leg appears to be two inches shorter than the right. Once church authorities in Constantinople displayed a full burial shroud, not just a face, artists and physicians would have noticed this disparity in the length of the legs. However, there having been no crucifixions in seven hundred years, they were unaware of the various techniques in the practice of crucifixion and could only conclude that Jesus had a shortened leg. That misconception now becomes a great gift to our era, because it proves in a novel way that the Mandylion/Shroud that was in Constantinople for 257 years is the same as the Shroud in Turin today.

The logic of circumstantial evidence does tell us much about the Man on the Shroud:

- The careful work of researchers Francis Filas and Alan and Mary Whanger is highly persuasive in establishing that coins on the eyes of the Man are datable to A.D. 29 or 30, so that a crucifixion of A.D. 33 becomes quite probable. It is now fairly certain that Jesus' crucifixion occurred on Friday, April 3, A.D. 33, according to Dr. Paul L. Maier in *First Easter* and *Pontious Pilate;* also, in his "Sejanus, Pilate and the Date of the Crucifixion," *Church History XXXVII,* 3/13, March 1968. Maier cites Finegan, W. E. Filmer, Frothingham, and Doyle as agreeing with this date. To the same effect in Brame in *The Augustan XXII:* 2, at p. 71, 1984, and H. W. Hoehner in *Chronological Aspects of the Life of Christ,* Zondervan, 1977 (and he cites concurrence by Goldstein).

- The burial practices of the first-century Jews, the crucifixion practices of the Romans in Palestine, and the pollen grains from the Dead Sea area found on the Shroud by Max Frei make Palestine a strong candidate for the site of the crucifixion.

- Jewishness of the Man seems well established. In addition to Weyland's artistic analysis (chapter 13), Harvard professor Carleton Coon, viewing 3-D profiles and other data, says the Man of the Shroud was "of a physical type found in modern times among Sephardic Jews and noble Arabs." Ian Wilson agrees with those who believe a certain dorsal feature from the head to the shoulder blades of the Shroud image is an "unbound pigtail." He concludes that is "the most striking Jewish feature" on the Shroud, since scholars report that it was a common fashion in Jesus' time for Jewish men to wear their hair caught at the back of the neck in a pigtail.

- Ridicule was part and parcel of a Roman crucifixion, so it was quite consistent that in Jesus' case there was the "crown" of thorns, the written legend "King of the Jews," the dressing of him in fine garments, the placing of a cane in his hand, and the verbal mockery—as described in the Bible. However, the crown of thorns in Jesus' case seems historically to have been a unique incident; in no other known crucifixion was there any kind of claim of kingship. Moreover, the Shroud markings show clearly that this was not a wreathlike arrangement, such as the Greeks fashioned of laurel leaves for their heroes, but rather was cap-like, and the thorns penetrated his entire scalp in a solid mass of wounds, especially lacerating the back of his head where it came in contact with the cross. All four Gospels relate that Jesus underwent severe beatings with fists and sticks and that the blows were aimed specifically at his head and face. Again, the Shroud markings are clear as to the multiple injuries in this area, including a large bruise on the right cheek, a burst lower lip, and an apparent broken nose, which of course is cartilage, not bone.

In spite of all the detailed data that has been developed about the Shroud, much of which relates to aspects not discernible to the naked eye and which depends upon the use of very sophisticated equipment, no data yet developed militate against the growing presumption that the Man on the Shroud was Jesus of Nazareth. If the Shroud *does* apply to Jesus, and if it has any meaning at all, it must certainly convey the fact that the heart was pierced, resulting in the loss of most of his body's blood. Thus he certainly was dead when removed from the cross. Medical experts from Italy, Germany, France, England, and America all agree, for a variety of reasons, that the Man of the Shroud was definitely dead before he was taken from the cross and that we are dealing with a real corpse that suffered real wounds of abuse and crucifixion.

The Shroud of Turin could be an authentic first-century burial shroud of a crucified man and still have not enwrapped Jesus. But here logical inference comes into play. And here the celestial oddsmakers have stacked the deck against the skeptic, for the compelling evidence with coincidence on top of coincidence must convince our minds beyond all reasonable doubt that this was the Shroud of Jesus.

See the scientific paper of this author, "Enigmas of the Shroud of Turin," pp. 39–49, *Sindon,* no. 33 (December 1984), Centro Internazionalle della Sindone, Turin, Italy, listing twenty-one enigmas of the Shroud images that the STURP members find scientifically inexplicable. Additionally, it should be noted that the blood flows from the wrist wounds along the arms angled and dripped off the arms precisely as would be expected by the effect of gravity. Yet, the principle of gravity was not understood until the seventeenth century—thus an artist of the fourteenth century or earlier would not likely have painted such exactly proper rivulets of dripping blood.

EIGHTEEN

ARE THERE PARALLELS TO THE SHROUD?

T HERE CAN be no doubt that cloth can survive for two thousand years or longer, if it is kept dry (chapter 11). Museums in Egypt have linens dated to 4000 B.C.—6,000 years ago—that are in fairly good condition. Burial shrouds more than 2,000 years old have been found in reasonably good condition. But no burial shroud, other than the one in Turin, has ever been found bearing an image on it.

Rumors and claims will sometimes suggest other such images—even citing respectable names. Shroud researcher Robert K. Wilcox[1] ran down one such claim. While in Turin, a Benedictine priest showed him a volume called *Annals,* written by French archaeologist-Egyptologist M. Gayet, relating to his excavations about the turn of the century near Antinoe, Egypt. On one page Gayet had written:

> Among these documents [meaning burial shrouds] the most important one is a face-veil, folded in four, and carrying the impression of the face to which it was applied. These imprints formed something like dark spots where the prominences of the face were, and show up black…. This image gives us the face of a dead man.

Drawings accompanying the text suggested that the face of the corpse had been covered by the veil, then the body was wrapped in a shroud and bound mummy-style. Wilcox was impressed and made photocopies of the text and drawings.

When he visited Paris, Wilcox went to the Coptic section of the Egyptian collection in the Louvre Palace Museum and asked to see the

Gayet group of Egyptian artifacts. The curator of the Coptic section told Wilcox that he was very familiar with all of the items of that group of artifacts, but there was no such item as a face-veil with the image of a face on it. Wilcox brought out the copies of the pages of Gayet's book and showed the curator Gayet's statement. After reading the passage through twice, he asked Wilcox to return the following day. The next day they went to the storage room together and laboriously examined every piece of cloth in the collection—three trunks with approximately seventy-five burial garments in each. There was no hint of a face or a body image on any of them. He did note that corpses wrapped in linen will leave stains of the body's decomposition on the cloth, and, if and when the cloth rots, it will discolor. Wilcox photographed some of the discolored and stained linens.

That would have been a somewhat unsatisfactory ending to the story, but later he happened to reread the last chapter of the book written by the Shroud's first scientist-researcher, Paul Vignon. In it Vignon describes several shrouds, shown him by the Egyptologist M. Gayet, as having on them some vague brown stains, devoid of shape or gradation. Vignon considered that they might prove the vast difference between ordinary, unremarkable stains on burial cloths and the Shroud of Turin, which he considered "equivalent to a portrait."

Although there are no other images on shrouds, there are parallels to the Shroud of Turin. Perhaps the best example is the image known as "Our Lady of Guadalupe." This is a cactus-fiber cloak enshrined in the Basilica of Guadalupe in Mexico City. The story, written in an Indian dialect in the sixteenth century, says that in 1531 the Virgin Mary visited a poor Indian villager, Juan Diego, several times. He told his bishop, but the bishop disbelieved Diego. On a subsequent visit to the bishop, Mary put her full image on Juan's rough cloak in an instant as he stood there. The cloak is now well cared for, but one wonders how protected it may have been in earlier years—yet the image as well as the cloak have survived for four and a half centuries. The abbot of the basilica authorized the commencement of scientific tests of the cloak in 1979, by the taking of infrared photographs. These were discussed at a scientific conference in 1980. Further testing is planned.

This is the story: On Saturday, December 9, 1531, as Juan Diego, age fifty-seven, was crossing the foot of a small hill called Tepeyac on his way to the town of Tlatelolco (a suburb of Mexico City), Mary the mother of Jesus, who came to be known in Mexico as Our Lady of Guadalupe, first appeared to him. Juan was a Nahuatl Indian who dropped his Indian name and was baptized in 1525, renamed himself Juan Diego, and was regarded as a devout Christian. On that Saturday morning he was on his way to the Franciscan monastery at Tlatelolco to attend mass and listen to the monks, as was frequently his custom. When he was beckoned to the summit of Tepeyac, he saw Mary "standing in the midst of glorious light." She spoke to him in his Indian tongue and told him who she was, and requested that a shrine be built there in her honor. Juan went straight to Fray Juan de Zumarraga, the Franciscan bishop in Mexico City, and told of his experience. The bishop told him to return on another day, apparently hoping to discourage the Indian.

Juan Diego returned the same day to Tepeyac Hill and again saw Mary, just as he had first seen her. He stayed in her presence until nightfall and then returned home. The following day, Sunday, Juan saw Mary again. He attended mass at Tlatelolco and then went immediately to Mexico City to see the bishop. After considerable delay, he was finally taken to the bishop, who questioned him in detail about the experiences. Hoping further to discourage Juan, the bishop requested a "sign" from the lady on the hill.

Juan returned immediately to the hill, saw Mary for the third time, and received her promise to grant the bishop's request the following morning. In the meantime, his uncle, Juan Bernardino, became seriously ill, and for this reason Juan was unable to return to the hill the following day, which was Monday. The next day, Tuesday, December 12, he was hurrying past the hill to summon a priest for his dying uncle when the lady came down the hill to meet him. She told him not to be concerned for his uncle, that he had her for all necessary health and protection. Also, she instructed him to go up to the hilltop and gather all the roses and other flowers he might find there, and return to her with them.

Although flowers were not to be expected on a hilltop in midwinter, he did as instructed and found a garden full of flowers. There were so many that he had to carry them folded into his *tilma,* a blanketlike cloak hand-woven from fibers of the maguey plant (also known as agave fiber), a form of cactus. He brought them down the hill to Mary, who rearranged them in the *tilma* and said, "These roses and flowers are the sign that you are to take to the bishop," and admonished him that no one else was to see what he carried in the *tilma.* As Juan proceeded on his errand to Mexico City, six miles away, Mary appeared to his uncle and healed him.

When Bishop Zumarraga finally agreed to see Juan Diego again, and Juan dropped the apronlike front of his *tilma,* a cascade of spring flowers, including roses, lilies, carnations, iris, furze, jasmine, and violets spilled into the bishop's lap. But even more miraculous was that the bare *tilma* now bore in full color a beautiful likeness of Our Lady of Guadalupe.

The bishop's doubts vanished at once. A new chapel, the Hermitage, was built at Tepeyac Hill, and on December 26, 1531, the Tilma with its picture of Our Lady was installed there, with Juan Diego in charge of the chapel. From 1622 to 1709, while the Basilica of Guadalupe was under construction in Mexico City, the *tilma* was moved temporarily to a nearby church. Upon completion of the basilica, the *tilma* was placed above the main altar, where it stayed until December 12, 1976, when a new shrine to Our Lady of Guadalupe was dedicated and the *tilma* was installed behind glass above the main altar.

At least two contemporaneous accounts of these incidents were written. One was by Bishop Zumarraga himself (first bishop of Mexico), a copy of which he took to Spain in 1532. The most comprehensive account was written by a native scribe, Don Antonio Valeriano (later governor of Mexico City for thirty-five years), who interviewed Juan Diego sometime between 1540 and 1545 (Juan Diego died in 1548), and whose record is known as the *Nican Mopohua.* There are still eleven *Annals* and two *Charts* in existence that record these occurrences. The whereabouts of the original of the *Nican Mopohua* is not known—it may be permanently lost. One exact copy does exist—it

Figure 1.
A close-up of the Guadalupe Madonna Face. Note the sensitivity of the face in spite of being created on a rough cactus-fiber cloak and its 450-year age, the first 100 of which it was unprotected. *(Courtesy Center for Applied Research in the Apostolate)*

was taken to Europe in 1867 by Jose Fernando Ramirez, minister of foreign affairs in the cabinet of Emperor Maximilian (and former director of the Mexican National Museum), upon the fall of the Mexican Empire. After Ramirez's death, his literary estate was sold at auction in London, and his copy of the *Nican Mopohua* and related documents were purchased by the New York City Public Library, in whose hands they remain today.

Art experts examined the figure on the *tilma* in 1666, 1751, 1778, 1956, and 1963. All experts have marveled at the quality of the picture, the enigma of the technique, and the remarkable state of its preservation. The medium used is still unknown. One group of experts said they favored neither oil nor tempura "because it seems to be one or the other, and yet it is not what it appears to be." Kodak Company experts in 1963 were also nonplussed. For its first 116 years the *tilma* was not covered by glass, as it is now. One expert commented that survival of the *tilma* was inexplicable because in Mexico's climate, where the atmosphere is charged with nitrous particles and humidity is high, the air is so hostile that it disintegrates buildings and even consumes iron. In Mexico, a cactus-fiber cloak is expected to survive only about twenty years before disintegrating. Another expert pointed to the deleterious effects of smoke from countless candles at the altar and seventy lamps burning, in addition to the rubbing and kissing of the image by millions of pilgrims. Moreover, Don Carlos Maria de Bustamente recorded a bizarre incident. Technicians cleaning the *tilma's* gold frame spilled a vial of etching fluid directly onto the image—yet it suffered no harm.

On the night of May 7–8, 1979, Dr. Philip Serna Callahan, an artist and research photographer of the University of Florida, Gainesville, was permitted to take the *tilma* from its frame for six hours and take many photographs of it, forty of them utilizing infrared photography. As an art historian specializing in Renaissance paintings, he was able to make a number of firm conclusions and a few educated guesses— but the latter can be validated only if chemical tests of the pigments are made sometime in the future. Callahan's report of his study has been published[2] by the Center for Applied Research in the Apostolate (CARA),[3] Washington, D.C. Subsequently, CARA sponsored a scientific conference on June 21–22, 1980, to consider further scientific tests of the image on the *tilma;* previously CARA had conducted literary research on the *tilma* image, reflected in its other publications.

Callahan's work developed several startling findings. First, he demonstrated that the image as we can see it today was executed in stages, with additions and one significant change. He considers that the original figure, as shown to Bishop Zumarraga by Juan Diego in 1531, consisted only of the face and hands, the rose robe, the plain blue mantle, and possibly a gray outcropping of rock on which the figure stood (the latter is no longer visible). This original figure he finds totally inexplicable. To him it is one of the great masterpieces of artistic facial expression in the world, and he states that he has observed no portraits that are executed in a similar manner. Concerning the nature or type of paint and the technique of application, he cannot even offer a conjecture. There was no undersketching that would be normal to guide the artist, there was no sizing put on the coarse-weave *tilma,* there are no marks of brush-strokes, and there was no protective coating of varnish over the final image. Yet despite all that, the robe and mantle have never been overpainted and are as bright and colorful as if newly painted. Even the face has no chips or blemishes. Some experts have suggested that different parts were painted in different media (oil, tempera, watercolor, and fresco). Callahan finds major objections to each.

He considers that the first additions were probably made in the sixteenth century by an Indian artist, who added a waist tassel and a crescent moon under the figure's feet, at least. This may also have been the time of the only major alteration of the original image—the fingers were shortened by a half inch, making them more appropriate for an Indian. Indeed, the olive-colored skin tone of face and hands and the figure's height could imply an Indian maiden as the subject.

Sometime later, probably in the early seventeenth century, Callahan believes the other additions were added, most of which he describes as Spanish Gothic. During the great flood of 1629 the portrait was taken by canoe to the cathedral in Mexico City for safekeeping and was not returned until 1634. The *tilma* may have been folded to simplify removal (some crease damage does exist), and it is quite possible that the edges got wet, especially the bottom of the *tilma,* including the lower part of the image. For whatever reason (possibly to cover water damage), lower folds were added to the robe and a small angel was added, ostensibly to hold up the moon (on which the figure now stands) on his outstretched hands. This addition obliterated the rock upon which Our Lady originally stood. A covering for water damage may also have been in part the reason for adding the white background and black border where none had existed. Other additions, possibly at the same time, were a background sunburst, gold sun rays, gold stars, and gold trim of the mantle. Gold and blue edges were also added to the mantle, plus a gold bracelet and fur cuffs.

Callahan concludes without hesitation that all the changes and additions, at whatever time, were man-made with conventional paints, readily identifiable, and that these efforts show their age and will continue to deteriorate. Conversely, the only significant damage to the original figure is where some of the mantle's blue is missing over the center seam of the *tilma*—likely caused by folding or careless handling during some of the moves. The *tilma* is now mounted (probably with glue) onto a large metal sheet, which may have been done at the same time the last additions were painted.

If the story of *Nican Mopohua* is to be believed (and many historians have accepted it), and if the artistic findings of Dr. Callahan are accepted (as they tentatively have been by teams of working experts), then the original image of the *tilma* and the image of the Shroud have commonality in the enigma of their creation and the probable superhuman source of such creation—though, of course, they have very basic significant differences. Callahan notes one similarity: As with the Shroud Face, the face of Guadalupe is not outstanding and impressive to look at until one is at least six or seven feet away.

One might reject the suggestion of a supernatural source for the original picture as being an unrealistic, unprovable conclusion based upon negative findings. One almost might attribute guile to Juan Diego and gullibility to Bishop Zumarraga. But, how do we resolve the enigma of the picture—which Callahan calls inexplicable—in the light of present-day, repeated artistic evaluation, and of the scientific findings? How was the original figure made on the *tilma*?

While in Tepeyac during the latter half of the sixteenth century, the *tilma* was cut to the size of the image (41 by 66 inches); the figure of Our Lady is 56 inches tall. Dr. Callahan observed that the rough texture of the cloak provides a 3-D aspect, and the imperfections in its weave are precisely positioned under the face of the image, so as to accentuate the shadows and highlights, conveying a high degree of realism.

The parallel of the image of the *tilma* to the Image of the Shroud was heightened in 1963 when the experts of Kodak de Mexico S.A. concluded that the *tilma* is "essentially photographic in character." That evaluation might seem a gratuitous conjecture, but there are two lines of collateral support. In 1936, two fibers from the image, one red and one yellow, were taken to Richard Kuhn, Nobel Prize winner in chemistry and director of the chemistry department at the Kaiser Wilhelm Institution in Heidelberg, Germany, for evaluation. After careful examination, Kuhn announced that there was no coloring of any kind in the fibers; the materials used to produce the colors were unknown to science, being neither animal, vegetable, nor mineral dyes. Synthetic coloring could not be considered because it was developed three centuries after the creation of the image. Professor Francisco Campa Rivera of Mexico came to the same conclusions during his examinations of the *tilma* in 1954 and again in 1966.

The second and stronger line of support for the Kodak conclusion concerns the results of magnification of the eyes of the image—especially the right eye. In 1929, photographer Alfonso Gonzales made an amazing discovery. His enlargements disclosed what appeared to be a human face in the eyes of Our Lady. Even more startling, in 1951, draftsman J. Carlos Salinas Chavaz was using a magnifying glass to examine an enlargement of the face of the image, when he found in the pupil of the right eye the bust of a bearded man!

This finding was confirmed by a special commission in 1955. The next year, occultist Dr. Rafael Torifa Lavoignet examined the eyes of the image directly with an ophthalmoscope and reported that "in the cornea of the eye a human bust can be seen. The distortion and place of the optical image are identical with what is produced in a normal eye." When the ophthalmoscope is focused into the pupil of a human eye, it is possible to obtain the image at the back of the eye. Lavoignet found the same light reflection in the eye of the image, but said that such a result is not possible from a flat surface, such as a picture. He examined various types of paintings with the ophthalmoscope and found not the least reflection, "whereas the eyes of the Blessed Virgin of Guadalupe give the impression of life." Conformance to the laws of optics was noted by a surgeon, Dr. Javier Torroella Bueno, in 1979: "The distortion of the reflected image [in the eye of Our Lady] is even more striking, for it is in perfect obedience to the laws of curvature of the cornea."

Beginning in 1962, Dr. Charles Wahlig extended these findings considerably, utilizing the collaboration of eight other specialists. By enlarging the eye areas 25-times, he first discovered two more faces reflected in the cornea of the eyes. Next, he set up a simple experiment to validate the phenomenon in life, by posing his eldest daughter, Mary, while he, his wife, and younger daughter faced her. When a photograph of Mary's face was developed, busts of the three family members were clearly seen in Mary's eyes. Then came Wahlig's detective work. The largest bust seemed clearly to be Juan Diego, based on various paintings, but neither of the other two seemed to resemble Bishop Zumarraga. In 1960, restoration of an old church resulted in discovery of a painting made in 1533 of Juan Diego's presentation to the bishop a year and a half earlier. This painting clearly showed that Diego was flanked by the interpreter, Juan Gonzales, and Bishop Fuenleal, and the three were facing Bishop Zumarraga. Dr. Wahlig speculates that Our Lady must have chosen to remain invisible while standing behind Zumarraga, but imprinted on Diego's widespread *tilma* is a picture of herself so accurate and complete that the three men facing her were reflected in her eyes, and that reflection was recorded in her picture on the *tilma*.[4]

A footnote is appropriate: Records of the missionaries in Mexico before and after 1531 clearly show that after 1531, evangelization increased and about 9 million Aztec converts were added, much "out of proportion to the increased evangelical workers." One also wonders how the growth of Christianity was affected during the Shroud's Edessa period, the Constantinople period, the Lirey-Turin period, and the post-Pia period, and how it will be affected by the scientific work of the recent past.

NINETEEN

The Shroud Face as a Portrait of Jesus

S INCE THE advent of modern photography, and especially since the 1931 Shroud photographs by Giuseppi Enrie, which gave face-only negatives of the Man of the Shroud, portrait artists interested in painting the face of Jesus have had a very special subject to copy. Because, if this image is indeed of Jesus of Nazareth in the tomb, then the face negative is in effect a death mask of Jesus. However, if the images were caused by a thermonuclear-type burst of Christ-energy, then the image is unique in the world and more intimate than an ordinary death mask could ever be.

This sort of rationale may have been in the minds of two modern portrait artists—Ariel Agemian and Ris Phillips—who each painted the Face of Jesus using a Shroud negative photograph as a guide. These portraits will be discussed later in this chapter.

Prior to the 1350s, artists, especially those working from the Image of Edessa/Mandylion or copies of it, knew instinctively that there was a supernatural factor in their subject and that at the same time there was a mysterious lack of naturalness (because it was a photographic negative), which of course they couldn't understand at all. Yet their strong reverence for their subject resulted in a slavish precision respecting detail, as they saw it. The result was a group of anomalies found in a dozen or so of the better portraits of Jesus that come to us from that period.

Over the years, researchers Paul Vignon, Edward Wuenschel, and Ian Wilson have noted fifteen to twenty nonartistic oddities in the mosaics, paintings, and icons that are suspected of having been copied from the Image/Mandylion/Shroud. These oddities resulted from portraying the cloth weave, wrinkles in the cloth, blood rivulets, or imperfections in the image. In each of these cases, the artist, wishing to be

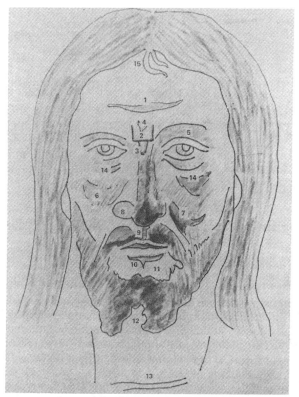

1. A transverse streak across the forehead
2. The three-sided "square" on the forehead
3. A V-shape at the bridge of the nose
4. A second V-shape, inside the three-sided square
5. A raised right eyebrow
6. An accentuated left cheek
7. An accentuated right cheek
8. An enlarged left nostril
9. An accentuated line between the nose and the upper lip
10. A heavy line under the lower lip
11. A hairless area between the lip and the beard
12. The forked beard
13. A transverse line across the throat
14. Heavily accentuated, owlish eyes
15. Two loose strands of hair falling from the apex of the forehead

Figure 1.

Dr. Paul Vignon's Iconography Face analysis, with Wilson's modifications. Many of the icons, mosaics, and paintings of Jesus created under Byzantine influence and dated roughly to the sixth through the thirteenth centuries were found by sindonologists Paul Vignon and Edward Wuenschel to contain up to twenty similar oddities that were unattractive and unartistic. More recently, historian Ian Wilson has made a similar evaluation and has identified an aggregate of fifteen such peculiarities, as noted on this sketch. *(Courtesy Ian Wilson)* totally faithful to the original, incorporated these oddities even though they are irrelevant to or detract from the naturalness of the face. The correlation of these repeated oddities on various early pictures of Jesus and their relationship to the Shroud Face has come to be known as Vignon's iconographic thesis. Typically, the pictures (like the Shroud) show an absence of ears, neck, and shoulders. Two blood rivulets on the forehead at the hairline are incorporated as curls. A cloth wrinkle across the middle of the forehead is included as if it were a scar. A bruised left eyebrow is shown with twice the vertical dimension as the right eyebrow. From nine to fourteen of these oddities in each of various pictures are too much for coincidence. All these artists must have copied from the same original, and all of them misunderstood the nature of these imperfections. They also made the eyes far too large, not realizing that the lids were closed by a coin—that their pattern was in fact a "death mask." Because they must have copied from the same "source," that original must have been the Shroud of Turin itself, even though custodians of it at various times were unaware of its true nature.

Figure 2.
The face of Jesus from the mosaic of the Transfiguration, St. Catherine's (left) and from an icon at St. Catherine's Mount Sinai. *(Courtesy Archbishop Damianos)*

Figure 3.
The face of Jesus from a Justinian II coin (left) *(Courtesy A. D. and M. Whanger)* and from a Constantine VII coin. *(Courtesy American Numismatic Society)*

Some of these distinctive features are definitely unartistic, as well as unnatural. For instance, between the brows is the troughlike marking of a three-sided square; attached just below it is a triangle, pointed downward. These features do appear on the Shroud face, though faintly; it is likely that these are blood traces that accidentally make that pattern. Also, many of the portraits show a space about three-quarters of an inch wide under the nose, between the two halves of the mustache—and in that bare space, the artists have put a dark, heavy, vertical line. It seems clear, with our present knowledge, that this was created by a rivulet of blood dripping onto the mustache from the septum of the nose. We notice that neither of these oddities are as noticeable on a photographic negative, but that was not an advantage the early artists had.

General features of many portraits of Jesus painted in the early centuries are largely consistent with each other and with the Shroud Face as well. These include an oval-shaped face, a prominent nose, deep-set eyes, long hair parted in the middle, and a forked beard. Uncommon features frequently involve overly large eyes, which one can speculate may have resulted from duplicating the swelling the Shroud exhibits from bruises and other injuries, or from the coins on the eyelids.

The work of Vignon, Wuenschel, and Wilson in pursuance of the iconographic thesis of identity has obviously been a laborious one of measurement and comparison to find the commonalities in more than a score of early faces of Jesus, which now appear to have been copied from the Shroud. They have doubtless painstakingly considered and rejected twice that many. Consequently, it is fascinating to reflect upon the impact that Dr. Whanger's "polarized image overlay" technique can have on these comparison studies (discussed in detail in chapter 11), since the comparisons he has made have detected from 33 to 74 points of congruence when matched with the Shroud Face. He concludes that the Byzantine icon face and the face on the Justinian II coin are so nearly identical to the Face of the Shroud that they *must* have been based on a copying from the Shroud by artists. Whanger believes that this overlay comparison is so accurate that the procedure should be considered as reliable as fingerprint identification.

Considering the logistical problems early artists faced, we must be truly amazed at the fidelity and accuracy they achieved. For instance, take the icon face (a painting in a monastery on a mountaintop at the southern tip of the Sinai Peninsula), and the Justinian II coin (minted in Constantinople). During the four-hundred-year period from about 550 to 944, the Image of Edessa was kept and frequently venerated in a church (and later a cathedral) in Edessa (which is situated between the headwaters of the Euphrates and Tigris Rivers, 150 miles east of the nearest Mediterranean port. Constantinople is approximately 600 miles northwest of Edessa and Mount Sinai about 600 miles southwest). When an artist reached Edessa, we can suppose he spent many days (or even weeks) taking careful and precise measurements of the Image and making many sketches, doubtless using a variety of lighting arrangements to bring more image definition to the Shroud Face. He must have been exceptionally talented, for each resulting work of art now has scores of points of congruence when overlaid with the Face of the Shroud in *a photographic negative,* which he could neither see nor understand!

It is typical of some of the earliest copies of the Image of Edessa that the eyes are closed. Interestingly, in the Genoa Church of St. Bartholomew is an Edessa image copy with eyes open. When x-rayed at successive depths (a process called tomography), it was found that the original icon had had closed eyes, but it was overpainted to show open eyes.

Vignon's early observation that lightness and darkness of the Shroud body image seemed to vary with the distance between the body and the cloth, led to the Jackson/Jumper work in 1975–77 (chapter 8) that validated Vignon and resulted in 3-D pictures projected by computer. Shortly thereafter, similar 3-D projection by computer was done in Italy by Tamburelli. Previously, however, in the middle 1960s, Leo Vala, a London artist and photographer, developed his own three-dimensional technique by projecting a transparency image with an epidiascope. He first made a lifesize transparency of the Shroud Face negative. Next he prepared a large lump of white modeling clay and projected the transparency image onto it. He then slowly and carefully molded the clay, conforming it to the shape indicated by the tones on the clay of the transparency image being projected. The result was incredibly lifelike and extremely faithful to the Shroud Face.[1]

Once the Shroud was known and well publicized throughout Europe (1357 and afterward), numerous artists utilized the Shroud's facial features. Rubens and Van Dyck did so more than once. A Rubens (1577–1640) painting of Jesus after the Shroud image shows nail wounds in the wrists.

In early 1984, I learned of the work of Thomas Goyne, a reconstructive artist employed by the State Police of Virginia. As a forensic sculptor he often is asked to create a face from a skull or other sketchy evidence to facilitate identification. Intrigued by the possibilities for Shroud research, I telephoned and then corresponded with Goyne and found that he was strongly interested in attempting a reconstruction of the face and bust of the Man of the Shroud from the Shroud of Turin.

Once his interest was well established by documents and preliminary materials that I provided, I put Goyne in touch with Rev. Albert R. ("Kim") Dreisbach, a retired Episcopal priest in Atlanta who is director of the Shroud of Turin Center and Exhibition there. Dreisbach was able to furnish Goyne with various scientific materials produced by the STURP project. Goyne approached the problem from two directions: First, he carefully examined and measured all of the ancient Palestine skulls available at the Smithsonian Institution in Washington, D.C.; then he used the Shroud image data to develop a computer program to guide his sculpting. The result was two busts, "before and after," of the Man of the Shroud—one as he probably appeared naturally, and the other, after the crucifixion, showing all the marks of his passion. Both busts are now the property of the Atlanta Shroud Center.

Thomas Heaphy, a prominent English painter, accompanied scientists in the mid-nineteenth century in reopening and exploring the Roman catacombs. Heaphy found a number of paintings of Jesus on the walls and ceilings of some of the rooms and passageways and made careful copies of them by candlelight, which he later published in the form of etchings that are preserved in the British Museum Library, London. There they lay untouched for more than a century. His work was rediscovered by Rex Morgan, a Shroud of Turin researcher/author, and photographs of the Heaphy material were included in Morgan's *The Holy Shroud and the Earliest Paintings of Christ*, 1985. Morgan later made photographs of the originals during a 1993 visit to the catacombs (they will appear in a future book). The full-face Heaphy copies of the Jesus face have been found by Alan and Mary Whanger to be overwhelmingly accurate (152 points of congruence) when compared with the Shroud Face. This Face, from the Domitilla Catacomb, has been dated to A.D. 40 to 60 and may well have been based on a Shroud face copy made in Edessa during its public period there, A.D. 33 to 57.

In May 1996, Morgan again visited the Domitilla Catacomb (specifically, the Orpheus Cubiculum chamber of same), together with his son, Christopher, a photographer, and Isabel Piczek, world-renowned artist and art expert. Of the several catacomb faces of Jesus, the one in this chamber is considered to be the best.

Most artists in recent times prefer to take artistic license, and thus only limited identity with the Shroud will be found. Two outstanding exceptions should be noted.

The first is a portrait of Jesus painted in 1935 by Ariel Agemian. An artist and linguist, Agemian was a scholarly Armenian educated in Venice by the Mechitarists, an order of monks of the Catholic Armenian Church, headquartered in Venice. Agemian's Face of Jesus is based

Figure 4.
This Face of Jesus, in the Orpheus Cubiculum chamber of the Catacomb of Domitilla, Rome, has been dated to about A.D. 45. This reproduction of the face was made in mid-nineteenth century by Thomas Heaphy. *(Courtesy Rex Morgan)*

Figure 5.
This profile Face of Jesus, from the Roman catacombs, cannot be scientifically compared with the Shroud Face. *(Courtesy Rex Morgan)*

directly on the Shroud Image. The face is basically in sepia and varying shades of brown, including brown eyes, hair, and beard. It is a very compelling and provocative face, with eyes that seem hypnotically to hold one's attention.

The Agemian Face is such an accurate duplicate of the Shroud's facial dimensions that the Holy Shroud Guild has used the two faces in commissioning a special "double effect" portrait for home study and inspiration. The result is superficially comparable to Dr. Whanger's scientific technique discussed in chapter 11. The Guild has mounted these two faces one on top of the other in a single frame, by a process known as a Super Xograph (a laser-controlled, three-dimensional technique). The surface of the portrait is ridged, or serrated. Remarkably, by tilting the portrait, the process permits the viewer to see first one face, then the other. Straight-on, one sees the Agemian face. If one side is pulled toward the viewer, at an angle of about 45 degrees, the Shroud face is seen. A tilt in between these two extremes results in a blurring of the two faces together, and the complete single identity of the features of the two can easily be seen.[2]

The other portrait of Jesus was painted in 1970 by American artist Ris Phillips of Phoenix, Arizona. Her portrait was commissioned under very unusual circumstances by Col. Frank O. Adams (Ret.) of Tucson. While lecturing in England in 1966 on the subject of meditation, his host showed him a photograph of the Shroud of Turin and told him its story in outline. Adams knew immediately that he had to learn more and that he had to devote himself significantly to publicizing the Shroud story in the United States. Slide-lectures from coast to coast became a part of his effort, but his reading of Shroud lore convinced him that a more meaningful Face of Jesus than was available should be painted, based on the dimensions of the Shroud face.

Adams's reading brought him into touch with a very esoteric little book titled *The Archko Volume,* edited by W. D. Mahan[3] and first published in 1887. Mahan, a Missouri preacher, became so intrigued by stories of old religious records that he consulted American experts, sailed to Europe, consulted with experts in England and France, hired researchers, translators, and clerks, and spent several months in the

Figure 6.
The face of Jesus, Christ Enthroned, a mosaic in the narthex of Hagia Sophia Cathedral, Istanbul (above). *(Courtesy Centro Internazionale della Sindone of Turin)* The face of Jesus, Christ Enthroned, sixth century, in Sant' Apollinare Nuovo Church, Ravenna, Italy (below left), and in the Palatine Chapel, Palermo, Sicily, twelfth century (below right). *(Courtesy John Gitchell)*

libraries of the Vatican and of the Mosque of St. Sophia in Constantinople, searching out and copying old records purporting to date from the days of Jesus. Adams knew very well that such material could not be validated; he was nonetheless fascinated by three of Mahan's documents, purporting to give eyewitness descriptions of Jesus, including the color of his hair and eyes. Knowing that Jesus was not described at all in the Bible, and finding these descriptions consistent with each other and with both apocryphal and mystical descriptions, Adams carefully copied the text of these descriptions. In part, the three excerpts from *The Archko Volume* are:

- From a letter written by Publius Lentulus, governor of Judea, to the Roman Senate and Tiberius Caesar: "He is a tall, well-proportioned man and there is an air of severity in his countenance which at once attracts the love and reverence of those who see him. His hair is the color of new wine, from the roots to the ears, and thence to the shoulders; it is curled and falls down to the lowest part of them. Upon the forehead it parts in two after the manner of the Nazarenes. His forehead is flat and fair; his face without blemish or defect and adorned with a graceful expression. His nose and mouth are very well proportioned. His beard is thick and the color of his hair; his eyes are *gray* and extremely lively."

- From a report by Gamaliel, teacher of Saul of Tarsus, addressed to the Sanhedrin, and quoting from a philosopher, Massalian: "He is the picture of his mother, only he has not her smooth, round face. His hair is a little more golden than hers, though it is as much from sunburn as anything else. He is tall, and his shoulders are a little drooped; his visage is thin and of a swarthy complexion, though this is from exposure. His eyes are large and a soft blue and rather dull and heavy. The lashes are long, and his eyebrows very large. His nose is that of a Jew."

- From a report by Pilate to Emperor Tiberias: "I observed in the midst of the group a young man who was leaning against a tree, calmly addressing the multitude. I was told it was Jesus. This I could easily have suspected, so great was the difference between him and those listening to him. His golden-colored hair and beard gave his appearance a celestial aspect. He appeared to be about thirty years of age. Never have I seen a sweeter or more serene countenance."

At the time, Colonel Adams was living in Virginia Beach, Virginia, where he was senior executive and lecturer for the Association for Research and Enlightenment. During his daily meditation period he heard a voice tell him to take the Shroud Face and these descriptions to the artist Ris Phillips for a painting of the face of Jesus. He had met Ris Phillips once, but felt that he hardly knew her. Nevertheless, at the first opportunity he visited her and proposed a portrait of Jesus based on the data mentioned. Phillips surprised him by saying that in a meditative period she had thought of Adams and felt that he would call on her. Accordingly, she undertook his commission to paint the face of Jesus.

Ris Phillips is a native of California who married a member of the U.S. Air Force and traveled with her husband and their children on his various assignments, including foreign tours. During his duty in Libya, events in Ris's personal life caused her to read the Bible intensively and delve deeply into religion. Mrs. Phillips is a self-taught artist, and three times she had been commissioned to paint the face of Jesus. However, when she began to work on Adams's special commission, with guidance from the Shroud Face dimensions and the detailed descriptions resulting from Adams's research, she realized at once that this was to be no ordinary work of art. "It was so much more meaningful that I put myself and my religious feelings into every stroke of the brush," she says.

Phillips's portrait for Adams presents a most striking visage. Handsome and perfectly proportioned, the face nevertheless seems totally masculine and virile. The reddish brown hair and beard and the medium blue eyes attractively set off the high forehead and strong-boned face. The mustache does not hide the well-formed lips. The eyes seem to look into the depths of the viewer.[4]

Apart from coloration, many apocryphal accounts seem to support the idea that Jesus was handsome. These include the "Life and Passion of St. Caecilius," the "Passion of Saints Perpetua and Felicitas," the "Actus Vercellensis," and "Acts of John"—the latter describes Jesus as "a handsome youth with a smiling face."

As to the reddish color of Jesus' hair and beard, as described above, it is interesting to note that during the trial of Templars de Molay and de Charnay, witnesses who described the "face" or "head" the Templars were accused of worshiping testified that the image had a red beard. Also (as covered in chapter 3), when a copy of the Templar face was found in a ruin in Templecombe, England, it did indeed have a red beard. There is no indication of why the Templars, who were apparently copying the Shroud face, thought the beard should be red; they had certainly looted many archives in Jerusalem and environs that might have persuaded them in that regard.

In the early 1970s authors O. Preston Robinson and Christine H. Robinson wrote an article in *Church News* about their research in the Cambridge (England) University Library, where they examined an old book with leather pages written in Latin. In the back of it was a complete translation into English. It purported to contain copies from ancient documents found in Palestine. One document was said to have been copied by Emperor Theodosius the Great from the public registers of Pontius Pilate. Among other things, the document contained descriptions of Jesus, saying that his hair was "the color of a hazelnut, almost ripe; it lies plain to his ears and then cutteth into rings ... and lies waving upon his shoulders." Another, attributed to Nicephorus's *Ecclesiastical History,* described his hair as "inclining to a yellow color, not very thick and curling at the ends ... his beard yellow, but not long. The hair of his head a considerable length because it had never been shaved or cut." This last is most interesting in view of the findings of American scientists that seem to support the suggestion (from the dorsal image of the Shroud) that the Man on the Shroud had hair down his back caught in ponytail fashion. With reference to Adams's use of the Lentulus description of Jesus (above), the Robinsons' report an old *Classical Dictionary* of 1841 by Charles Anthon that lists Gaetulicus

Lentulus as consul at Jerusalem in A.D. 26, who was later executed by Emperor Caligula for "conspiracy."

Apart from coloration, both of the faces of Jesus featured in this chapter are extremely accurate as to the contours of the face of the Man on the Shroud. However, the suggestion of a tall Jesus, with chestnut or reddish hair and beard and eyes of gray or blue, may bother some persons who feel that all Jews of that period must have been short, with curly black hair and black or brown eyes. Not necessarily. Archaeologists have shown that many of Jesus' contemporaries were six feet or more in height. This was not uncommon. As to coloration, we must remember that some seven hundred years before Jesus' time, Assyria carried off most of the northern ten tribes of Israel and brought

Figure 7.

The face of Jesus, twelfth century, Martorana, Palermo, Sicily (below); on the cross, early-thirteenth-century painting at the Church of the Mother of God (left), Studenicia, Yugoslavia. *(Courtesy John Gitchell)*

other captive peoples into Israel to repopulate the land by forced inter-marriage with the remaining Jews. The latter, intermarried, were the Samaritans of Jesus' time. As Jews of mixed blood drifted back to Israel, Galilee, and Judea over those seven centuries, it is a fact that some of them were blondes and redheads.

For some, the negative Shroud Face can be a very powerful focus and inspiration in times of prayer and meditation, particularly for those who are most comfortable with an imprecise and mysterious image. Others (especially the "visualizers") may prefer a truly natural and life-like image of Jesus, and they may find a more compatible inspiration in the Agemian or Phillips portraits. Either unadorned or "brought to life" by an artist's talents, the Shroud Face is claimed by many to evoke

Figure 8.
The face of Jesus, the Spas Nereditsa, Moscow (left) *(Courtesy John Gitchell)*, and a statue of Parthian King Uthal of Hatra, in Baghdad. Note the trel-liswork pattern of his robe, similar to that surrounding the Spas Nereditsa, which may have been used to trans-form the Shroud of Gareb Hill (Jeru-salem) into the Mandylion of Edessa and Constantinople. *(Courtesy Dept. of Antiquities, Baghdad)*

the Christ presence in their "quiet time," and this after all may be what Pope Paul VI had in mind when he expressed the wish that for Christians, the Shroud might "introduce them to a more penetrating vision of His inmost and fascinating mystery."

TWENTY

CONCLUSIONS: SCIENTIFIC, RELIGIOUS, AND PERSONAL

A T THE time the Shroud of Turin was first publicly presented in Lirey, France, in 1357, the only form of Christianity in Western Europe was Roman Catholicism (there were Eastern Orthodox churches in Russia and Asia Minor). Protestantism was nearly two hundred years in the future, and independent Christian denominations much farther than that. Thus, the private owners of the relic would of necessity be Roman Catholics. But, it cannot be said that the Shroud is strictly a Catholic relic. The Shroud is a Christian relic in the broadest sense, and the entire human race should be interested. For that reason, this presentation has been made as comprehensive as possible, and I have endeavored to keep the influence of my personal biases to a minimum.

The reasonable meaning and effect of so broad a presentation is difficult to assess in a simple manner. As an initial summary, the British churchman Dr. John A. T. Robinson has put it well. Regarding the possibility that this was the actual cloth that wrapped the body of Jesus of Nazareth, Robinson says that the Man of the Shroud image was "almost certainly a Jew, of the right age, who suffered death by crucifixion. Though most of the marks of this barbarous punishment would not point distinctively to this one man, the evidence of severe injury to the scalp by a 'crown of thorns' surely cannot reasonably be posited of any usual victim: it was a mock coronation as King of the Jews.... If then everything else were to prove positive, there must be a strong presumption that it belonged to this man. We cannot say more, but neither, I think, can we say less. If then it were this very cloth, what difference would it make?"[1]

There seems to be a solid consensus among the medical experts that the Man of the Shroud was 30 to 40 years of age, 175 to 185 pounds, and six feet tall (plus or minus two inches). He was well built and muscular—a man accustomed to manual labor. The coins on his eyes indicate that his death occurred probably between 29 and 36, during the governorship of Pontius Pilate as procurator of Palestine. But there was no painting of Jesus made from life, and the Bible gives no physical description of him, nor does it note any deformities or special physical features, and no hair and beard style is indicated. (Of course, blood type, dental record, fingerprints, and facial type are unknown.)

The Shroud images are unusual in several respects:

- the body images are photographic negatives;

- they are superficial and run only one or two fibrils deep into the threads;

- the images encode three-dimensional data that a computer can translate into a relief image;

- the images are non directional, showing a total absence of brush-strokes or other indication of physical application;

- they are pressure-independent, with front and back views compatible;

- there is a lack of image saturation;

- variation is by shading and density without change in color;

- there is exact anatomical and pathological data and lack of distortion;

- they were not made by paint or other additive;

- they have been unaffected by heat or water;

- actual primate blood, probably human, has made the photographically positive blood images;

- the blood in many areas has penetrated to the reverse side of the cloth;

- the bloodstains relate to four different periods covering about twelve hours;

- bloodstains and blood clots, whether fresh or dried, are unbroken and unsmeared (experimentation proves there is no way a cloth like the Shroud could be *lifted* from a body or a statue without either smearing or breaking bloodstains or blood clots that are thirty-six hours old or less);

- the Shroud images are consistent with medical and pathological knowledge, with Roman practices, with Jewish ritual, with history, and with the Bible;

- scientifically, this is not the image of a man lying on his back, but the image of a man upright but not standing;

- the image is consistent with known scientific data *only* if it be postulated that the image was imprinted on the cloth as the upper half of same *fell through* the body space.

The Shroud body image is a true "mirror-image," and so, if the "rays" of the body had come *up* to the cloth they would have made this image that *does* exist, *only* if the cloth had been *flat and stiff* as a board lying atop the body. Any draping or curvature of the cloth would have distorted the image as a funhouse mirror does.

Of course, the suggestion remains that this is the Shroud of Jesus and that the images on it were made without physical explanation and by a spiritual energy as part of a spiritual event we call the Resurrection. This explanation will never be proven, but I personally believe it.

Textile analysis of the Shroud cloth resulted in conclusions that:

- the weave (3-to-1 herringbone twill) had been used in the Middle East of the first century, but was at that time unknown in Europe;

- cotton traces in the linen cloth meant that it had been woven on a loom previously used to weave cotton cloth—virtually precluding European production;

- it almost certainly was made in the Near East (Syria to Mesopotamia to Egypt) and could have been made in the first century;

- the Z-twist thread was distinctive of the Near East of the first century, but was then unknown in Europe.

The pollen studies of Dr. Frei seem to establish beyond doubt that the Shroud was exposed to the air in Palestine, southern Turkey, and western Turkey, and that this clearly could have occurred in the first century.

A type of *light* radiation rather than *heat* radiation seems most strongly indicated as the agency making the Shroud image. The points that elude us are the exact technique that created the images, knowledge and capability to replicate the images, and the identity of the person on the Shroud.

Dr. Eric Jumper has said: "We can conclude that the Shroud image is that of a real, human form; of a scourged, crucified man. It is not the product of an artist. The bloodstains are composed of hemoglobin."

William Deerfield, *Guideposts* associate editor, said: "For the Doubting Thomas in each of us, could it be that Jesus Christ did leave something in the tomb on that first Easter morning—a faint, straw-yellow image on a fragile linen cloth—a kind of 'affidavit'?"[2]

Concerning the work of her peers at Turin, one scientist commented: "Regarding the Shroud of Turin, I think Albert Einstein indirectly but perfectly explained how the Shroud was made. $E=Mc^2$ succinctly states that matter and energy are interconvertible. Perhaps Christ did demonstrate the cosmic circus trick—he dematerialized and became energy. Perhaps in the process, an image was formed from the release of such energy before it was dispersed into the atmosphere.... Some of the mysteries of the universe may be locked within the force that created the markings on a piece of linen nearly 2,000 years ago."[3]

A prominent member of the STURP team, Ray N. Rogers of the

Los Alamos Scientific Laboratory, has mused philosophically: "What better way, if you were a deity, of regenerating faith in a skeptical age, than to leave evidence 2,000 years ago that could be defined only by the technology available in that skeptical age?"

The Shroud data is strong enough to *permit* a belief that it is the burial shroud of Jesus, but that data will not *compel* such a belief. The subject does not permit many certainties. Thus it is wholly inappropriate to speak of "proof" or "failure of proof" as to the identity of the Man of the Shroud. Some small areas of investigation of the Shroud permit limited scientific certainty, and several general negatives have been possible in the course of this scientific inquiry; the scientists of STURP have wisely confined themselves to these areas. No current STURP member has made claims as to the Man's identity.

One of the strongest logical arguments, advanced by Herbert Thurston, a British Jesuit, affirming that the Shroud did enwrap Jesus of Nazareth, is the suggestion that (with so many details on the Shroud fitting Jesus and apparently fitting no one else *totally*) if this Shroud was not made in some paranormal way by Jesus the Christ, then it must have been fabricated and faked to make it appear to be Jesus. No other alternatives seem reasonable. Yet the scientific evidence makes abundantly clear that this Shroud is *not* a fabricated fake!

In any event, the scientific data and conclusions of the STURP evaluations seem, on the basis of today's science, to leave us no alternative but a supernatural cause for the Shroud images (which is beyond the purview of science to explain)—thus taking us back to the tomb of Joseph of Arimathea on that first Easter.

Thus two crucial questions remain: Considering the facts that have now been established about the Man on the Shroud, could the man have been anyone other than Jesus of Nazareth? Considering the inexplicable nature of the Shroud image, could it have been imprinted on the linen in any manner except by a miracle performed by Jesus the Christ?

Regardless of the answer to these questions, we must acknowledge that there will never be an exact identification of the Man on the Shroud by direct evidence.

Perhaps a restatement of definitions of the word "resurrection" may help our perspective. First, "human resurrection" is a simple transition through the door of "death" from earthly life to heavenly life; movement to an altered state of consciousness involving a dropping of the physical body and a freeing of the spiritual body. This occurred to Jesus on the cross, just before the soldier's spear thrust. Second, Jesus was Christed, probably at Jordan. Third, "christological resurrection" may have happened only once in history; it must have happened on Easter morning in Jesus' tomb. It was apparently marked by a subatomically-generated blast of power, the results of which included the dematerialization of Jesus' physical body, the nuclear photography of the images on the burial shroud, the blast of the boulder from the door of the tomb, and the earthquake. The purpose and reasons can only be speculated upon.

The Greek mystic-poet-author-philosopher-politician Nikos Kazantzakis, wrote:

> Christ… leans over, blows on the worms, and the air fills with butterflies. That's the meaning of resurrection—the worms must become butterflies, and not simply be turned into immortal worms.

Speaking of the Shroud of Turin, the Reverend Adam J. Otterbein, president of the Holy Shroud Guild, has said:

> We have to start with the fact that there are two kinds of thinking—*cognitive thinking,* where evidence is measured and proof is possible, and *faith thinking,* where you feel responsibility to act or take a stand but there is no way to obtain compelling proof. Relics are in the realm of faith thinking. The great value of a relic is that by making demands on faith, it gets *faith thinking* started. A relic is a stimulator to devotion. Seeing the Shroud makes us realize better how Christ suffered for us.

Along the same lines, Christianity does not *require* such signs as the Shroud of Turin. Christianity is a matter of faith and must always remain so. But, how many Christians have faith so solid and unfalter-ing, so infallibly certain, that they would not benefit by the Shroud's demonstration of a reality that transcends scientific explanation?

How many Christians have such faith that, with open minds they would not be struck by the brilliance of the Shroud's mystical vision? Christianity has many pitfalls: complacency in a religion that demands too little; agnosticism in a religion that does not answer the hard ques-tions; faltering faith in a religion that seems impractical. The reality of the Shroud can jolt the Christian, high and low, out of such pitfalls.

That Jesus of Nazareth was a very special son of God, I have no per-sonal doubt. That he was totally unique, the "only begotten Son"—that his conception, birth, baptism, message, and life were totally unique—are matters on which I have no special authority or competence to speak to others, and on which I feel no compelling need to resolve for myself. Answers for them depend too much on words and the mean-ing of words and are not fully relevant to my conviction as a Christian. The Easter Resurrection of Jesus the Christ I consider crucial to my faith, and on the Shroud of Turin I see that phenomenon meticulously pictured. That action has not been paralleled in the knowledge of man, and the Shroud, as a probable relic of that event, is totally unique in the world. Moreover, intrinsically and extrinsically, the Shroud's own testi-mony must be highly compelling to any thinking person, and none of the evidence of any kind concerning it militates in the slightest degree against its presumed authenticity, or its identification with Jesus.

If one asks of the scientific data,—"Is the Shroud authentic?"—the answer must be "Yes" because it is not a fraud, not made by trickery or clever artifice; it is not great art made by the hand of man, nor a process of nature that might be expected to happen again. Therefore, *it is an authentic artifact.*

However, when one asks the more difficult questions of the scien-tific data—What is the Shroud image? Who was the pattern for the figure on the Shroud? Was it Jesus of Nazareth? How were the images made? Did the Christ-power of Jesus' spirit create the images? Can it be duplicated?—the answers, if there are any, may be negative, and will be more limited and qualified, and of the "don't know" genre. There will be less certitude, and some, understandably, may even say that science will never give us these answers about the Shroud of Turin.

And yet, if one should ask these questions of the heart—of one's own soul—for the Christian, certainly, upon examining the solid evidence and the compelling logic now available respecting the Shroud, he will see that only a small leap of faith is required from this pedestal of knowledge—and the *knowing* will be one of confidence.

The evidence of the Shroud is imperfect and incomplete, but this is the way with most situations in life where one makes judgments and decisions. If the reader wishes to evaluate the evidence of the Shroud, he might do well to consider himself in the situation of a juror. In most court cases the jury must render its judgment on the basis of conflicting and incomplete evidence, because perfect and complete proof is not possible. Experts for the plaintiff and the defendant swear to opinions exactly opposite to each other. On the same evidence, handwriting experts disagree as to the author of a disputed document; fingerprint experts disagree as to whether a print was made by a certain person; chemical engineer experts reach opposite conclusions as to a substance and its effect; doctors disagree as to whether an injury will be disabling; and so it goes. But a judgment can be, and is, rendered by the jury. Similarly, you, as a juror before the Shroud, can decide if the evidence is reasonable or meaningless, is believable, is convincing or unimpressive, is overwhelming. Is the Shroud plausible and probable? Is its message sensible and meaningful? What is your judgment?

Author's Afterword:
A Fourteenth-Century Cloth?
Don't You Believe It

If today's greatest artists, artisans, technicians, and scientists, individually or in concert, cannot create a Shroudlike image on cloth, why should we believe that an unknown expert of the fourteenth century could have done it? This Shroud, with its mystical images, is an archaeological artifact of ancient provenance, and it presents a collection of anomalies that modern science cannot explain—an enigma to us all.

In the five years following the carbon-dating announcement of October 13, 1988, seven major scientific symposia were held, which included powerful papers supporting authenticity claims on behalf of the Shroud, and several of those papers are summarized in the Special Introduction to this edition.[1]

What do I mean by "authenticity"? The scientific, historical, and other technical data that I refer to as supporting authenticity do unequivocally support the probability of a first-century or very early date for this Shroud and its enigmatic images, and as having originated in the Near East (likely Palestine). Science has not *proven* (and in my opinion will never categorically prove) this to be specifically the Shroud of Jesus of Galilee. Believers will always need a small leap of faith from the pedestal of knowledge Shroud research has provided. But that research has established that the Shroud images cannot have been man-made by any technique of art or science recorded throughout history, nor by any natural process ever observed or deduced. And *all* alternative theoretical or suspected methods of image-creation suggested by the critics have been carefully and totally demolished by Shroud scientists as *not possible*. As to "authenticity," we know this Shroud with its images is not a phony, a fake, a fraud, an imitation, a copy, to any degree or in any respect; it was not made in the past thousand years; a fourteenth-century origin is virtually *impossible*. Science still does not know how the images were "imprinted" on the Shroud.

The full, official scientific report of the carbon-dating of the Shroud was published in London's pretigious scientific journal *Nature* in February 1989. But has that report satisfied the scientific community? It has not! Hardly had the dust settled (the C-14 fallout?) from that report before science specialists worldwide began pointing out sizable and very basic flaws in the entire carbon-dating activity. *Nature* for May 31, 1990, and *Science News* for June 9, 1990, reported on recent evaluation of ocean floor cores of corals in the Barbados that seems to establish that "the carbon-14 clock has been running fast"!—one reason being that "the ice-age atmosphere [was] holding up to 40 percent more carbon-14 than today's"; also, "because the half-life used... is 3 percent too small, but most of it is caused by an increase in atmospheric C-14 activity over time." Even more serious and more basic has been the suggestion that the statistical speculation relating to C-14 decay-rate is based on the time structure of Newtonian physics—the validity of which is now put seriously into question by the new time scenario in modern physics.

Nor can the laboratories' competence any longer be presumed as beyond question. J. Erwin in his 1983 article "Materials of Terrestrial Origin Used for Radiocarbon Dating" (PACT 8:235–276) states:

> ...The samples to be dated should contain carbon. However, the mere presence of this chemical element is not sufficient to produce a valid result. After many years of C-14 dating it has been shown that numerous results are in error or are erroneously interpreted, often because of lack of knowledge about the value of the material selected for dating."

And recent reports of outrageous errors rampant in carbon-dating generally tell us much about reliability of the process.

1) *Science* magazine, December 1988, reported that *live* snails, still in their shells, were carbon-dated to 26,000 years ago.

2) *Antarctic* periodical recently reported that a freshly killed seal was carbon-dated as being dead for 1,300 years.

3) *Radiocarbon* magazine announced that the skin of a mammoth that had lived 26,000 years ago was carbon-dated to 5,600 years old.

4) The British Research Council gave 38 laboratories around the world an object of known age for testing by C-14 techniques; only seven labs gave acceptable results.

5) The Zurich laboratory (involved in the Shroud exercise) tested a lady's linen handkerchief, known to be no more than 50 years old, and recorded for it an age of 350 years.

6) The Tucson laboratory (also involved in the Shroud exercise) dated a Viking horn of A.D. 2006—the animal hadn't yet been born!—and this list of horrors can be multiplied by dozens more examples.

Although others have done so both generally and specifically, I am not presently questioning the honesty, propriety, and judgment of those acting for the Church, the British Museum, and the three laboratories involved in the 1988 dating exercise. The issues I do raise are the weaknesses and inadequacy—and possible inappropriateness—of the C-14 tools utilized, and of the probable laws of the 1988 exercise. In these connections it is relevant to note that science—just because it is science—should not be deemed beyond question and evaluation. In an editorial of July 6, 1989, the *Washington Post* cited "a whole range of questionable scientific practices including outright fraud, fudging or sloppiness in the lab, ordinary error… financial conflict of interest… lies about results… more pressures besides simple criminality driving sciences to cheat"—peer review and self-policing is no longer enough.

At the Rome Symposium on the Shroud of Turin, June 10–12, 1993, we attendees were treated to several very impressive scientific papers that addressed the flaws in the carbon-dating exercise of 1988 and the weaknesses in the basic process. Dr. Marie-Claire Van

Oosterwyck-Gastuche, an expert from the Royal Museum of Central Africa, explained that many of the contaminants known to be on the Shroud *do* resist the chemical cleaning procedures essential to the laboratory process; also, that no laboratory experience exists in the dating of linen cloth. Andrey A. Ivanov of the Lenin Institute in Russia criticized both the scientific assumptions and the statistical evaluations made by the three labs that use the "accelerated mass spectrometer" (AMS) technique to test the samples taken from the Shroud cloth in 1988. He stated that flax (from which linen is made) varies widely from one climate and soil to another; also, in flax-spinning the stems are routinely eliminated (which would eliminate lipids and proteins) and the resulting linen fibers (97 percent cellulose) thus will contain much more carbon-14 than the living plant, so that the cloth when tested appears much "younger" than it actually is. He concludes that the radiocarbon method will always find "impossibilities" when used for textile dating. And most important, Dr. Leoncio A. Garza-Valdes of San Antonio, Texas, explained that a natural microbe, the "isodiametric," frequently found on ancient artifacts, exudes a gel known as "lichenothelia varnish," which he found on pieces of cloth and on fibers removed from the Shroud by Scotch tape in 1978. The relevance of this finding is the high carbon-14 nature of the varnish, which could easily skew the carbon-dating of the Shroud by a thousand years or more. Unfortunately, the labs that did the 1988 dating made no microscopic examination of their Shroud samples before testing; Garza-Valdes lists eleven pre-test examinations they could have made. Dr. Remi Van Haelst, a statistician from Belgium, agreed with Oosterwyck-Gastuche and Ivanov that the laboratories' statistics were significantly faulty, and that same were *meaningless* because they did not use "blind testing."

Dr. Garza-Valdes's arguments were further buttressed by reports at a special C-14/Shroud symposium held in San Antonio in September 1993, and in four subsequent symposia.

As to the *impossibility* of a fourteenth-century date for the Shroud, it is worthy of special note that historians, especially Daniel C. Scavone and Ian Wilson among others, have now demonstrated by impressive evidence the ancient documents and art that *this* Shroud, bearing the *full* image of a crucified man, existed in Constantinople in A.D. 944 and was known by art copies in Egypt in the mid-sixth century.

As was alluded to by Father Rinaldi in the Special Introduction to this edition, the carbon-dating report of 1988 merely "expanded and extended the multi-faceted controversy which has raged about this Shroud" (under its various names, the "Face of Edessa," "the Mandylion," "the Shroud of Turin") since at least the year A.D. 944. On the very day, August 15, 944, that it was brought to the Byzantine emperor by his military task force, the emperor's sons, Stephen and Constantine, who upon viewing the image-on-cloth, promptly expressed disdain for so vague and unnatural a human face. But Constantine Porphyrogenitus, who would become emperor in just a few months, was an artist, and said that as an artist he could discern Jesus' portrait clearly (though of course it was a photographic negative picture, then nine hundred years before the invention of photography; see chapter 2).

The news media promptly and fully reported the carbon-dating announcement of 1988. Yet the seven subsequent international symposia that have presented strong data for Shroud authenticity have hardly (if at all) been mentioned. One is tempted to suppose that the media operate on the philosophy "If it's not negative, it's not news."

Almost all skeptics and critics of the Shroud of Turin image claim or assume that it was a medieval painting. At several of the scientific symposia on the Shroud during the past two decades, including the one in Rome in 1993, Isabel H. Piczek of Los Angeles has presented highly impressive papers on this subject. Piczek is a professional monument-artist with a degree in draftsmanship. She has executed artworks in every ancient and modern technique known, including nearly five hundred giant-size items in public buildings throughout the world. Piczek, in her professional papers respecting the Shroud image has analyzed every aspect of the image, and concluded that *it is not and cannot be* a painting of any sort, technique, or medium. This conclusion is doubly important because, she cautions, the Shroud and its image *must not* be conserved *as a painting would be,* "or else we may destroy the only object on earth which is a blueprint of the future of our cosmos."

At the Shroud of Turin International Symposium of June 18–20, 1999, held in Richmond, Virginia, there were researchers in attendance from 16 countries and the U.S.A., with 35 of them presenting papers.

The 1969 work of Dr. Max Frei, claimed to establish that more than 50 varieties of pollen found only in the Near East had been lifted from the Shroud and identified. In the late 1990s, that work was validated, seemingly beyond question, by Professor Avinoam Danin of Hebrew University, Jerusalem, and botanist Uri Baruch of Jerusalem. They spent time with Dr. Whanger at Duke University and verified that more than two dozen of the pollen varieties found on the Shroud grow only in an area within 30 miles of Jerusalem, and pollinate in the months of March and April. Dr. Whanger reported this data at Richmond.

On August 2, 1999, Danin and Baruch reported these findings with further details to the International Botanical congress meeting in St. Louis, Missouri. They further reported that pollen grains of these species were also found on the Facecloth of Oviedo, and that both the Facecloth and the Shroud carry type AB blood.

* * *

[*Note added in press:* Two very recent news stories appearing on the Internet describe the status of the 1988 Carbon-14 testing of the Shroud. Readers should also see the official web site of the Shroud of Turin at http://sindone.torino.chiesacattolica.it/en/welcome.htm. General Editor]

NEW STUDY CONFIRMS ANCIENT ORIGIN FOR SHROUD OF TURIN

http://www.cwnews.com/news/viewstory.cfm?recnum=34747

Jan. 19, 2005 (CWNews.com [Catholic World News])—New scientific tests on the Shroud of Turin have confirmed that the cloth dates back to around the time of Christ. The results dismiss a 1988 study that claimed the cloth was manufactured in the 13th or 14th century.

The American Shroud of Turin Association for Research (AMST AR) found that the tests done in 1988, using carbon-14 dating techniques, were actually performed on a patch that had been skillfully woven onto the original cloth of the Shroud.

Tom D'Muhala, the president of AMSTAR, says that new chemical tests have shown that the main cloth of the Shroud is "actually very old—much older than the published 1988 radiocarbon date."

Chemist Raymond Rogers, a fellow of the Los Alamos National Laboratory in New Mexico, dismisses the results of the 1988 test in a study published in *Thermochemica Acta,* a peer-reviewed scientific journal. He reports finding that the cloth used for those tests "was not part of the original cloth of the Shroud of Turin." Rogers added: "The radiocarbon sample has completely different chemical properties than the main part of the Shroud relic."

PROMINENT LOS ALAMOS SCIENTIST PROVES 1988 CARBON-14 DATING OF THE SHROUD USED INVALID REWOVEN SAMPLE

By Barrie M. Schwartz
Shrouds of Turin Website
January 21, 2005

http://www.shroud.com/latebrak.htm#rogers

A new, peer reviewed scientific paper by Raymond N. Rogers, retired Fellow of the Los Alamos National Laboratory, was published on January 20, 2005, in the latest issue of the journal *Thermochimica Acta,* Volume 425, Issues 1–2, Pages 189–194. Titled "Studies on the radiocarbon sample from the Shroud of Turin," the paper concludes: "As unlikely as it seems, the sample used to test the age of the Shroud of Turin in 1988 was taken from a rewoven area of the Shroud. Pyrolysis-mass spectrometry results from the sample area coupled with microscopic and microchemical observations prove that the radiocarbon sample was not part of the original cloth of the Shroud of Turin. The radiocarbon date was thus not valid for determining the true age of the Shroud."

In a press release earlier this week, Rogers stated, "The radiocarbon sample has completely different chemical properties than the main part of the Shroud relic. The sample tested was dyed using technology that began to appear in Italy about the time the Crusaders' last bastion fell to the Turks in AD 1291. The radiocarbon sample cannot be older than about AD 1290, agreeing with the age determined (for the sample) in 1988. However, the Shroud itself is actually much older."

As a result of his own research and chemical tests, Rogers concluded that the radiocarbon sample is totally different in composition from the main part of the Shroud of Turin and was cut from a medieval reweaving of the cloth. Rogers was also the leader of the chemistry group for the Shroud of Turin Research Project (STURP), the scientific team that performed the first in-depth scientific examination of the Shroud in 1978.

You can access the journal paper (or at least the abstract) at the following link: http://dx.doi.org/10.1016/j.tca.2004.09.029. Once there, if you click on the link to "Volume 425, Issues 1-2" at the bottom left of the page, it will open the table of contents for this volume. In the table of contents, scroll down to number 26, Ray's paper, and click on the "Summary Plus" link. That will take you to the entire paper, which is currently available gratis, but that will probably change very soon. In future, one will have to register and pay a fee to access the full text and illustrations. However, the free link to the abstract is permanent.

Rogers' new research clearly disproves the 1988 findings announced by British Museum spokesperson, Michael Tite, when he declared that the Shroud was of medieval origin and probably "a hoax." The British Museum coordinated the 1988 radiocarbon tests and acted as the official clearing house for all findings. Interestingly, the original carbon-14 dating protocol had called for chemical analysis of the samples prior to their destruction during the testing. However, that analysis was never performed by any of the three dating laboratories. Each lab was given a small portion of the single sample cut from a corner of the Shroud specifically for the tests. It is difficult to predict whether the anomalous nature of the sample would have been detected had the chemical analysis been performed, but it might have led the laboratories to request additional samples be taken from other areas of the Shroud to validate the accuracy of their results. As it was, the three laboratories concluded that their results were correct to a 95% certainty, a claim that, according to some experts, is difficult to support based on the single sample tested.

Another issue that arose in Ray Rogers' study was the finding of cotton fibers in the sample used for C-14 dating. There was no cotton found in any of the samples taken by the STURP team from the main body of the Shroud cloth in 1978. Yet even the Oxford lab, one of the three labs that performed the C-14 dating in 1988, reported they found cotton in the fibers of the sample they tested. My thanks to Rev. Albert "Kim" Dreisbach, Jr., for providing me with the additional information and several references to this cotton issue in an e-mail today. I have included his comments at the following link: Cotton Fiber in C-14 Sample:

http://www.shroud.com/pdfs/cotton.pdf

Almost immediately after the results were released in 1988, Shroud analysts questioned the validity of the sample used for the dating. In fact, one researcher with considerable experience in radiocarbon dating ancient artifacts, University of Hong Kong based archaeologist William Meacham, presented a paper in 1986, two years before the infamous dating, outlining his concerns. Titled, "Radiocarbon Measurement and the age of the Turin Shroud: Possibilities and Uncertainties" <http://www.shroud.com/meacham.htm> it suggested that contamination could easily skew the results.

Unfortunately, it went largely unnoticed. In light of Rogers' recent work, it is undoubtedly well worth re-reading.

More recently, researchers M. Sue Benford and Joseph Marino, using high-resolution photographs of the Shroud and enlisting the aid of textile experts, found indications of an "invisible" reweave in the area used for the C-14 testing. They presented a series of controversial papers at Shroud conferences that revealed their results, including *Evidence for the Skewing of the C-14 Dating of the Shroud of Turin Due to Repairs* <http://www.shroud.com/pdfs/marben.pdf> in 2000 and *Historical Support of a 16th Century Restoration in the Shroud C-14 Sample Area* <http://www.shroud.com/pdfs/histsupt.pdf> and *Textile Evidence Supports Skewed Radiocarbon Date of Shroud of Turin* <http://www.shroud.com/pdfs/textevid.pdf> in 2002.

It is interesting to note that when Ray Rogers first saw the Benford/Marino papers, he believed he could "disprove their theory in 5 minutes." Of course, that was not to be the case. In essence, Benford and Marino's findings stimulated him to do the research that ultimately led to today's stunning announcement. In fact, in a classic example of how science is truly self-correcting. Ray ultimately proved that Sue and Joe were correct! Ironically, it should be noted that the 1988 C-14 dating results were also technically correct: the only sample they tested was in fact, medieval. Unfortunately, it did not represent the main body of the Shroud cloth. Years later, when Prof. Luigi Gonella, Official Scientific Advisor to the Archbishop of Turin (and the man who approved the decision to take only a single sample) was asked why this was allowed to occur, he responded with a single word, "expediency." Unfortunately, that ill-fated decision caused seventeen years of turmoil and chaos in the study of what is arguably the most important relic in all of Christianity.

During the course of his research, Ray enlisted the aid of professional microscopist Dr. John L. Brown to independently examine some of his samples. See the article Dr. Brown wrote exclusively for the Shroud of Turin Website below:

[http://www.shroud.com/pdfs/brown1.pdf].

—*Frank C. Tribbe*
Valley of the Shenandoah, Virginia

NOTES

Chapter 1

1. Otterbein is author of "A Brief Appreciation of the Holy Shroud," pp. 187–89, *New Catholic Encyclopedia,* vol. XII, McGraw-Hill, 1967. Edward A. Wuenschel, C.SS.R., was one of the few American scholars who published articles about the Shroud in both ecclesiastical and secular publications during the 1930s. His *Self-Portrait of Christ* (Holy Shroud Guild, 1957) is still a respected standard work; his articles included one with Paul Vignon, published in 1937 in *Scientific American.*

2. The Guild distribution offices are at 294 East 150th Street, Bronx, NY 10451. The successor of Father Otterbein, president of the Guild, may be reached at P.O. Box 342, Canandaigua, NY 14424.

Chapter 2

1. A more detailed telling of the Abgar legend, with illustrations, is found in *The Icons,* vol. I (Monastery of St. Catherine at Mount Sinai) by Kurt Weitzmann, Princeton University Press, 1976.

2. A.D. 284—Diocletian declared the Roman Empire to be in four sections: two in the east and two in the west.
   A.D. 330—Constantine moved the "united" kingdom from Rome to Byzantium and renamed it Constantinople.
   A.D. 337—The division of east and west was resumed on the death of Constantine.
   A.D. 395—The division of the empire became permanent.
   A.D. 476—The end of the empire in the west.
   A.D. 756–1880—Papal States established.

3. Edessa was taken from the Moslems in 1097 by a crusader from Boulogne who, in 1100, became Baldwin I, king of Jerusalem, and reigned until 1118. His cousin from Le Bourg became count of Edessa in 1100 and became Baldwin II, king of Jerusalem in 1118, ruling until 1131. Crusaders ruled Jerusalem until 1187, when it fell to Saladin the Moslem. Edessa was retaken by the Moslems in 1144, and passed to the Turks in 1637.

Chapter 3

1. "Sindon in the Old French Chronicle of Robert de Clari," in vol. 1, no. 2 of *Shroud Spectrum International.*

2. Personal consultation.

3. House of Capetians, France:
   1285–1314 Philip IV
   1314–1317 Louis X
   1317–1322 Philip V
   1322–1328 Charles IV
   House of Valois (Capetians), France:
   1328–1350 Philip VI
   1350–1364 John II (the Good)
       (1336–60, John was in captivity in England; the dauphin was regent, and he later became Charles V)
   1364–1380 Charles V
   1380–1422 Charles VI
   1422–1461 Charles VII
       (1429, Joan of Arc made her stand)
   1461–1483 Louis XI

4. The theories of a "Knights Templar connection" are inspired by the historical research of Ian Wilson as reported in his book *Shroud of Turin,* Doubleday, 1978. However, *theory* is now replaced by historical documents discovered by the research of Dr. Daniel C. Scavone, historian of the University of Southern Indiana, which demonstrate the Shroud's Athens/Besancon/Lirey itinerary. Supplementing those data are the findings of Rex Morgan, Noel Currer-Briggs, and Ian Wilson concerning the Templecombe (England) Shroud Face copy which, when juxtaposed with the trial testimony against the Knights Templar, seem strongly to suggest that during the 1208 to 1343 "Besancon period" the Templars (whose base was nearby in the Champagne Province of France) had dozens of artists' copies of the Shroud Face made to facilitate religious ceremonies at their many orientation centers (including the one at Templecombe). There is no reason to suppose that those ceremonies were in any way improper, as the prosecutors of King Philip IV suggested, and the Templars stubbornly respected their vows of secrecy and went to martyrs' deaths.

5. Rev. Patrick O'Connell and Rev. Charles Carty, *The Holy Shroud and Four Visions,* Tan Books, 1974.

6. As reported by Peter M. Rinaldi, *It Is the Lord,* Warner Books, 1973, pp. 44–45.

Chapter 4

1. *Catholic Encyclopedia,* 13, 1912, pp. 762–63.

2. Early conferences on sindonology:

    a. National Congress, Turin, 1939.
    b. First International Congress, Rome, May 1–4, 1950; Turin, May 5–6.
    c. U.S. Conference, Albuquerque, March 23–24, 1977.
    d. Second International Congress, Turin, October 7–8, 1978.
    e. Second U.S. Conference, New London, Conn., October 10–11, 1981.
    f. Symposium, Canadian Society Forensic Science, August 24–28, 1981.
    g. Congress on Shroud and Science, Bologna, Italy, Nov. 27–29, 1981.

Chapter 5

1. *American Medical News,* April 13, 1979.

2. *Rivers in the Desert,* Farrar, Straus & Cudahy, 1959, p. 31.

3. From chapter 5, by Robinson, in *Face To Face with the Turin Shroud,* edited by Peter Jennings, Mahew-McCrimmon, London, 1978.

4. *The Month C I,* 1903.

Chapter 6

1. 1950; English translation in Doubleday/Image edition.

2. *Science News,* 119/17, April 25, 1981.

3. His article at p. 57 in *Face To Face with the Turin Shroud,* edited by Peter Jennings, Mayhew-McCrimmon, London, 1978.

4. *The Cross and the Shroud,* Angelus Books, 1982.

5. No. 30, Turin, December 1981.

6. Reported to the American Chemical Society symposium, September 15, 1982 (full identification footnoted in chapter 9).

Chapter 7

1. "The Dating of the Shroud of Turin from Coins of Pontius Pilate," 1980, privately published, Francis L. Filas, S.J.; revised 1981, 1982.

2. Studies of remains of first-century Jewish cemeteries confirm that the Jews did place coins on the eyes of their dead; see *First Century Jewish Burial Customs,* Father Joseph Marino, Saint Louis Priory, St. Louis, MO.

Chapter 8

1. *The Shroud of Christ,* Westminster, 1902 (English translation from French).

2. Available from the Holy Shroud Guild, 294 East 150th Street, Bronx, NY 10451.

3. STURP press release, New London conference, October 11, 1981.

4. Pellicori notes that there is no difference in image density between the frontal and dorsal images (see note 1, item 12, in chapter 9).

5. x-rays are invisible rays, just shorter in wavelength than ultraviolet rays, which can cause substances to emit (fluoresce) visible light. Overexposure to x-rays can be harmful to humans. Through the use of a fluoroscope, the x-ray penetration of a solid object can be observed, thus giving data about the object's internal structure, by means of the "fluorescing" of the x-ray; some of the x-rays beamed into the object cause emission, and that secondary emission can reveal exactly which elements are present, and whether they are constituents of a painter's pigments, organic substances, etc. The higher-energy radiation (invisible x-rays in this case) stimulates the atoms, which then emit light as *visible* colors; such colors will be characteristic of the atom stimulated.

6. When a beam of white light is broken into its component parts, as through a prism, each color is seen separately in sequence arranged by wavelengths, usually, for instance, from ultraviolet (the shorter waves), which is barely visible at one end, through the colors of visible light, to infrared (the longer waves), which is barely visible at the other end. A spectroscope is an electronically enhanced optical instrument used for examining a spectrum or part thereof. Spectroscopy is the scientific discipline of spectroscopic study, including the evaluation and measurement of materials when viewed in spectroscopically controlled light—it involves electromagnetic spectra from either emission or absorption of radiant energy by the substances examined.

7. A special camera that, in the infrared range, will photograph the image of an object on Polaroid film, utilizing the radiation emissions in that range.

Chapter 9

1. (1) Giovanni Tamburelli, "Some Results in the Processing of the Holy Shroud of Turin," *IEEE Transactions on P.A.M.I.*, 3/6, November 1981, IEEE Computer Society.

    (2) S. F. Pellicori, "Spectrochemical Results of the 1978 Investigation," *Sindon*, XXIII/30 (Centro Internazionale di Sindonologia), December 1981.

    (3) J. H. Heller and A. D. Adler, "A Chemical Investigation of the Shroud of Turin," *Canadian Society of Forensic Scientific Journal*, 14/3, 1981.

    (4) J. H. Heller and A. D. Adler, "Blood on the Shroud of Turin," *Applied Optics*, 19/16, August 15, 1980.

    (5) S. F. Pellicori and R. A. Chandos, "Portable Unit Permits UV/vis Study of 'Shroud,'" *Industrial Research & Development*, February 1981.

(6) R. A. Morris, L. A. Schwalbe, and J. R. London, "x-ray Fluorescence Investigation of the Shroud of Turin," *X-Ray Spectrometry,* 9/2, April 1980.

(7) R. W. Mottern, R. J. London, and R. A. Morris, "Radiographic Examination of the Shroud of Turin: A Preliminary Report," *Materials Evaluation,* 38/12, December 1980.

(8) S. Pellicori and M. S. Evans, "The Shroud of Turin Through the Microscope," *Archaeology,* January–February 1981.

(9) V. D. Miller and S. F. Pellicori, "Ultraviolet Fluorescence Photography of the Shroud of Turin," *Journal of Biological Photography,* 49/3, July 1981.

(10) Roger Gilbert Jr., and Marion M. Gilbert, "Ultraviolet-Visible Reflectance and Fluorescence Spectra of the Shroud of Turin," *Applied Optics,* 19/12, June 15, 1980.

(11) J. S. Accetta and J. Stephen Baumgart, "Infrared Reflectance Spectroscopy and Thermographic Investigations of the Shroud of Turin," *Applied Optics,* 19/12, June 15, 1980.

(12) S. F. Pellicori, "Spectral Properties of the Shroud of Turin," *Applied Optics,* 19/12, June 15, 1980.

(13) Eric J. Jumper and Robert W. Mottern, "Scientific Investigation of the Shroud of Turin," *Applied Optics,* 19/12, June 15, 1980.

(14) L. A. Schwalbe and R. N. Rogers, "Physics and Chemistry of the Shroud of Turin," *Analytica Chimica Acta,* 135 (1982) 3–49.

(15) J. P. Jackson and E. J. Jumper, "Space Science and the Holy Shroud," *La Sindone e la Scienza,* Proceedings, II Congresso Internazionale di Sindonologia, 1978.

2. This proceedings is available from the Holy Shroud Guild, 294 East 150th Street, Bronx, NY 10451. Two earlier Proceedings of Shroud conferences are also available: (1) The 1977 *U.S. Conference of Research on the Shroud of Turin* (from the Holy Shroud Guild); and (2) *La Sindone e la Scienza,* from the International Center in Turin.

3. This paper was presented at the Seventh Symposium on Archaeological Chemistry of the American Chemical Society, September 14–15, 1982, Kansas City, titled "A Comprehensive Examination of the Various Stains and Images on the Shroud of Turin," and was authored by Eric J. Jumper, Alan D. Adler, John P. Jackson, Samuel F. Pellicori, John H. Heller, and James R. Druzik; it is appearing in *A.C.S. Advances in Chemistry,* "Archaeological Chemistry," vol. 3, 1983 (discussed in chapter 10).

4. Presented by John P. Jackson, Eric J. Jumper, and William R. Ercoline at the IEEE International Conference on Cybernetics and Society, October 28–30, 1982, in Seattle; it will appear in a 1983 proceedings of the IEEE (discussed in chapter 10).

5. Usually annually; Nos. 27 (June 1978), et seq., being the most relevant to the modern scientific studies. Available (donation suggested) from Centro Internazionale della Sindone, Via S. Domenico 28, Torino 10122, Italy.

6. From the Indiana Center for Shroud Studies, Route 3, Box 557, Nashville, IN 47448; fifteen dollars per annum.

7. (1) "The Mystery of the Shroud," by Kenneth F. Weaver, *National Geographic,* June 1980.

   (2) "Shroud of Mystery," by Annette Burden, *Science* 81, November 1981.

   (3) "Science and the Shroud of Turin," by Virginia Bortin, *Biblical Archaeologist,* Spring 1980.

   (4) "Shreds of Evidence," by Cullen Murphy, *Harper's,* November 1981.

8. (1) "New Light on the Shroud," by William Deerfield, *Guideposts,* November 1981.

   (2) "Scientists Say Authentic Burial Cloth," *Catholic Sentinel,* April 24, 1981.

   (3) "The Turin Shroud: Miracle or Forgery?" by J. Robert Wright, *Living Church,* March 4, 1979.

   (4) "Toward Unhoaxing the Turin Shroud," by Robert Hudson Dinegar, *Living Church,* February 10, 1980.

   (5) "The Shroud of Turin: A Look at the Overall Picture," by Robert Hudson Dinegar, *The Living Church,* May 17, 1981.

9. Newspaper stories quoting interviews with W. McCrone of McCrone Research Institute, Chicago, and based on three articles authored by him in the 1980–81 issues of *The Microscope* (see note 11, below).

10. Considered as the first of four broad, formal reports by STURP, the panel presentation on behalf of STURP is published as "A Chemical Investigation of the Shroud of Turin" in the *CSFS Journal,* 14/3, 1981; see item 3 of note 1, this chapter.

11. Holy Shroud Guild newsletter, February 1981.

12. *Sindon,* No. 30 (see note 1, item 2); earlier paper, see note 1, item 12.

13. See note 1, item 5.

14. See note 1, item 10.

Chapter 10

1. Note 1, item 9, chapter 9.

2. Note 1, item 6, chapter 9.

3. Note 1, item 11, chapter 9.

4. See definition in note 6 of chapter 8.

5. See definition in note 7 of chapter 8.

6. Note 1, item 7, chapter 9.

7. Note 1, item 8, chapter 9.

8. Note 1, item 14, chapter 9.

9. See chapter 9.

10. Note 1, item 3, chapter 9.

Chapter 11

1. Proceedings of J. B. Bird Pre-Columbian Textile Conference, 1981.

2. March/April 1981, 34/2, "La Galgada: Peru before Pottery," by T. Grieder and A. B. Mendoza.

3. *Frontiers of Science,* May/June 1981.

4. *Archaeology,* May/June 1981, 34/3, "Nubia's Last Christians," by D. P. Van Gerven.

5. News item.

6. Report of the Turin Commission on the Holy Shroud, 1976.

7. Slides of these images and related data may be obtained from the Holy Shroud Guild.

8. News item.

Chapter 12

1. See *It Is the Lord,* by Peter Rinaldi, pp. 43–45.

2. *The Secret Vaults of Time* by Stephan Schwartz, Grosset & Dunlap, 1978; *Extrasensory Ecology* by Joseph K. Long, Scarecrow Press, 1977; and *Visions of Time* by David E. Jones, Quest Books, 1979.

3. McNair's evaluation is contained in *Face To Face with the Turin Shroud,* edited by Peter Jennings, Mowbrays & Mayhew & McCrimmon, Oxford and Great Wakering, England, 1978.

4. Cameron also has a chapter in *Face To Face with the Turin Shroud.*

5. *Ampleforth Journal,* spring 1969.

6. *Etude Critique sur l'origine du Saint Suaire,* Paris, 1900.

7. Holy Shroud Guild newsletter, February 1981.

8. "STARBABY," by Dennis Rawlins, *Fate,* October 1981, pp. 67–98.

9. "Pseudoscience? or Pseudocriticism?" by Theodore Rockwell, *Journal of Parapsychology* 43(3) 1979, pp. 221–31.

10. Author of *The Shroud of Turin* (Germany, 1955), Bruce Publishers, Milwaukee, 1957.

11. Comments of Werner Bulst, September 9, 1982.

Chapter 13

1. *Shroud,* by Robert K. Wilcox, Macmillan, 1977, p. 136.

2. See chapter 19.

3. *Shroud,* by Wilcox, p. 131.

4. Peter M. Rinaldi, *It Is the Lord,* Warner Books, 1973.

Chapter 14

1. New International Version.

2. See *The Humble Approach* by John Templeton, Seabury Press, 1980.

3. For related reading, see: *Miracles* by C. S. Lewis, Macmillan, 1947, 1960; *Miracles,* edited by Martin Ebon, NAL/Signet, 1981.

Chapter 15

1. Rinaldi, *When Millions Saw the Shroud: Letters from Turin,* Don Bosco Publications, 1979.

2. As reported by Rev. Patrick O'Connell and Rev. Charles Carty in *The Holy Shroud and Four Visions,* Tan Books, 1974.

3. Robinson's views are more fully expounded in the book, *Face To Face with the Turin Shroud,* Mayhew-McCrimmons, 1978, p. 69, which is the source for the words quoted and italicized above.

4. Pages 171–73 of his book *Shroud,* Macmillan, 1977; quoted with permission.

Chapter 16

1. Initially presented in the *Catholic Medical Guardian,* May 1931, O'Gorman's ideas were expanded in a London speech that was printed in the *American Ecclesiastical Review,* Vol. CII, 1940. Researcher Wilcox deserves credit for discovering this material and bringing it to sindonologists' attention.

2. *When Millions Saw the Shroud* by Peter Rinaldi, Bosco, 1979, p.137.

3. *The World of Ted Serios,* Morrow, 1967.

4. *Blueprint for Immortality* by H. S. Burr, Neville Spearman, London, 1972; American title, *Fields of Life*, Ballantine, 1973.

5. *A New Science of Life,* by Rupert Sheldrake, Frederick Muller, London, 1981; American edition, J. P. Tarcher, 1981.

6. *Shroud of Turin*, Doubleday, 1978, p. 209.

7. *The New Yorker*, August 31, 1946; *Hiroshima*, Knopf, 1946.

8. *Hiroshima-Nagasaki: A Pictorial Record,* Hiroshima-Nagasaki Publishing Committee, Tokyo, 1978.

9. Abingdon Press, 1967 and 1968.

10. *Picture Windows on the Christ,* Magian Press, 1979; all three volumes by Wise are available from Magian Press, P.O. Box 117, Penn Laird, VA 22846.

11. Gardner Murphy, J., ASPR, 1963, 1966, 1967. Also see Charles T. Tart, *Altered States of Consciousness,* Doubleday/Anchor, 1972, and *States of Consciousness,* Dutton, 1975; John W. White, *Frontiers of Consciousness,* Avon Books, 1975; Ken Wilber, *The Spectrum of Consciousness,* Quest, 1977; Robert E. Ornstein, *The Psychology of Consciousness,* Viking, 1972; and *The Nature of Human Consciousness,* Freeman, 1973; Frances E. Vaughan, *Awakening Intuition,* Doubleday/Anchor, 1979.

Chapter 18

1. Author of the excellent book *Shroud,* Macmillan, 1977.

2. *The Tilma under Infrared Radiation,* 1981, a booklet of C.A.R.A., P.O. Box 29150, Washington, DC 20017.

3. A Catholic Church organization whose mission is to discover, promote, and apply modern techniques and scientific informational resources for practical use in a coordinated and effective approach to the Church's social and religious mission.

4. Further references include: *A Handbook on Guadalupe,* by Dr. Charles Wahlig, Franciscan Marytown Press, 1974; and *The Wonder of Guadalupe,* by Francis Johnston, Tan Books, 1981.

Chapter 19

1. "The Holy Shroud of Turin: Is It a Photographic Phenomenon?" *Amateur Photographer,* London, March 8, 1967.

2. Various sizes of this "double effect" portrait may be purchased from the Holy Shroud Guild.

3. Keats Publishing, 1887, 1975.

4. Copies of the portrait may be purchased (colored prints, 8x10 and 16x20) from Patrick Walsh Press, 2206 S. Priest, Suite A, Tempe, AZ 85282. That publisher, in 1982, released *Sindon: A Layman's Guide To the Shroud of Turin* by Frank Adams, describing his personal pilgrimage respecting the Shroud.

Chapter 20

1. From chapter 5, *Face To Face with the Turin Shroud,* Mayhew, McCrimmon & Mowray, 1978.

2. *Guideposts,* November 1981.

3. Cynthia L. Theall, *Science News,* letters section, October 24, 1981.

Afterword

1. These symposia were the Section on the Carbon-dating Controversy, Second Annual Humanities, Science and Technology Conference, Ferris State University, Big Rapids, Michigan, April 7–8, 1989; the International Conference on the Shroud and Iconography, Bologna, Italy, May 6–7, 1989; the Paris (France) Symposium on the Shroud of Turin, September 7–8, 1989; Sardinia Shroud Symposium at Cagliari, Italy, April 1990; Symposium on the Shroud of Turin, Columbia University, New York, March 2–3, 1991; St. Louis Shroud Symposium, Saint Louis University (Missouri), June 22–23, 1991; Rome Shroud Symposium, June 10–12, 1993.

SELECTED BIBLIOGRAPHY

Classical Writings on the Shroud

Adams, Frank O. *Sindon: A Layman's Guide To the Shroud of Turin.* Tempe, Ariz. Patrick Walsh Press, 1982.

Barbet, Pierre. *A Doctor at Calvary.* New York: Doubleday, 1950, 1963.

Bulst, Werner. *The Shroud of Turin.* Milwaukee: Bruce, 1957.

Cheshire, G. L. *Pilgrimage to the Shroud.* New York: McGraw-Hill, 1956.

Guscin, Marc. *The Oviedo Cloth.* Cambridge, England: Lutterworth Press, 1998.

Haralick, Robert. *Analysis of Digital Images of the Shroud of Turin.* Blacksburg, Va: Virginia Polytechnical Insitute, 1983.

Jennings, Peter, ed. *Face To Face with the Turin Shroud.* Great Wakering, England: Mayhew-McCrimmon & Mowbray, 1978.

Manton, Lennox. *Byzantine Frescoes and the Turin Shroud.* Manly, N.S.W., Australia: Runciman Press, 1994.

Marino, Fr. Joseph. *First Century Burial Customs of the Jews.* St. Louis: Saint Louis Priory, 1992.

Morgan, Rex. *Perpetual Miracle.* Manly, N.S.W., Australia: Runciman Press, 1982.

———— *The Holy Shroud and the Earliest Paintings of Christ.* Manly, N.S.W., Australia: Runciman Press, 1986.

Petrosillo, Orazio, and Marinelli, Emanuela. *The Enigma of the Shroud: A Challenge to Science.* Malta: Publishers Enterprises Gp., 1996.

Rinaldi, Peter M. *It Is the Lord.* New York: Warner Books, 1972.

————*When Millions Saw the Shroud.* New Rochelle, N.Y.: Don Bosco, 1979.

Scavone, Daniel C. *The Shroud of Turin.* San Diego: Greenhaven Press, 1988.

Vignon, Paul. *The Shroud of Christ.* New York: Dutton, 1902.

Volckringer, Jean. *The Holy Shroud Confronts the Image.* Manly, N.S.W., Australia: Runciman Press, 1991.

Weyland, Peter. *A Sculptor Interprets the Holy Shroud of Turin.* Esopus, N.Y.: Mission Press, 1954.

Whanger, Mary and Alan. *The Shroud of Turin: An Adventure of Discovery.* Franklin, TN: Providence House, 1998.

Wilcox, Robert K. *Shroud.* New York: Macmillan, 1977.

Wilson, Ian. *The Shroud of Turin.* New York: Doubleday, 1978.

———- *Holy Faces, Secret Places.* New York: Doubleday, 1991.

Wilson, Ian, and Vernon Miller. *The Mysterious Shroud.* New York: Doubleday, 1986.

Wuenschel, Edward A. *Self-Portrait of Christ.* Esopus, N.Y.: Redemptorist Fathers, 1954.

Zugibe, Frederick T. *The Cross and the Shroud.* Garnerville, N.Y.: Angelus Books, 1982.

RECOMMENDED BOOKS ON THE SHROUD

The Botany of the Shroud by Alan D. and Mary Whanger. Dr. Alan D. Whanger and his wife, Mary Whanger, created the Council for the Study of the Shroud of Turin, which they have operated in Durham, North Carolina, for more than three decades. In recent years they have concentrated on the evaluation of the botany of the Shroud, which involved pollen grains and fiber lifted from the surface of the cloth, plus the enlargement of Shroud photographs that disclose leaves and flower blooms that had been placed on the Shroud during the Man's burial. Both the pollen and the blooms have been precisely identified by experts from Jerusalem who are certain that a large percentage of them are uniquely limited to growths in the Jerusalem area, and which bloom in the spring at the time of Jesus' burial. With cooperation from the university staff, this book has now been published by the Claude E. Phillips Herbarium of Delaware State University, Dover, Delaware. This illustrated book is fifty-three pages, 8.5 by 11 inches in size; 2004.

The earlier book by Mary and Alan Whanger, *The Shroud of Turin: An Adventure of Discovery,* Providence House, 1998, primarily features their unique use of Polarized Image Overlay Technique to compare the Shroud Face with historically noteworthy paintings of the Face of Jesus (first through ninth centuries). Image-Overlay was a method developed by the FBI for use in court, and the courts have accepted such evidence. The Whangers matched their photos (one of the Shroud Face and the other an ancient painting reputed to be of Jesus' face) using two projectors focused onto a single screen, and laboriously counted the points of congruence. Their results have greatly exceeded the standard established by the FBI and accepted by the courts.

In 2003, Swiss specialist in historic textiles, Dr. Mechthild Flury-Lemberg, was employed on authority from the Vatican to perform restoration and conversion work on the Shroud of Turin. Her work is described in her book *L'intervento Conservativo-Preservation,* published in 2004 by Editrice O.D.P.F., Torino, Italy. She removed and replaced the five-hundred-year-old backing cloth and burn-hole patches on the back of the Shroud, and by careful reweaving restored all damage to the back of the cloth. In the course of her work, Flury-Lemberg, among other discoveries, found that the hidden accumulations of soot in the burn-holes may well have skewed the carbon-dating in 1988. Perhaps, and most important, she discovered that some of the original weaving was of a style known and used only in the Holy Lands of the first century.

In the Catacombs and the Early Church author Sylvia Bogdanescu (Runciman Press, Manly, Australia, 1998; Rex Morgan, series editor) presents wall paintings of the first century, two of which were found by Dr. and Mrs. Whanger to have been so closely identical to the Shroud Face that it must have been available at that time for the artist's copying.

The Orphaned Manuscript by the late Dr. Alan D. Adler (Effata Editrice, 2002). Adler was the foremost chemical expert on the Shroud of Turin, and these thirteen articles cover his primary points of interest in the cloth.

The DNA of God? (Doubleday, 1999) is by Dr. Leoncio A. Garza-Valdes, professor of microbiology at the University of Texas. By examination of pieces of the Shroud cloth, Dr. Garza-Valdes discovered that, like many ancient cloths, the Shroud has an *organic* "plastic coating" (bacteria) that increases over time and is high in carbon content, so that every century of the cloth life the carbon for carbon-dating procedures will record a *more recent* date for the origin of the cloth.

Flora of the Shroud of Turin by Alan and Mary Whanger (Missouri Botanical Garden Press, 1999), with assistance from Messrs. Danin and Baruch, Israeli scientists. Magnified photographs of blooms from the Shroud image have been identified as from the Middle East, and some from the area of Jerusalem that bloom in March–April and were growing before the eighth century. Some blooms were picked between 3 and 4 P.M. on the same day they were placed on the Shroud.

The Turin Shroud: The Illustrated Evidence (Barnes & Noble, 2000) by Ian Wilson and Barrie Schwortz. Schwortz was official photographer for the 1978 five-day examination of the Shroud in Turin. This book is enhanced by more than two hundred color photos, most taken by Schwortz.

The Burial of Jesus of Nazareth and the Shroud of Turin by Joseph Marino (published by Jeff Richards, Anaheim, California, 1999). A historical summary of the Shroud data from a religious viewpoint.

Index